FIDDLING FOR NORWAY
REVIVAL AND IDENTITY

Chris Goertzen

THE UNIVERSITY OF CHICAGO PRESS / CHIC⟨ ⟩ON

Chris Goertzen is assistant professor of music at Kenyon College.

The University of Chicago Press, Chicago 60637
The University of Chicago Press, Ltd., London
© 1997 by The University of Chicago
All rights reserved. Published 1997
Printed in the United States of America
06 05 04 03 02 01 00 99 98 97   5 4 3 2 1

ISBN (cloth): 0-226-30049-8
ISBN (paper): 0-226-30050-1

Library of Congress Cataloging-in-Publication Data

Goertzen, Chris.
    Fiddling for Norway : revival and identity / Chris Goertzen.
        p.   cm. — (Chicago studies in ethnomusicology)
    Includes bibliographical references and index.
    ISBN 0-226-30049-8. — ISBN 0-226-30050-1 (pbk.)
    1. Folk music—Norway—History and criticism.   2. Fiddling.   3. Fiddle
tunes—Norway—History and criticism.   4. Music—Competitions—Norway.   I. Title.   II. Series.
ML3704.G64   1997
787.2'1623982—DC21   97-7385
                                                            CIP
                                                            MN

⊗ The paper used in this publication meets the
minimum requirements of the American National Standard
for Information Sciences—Permanence of Paper for
Printed Library Materials, ANSI Z39.48-1984.

CONTENTS

FIGURES

Plates follow page 58

PREFACE AND
ACKNOWLEDGMENTS

Norway has two types of folk fiddle. The "normal fiddle" *(van-lig, or vanleg, fele)*—the subject of this book—is called that to distinguish it from the more famous (but not more common) Hardanger fiddle *(hardingfele)*, played mainly in Norway's central and western mountains.[1] I will in most cases call the normal fiddle simply the "fiddle" in this book, following current practice in the Norwegian folk music milieu. The Hardanger fiddle's distinctive appearance (a decorated body, four played and four sympathetic strings), whispery and nasal sound—to its fans, mystical and haunting—its complex music, and, above all, the instrument's uniqueness to Norway have made it a national symbol. The Hardanger fiddle has been intensively studied by both Norwegians and foreigners, while the fiddle has received much less scholarly attention from Norwegians and none from outsiders. The fiddle—physically the same as the violin—is played in the east, north, and in some parts of coastal Norway by as many fiddlers as devote themselves to the Hardanger fiddle, or more (see Fig. 1). Its tradition is at least as long as that of the Hardanger fiddle, and arguably more vigorous. And its music, while consisting almost exclusively of short, bipartite dances, can be remarkably attractive in both bold and subtle ways.

My first substantial contact with Norway's fiddle was during 1988–89, when I was teaching courses on American and Latin American music at the University of Trondheim as a Fulbright Lecturer. Soon after arriving in Norway, I attended the District Fiddle Contest *(dis-triktskappleik)*, the largest annual contest specifically for the normal fiddle, which took place that year in Røros, an old copper-mining town in the mountains, two hours by train south of Trondheim. It was

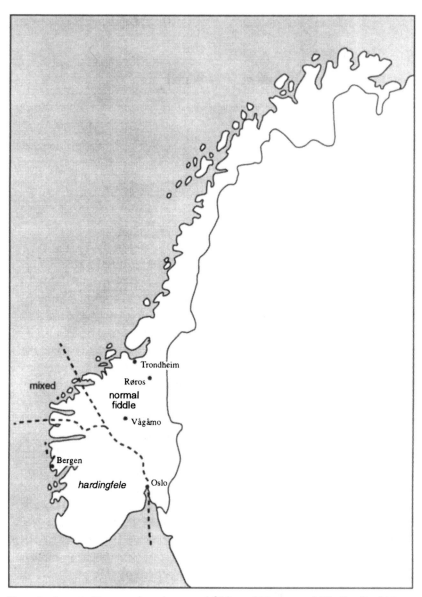

Figure 1. Areas in Norway where the normal fiddle and Hardanger fiddle (*hardingfele*)
are played, and an area where both instruments are employed

held in the Røros community center, a typical small-town multipurpose building with a few small rooms and two auditoriums. During
the competition, individual fiddlers wearing traditional regional costumes each played two contrasting tunes (many of the transcriptions
given in the Tune Anthology of this book are of tunes I first heard at
this event). These same fiddlers, along with less-skilled colleagues,
also competed in large ensembles, that is, their home fiddle clubs with
which they practice weekly and which occasionally accompany dances
and concertize. Dancers also competed in Røros. After two days of
watching and listening, I carried my tapes and field notes home and
tried to make sense of what I had observed, drawing on my experi-
ences as a student of American fiddling and occasional judge at American fiddle contests. Some observations were easy: there clearly were
regional styles, and players in their twenties seemed especially proficient, as in the United States. But why did the fiddlers seem (to my
admittedly inexpert ears) more skilled overall than my American sub-
jects? Why could I, an outsider versed in contemporary American
fiddling, predict much of the order in which contestants scored, but
not the winner? Why was the selection of dance genres so much wider
in the evening's recreational dancing than during the competition, and
why were some instruments then added to the groups I had heard
earlier in the day? And why were the audiences so quiet? Transcribing
the tunes answered some questions, but provoked even more. Over the
course of the year, I made many more such excursions, and returned to
Norway during the summers of 1991 and 1993. I conducted interviews, made field recordings, and listened to hundreds of hours of
past interviews and field collections that were assembled in the largest
archive of music for the fiddle, the Council for Folk Music and Folk
Dance (Rådet for Folkemusikk og Folkedans). It was my good fortune
that this organization is located where I was teaching, at the University of Trondheim.

Norwegian scholars who study fiddling have concentrated nearly
exclusively on recording the oldest fiddlers, documenting the most
venerable repertoires, and writing intimate histories of local traditions, in general treating the present as a window on what is considered to be a richer past. There is some room for foreigners in this
research world, simply because Norwegian funding can never sponsor
enough of this valuable, meticulous work. But I came to believe that
a visitor such as myself would be better advised to investigate topics
complementary to those that Norwegian scholars so ably pursue. This
book is about recent and current fiddling in a revival milieu that in

many ways parallels contemporary folk institutions and festivals elsewhere in the industrialized West, including American fiddling. When I look at fiddling of the past, it is mainly to understand the present better. This is a book with an outsider's point of view, aimed primarily at other non-Norwegians, though I hope some in Norway will find parts of it of interest.

This volume falls into two parts. Part one concerns people and events important in Norwegian fiddling. Developments before World War I are treated in a single introductory chapter. In it I briefly introduce those aspects of Norwegian geography, history, and psychology that bear on fiddling, the formation of Norway's central instrumental folk music and dance genres, influential nineteenth-century fiddlers, and, most important, how Norway's continuously evolving balance of national and local identity brought the fiddle into a folk music revival initially dominated by the Hardanger fiddle. The second chapter concerns the twentieth-century growth and diversification of the Norwegian folk-music revival, the contests spearheading this revival, and how concerts (just one of many symptoms of art orientation) and dances (a function at once old and recast) came to fit into a revival environment first defined by competition. That chapter will follow the National Fiddle Contest through the 1970s, when it assumed its current shape.

The next few chapters concern aspects of fiddling in contemporary Norway. Chapter 3 describes how fiddlers learn their craft today and why they choose to fiddle, and follows several local fiddle clubs and their activities. Chapter 4 covers contests and concerts on the local, regional, and national levels, and takes as close a look as possible at judging and at how occasionally conflicting emphases—local versus national identity, and tradition versus aesthetics—have transformed the artistic and social network nourishing Norwegian folk music. And Chapter 5 narrates a recent upheaval in Norwegian folk music, the debate and turmoil accompanying the introduction of newer genres (which are less specifically Norwegian) into official folk music venues. These newer genres, grouped under the rubric *gammaldans,* remain controversial: Are they really folk music? Do they deserve official support?

Part two consists of three chapters about the music of fiddling. Those chapters are centered on a sample of transcriptions of fiddle tunes most of which are in the older genres, the ones allowed in most contests. Each melody from this Tune Anthology (placed at the end of the book) is chosen to illustrate important aspects of the repertoires of which it is a part, repertoires associated with individual performers, with regions, and with the whole fiddle district (i.e., the areas where the fiddle is played). In that section of the book I address such issues as performance practice (physical adjustment of the instrument, bowing, ornamentation of melodies, rhythmic conventions), mode (major vs. "older" modes, historical associations of certain modes, the shaping of modes in part by specific tunings and by physical characteristics of the fiddle), melodic gesture and form, tune identity (multiple versions of pieces, when a tune is sufficiently distinctive to be considered a separate tune, sorting a "saturated" repertoire), and regional styles (of varying ages, musical characteristics of each, emphasizing contest or dance and egalitarian versus elitist ethos). The final chapter is a speculative summary, addressing the relationship between the music and the support system of the fiddle today, and between this complex and central Norwegian values.

Ola Kai Ledang of the Music Department of the University of Trondheim wrote the Fulbright job description that brought me to Norway, was an exemplary host and sounding board during my stay, and, along with his wife, Marit, helped in other ways during my stay and Norway and since. Bjørn Aksdal, Egil Bakka, and Erling Flem of the Council for Folk Music and Folk Dance allowed me easy access to the largest collection of music tapes for the fiddle in the country and advised along the way. Ivar and Frøydis Schjølberg, Mary Barthelemy, and Arild Hoksnes were of special help within the contemporary folk music milieu. Most of them, and Tor Erik Jenstad and Olav Sæta, were kind enough to comment on drafts of chapters. Through their help, I have avoided some errors of fact and many in spelling—most remaining inconsistencies will be the result of remaining faithful to various Norwegian dialects. All translations are mine. And dozens of fiddlers put up with my tape recorder and endless questions. Many of these fiddlers then were kind enough to look over my transcriptions of their playing. I thank them all.

PART *I*

Fiddlers

CHAPTER ONE

Introduction

Geography, History, and Norwegian Identity

Imagine yourself in Norway. You probably will picture a fjord or river in front of mountains, with a village or small town, and a scattering of more distant houses in the narrow strip of arable land between water and rock. The homes are not large, but they are quietly stylish, sturdy, and well kept. The people you see move with purpose but without strain. They know many or most of the people they see at the grocery store. Notably absent in this picture is evidence of poverty, sloth, crime, and other social ills. Air and water seem clear, and, while our view of the community includes a few businesses and perhaps a factory or two, industrial detritus is notably absent.

Is this some willfully concocted pastoral ideal? If so, it is not the exclusive property of outsiders: more than a few Norwegians believe this is what Norway is, and innumerable locations indeed fit the description. Nature is far from kind—resources are few, and weather often brutal—but Norwegians are used to coping. (A common aphorism has it that "there is no bad weather, only bad clothing.") The mountains and watercourses are beautiful, they are everywhere, and they are everywhere loved. Many a Norwegian placed by work or other circumstance in a city leaves his or her heart—and some relatives—in a rural hamlet, and returns there whenever possible. And many own or have ready access to a *hytte* (cabin), or at least a boat, and nearly everyone skis (during the weeks around Easter, so many Norwegians are skiing that the economy seems to be on vacation too).

That our idyllic-appearing community is Norwegian is made explicit by more than the combination of spectacular landscape, dignified architecture, and the inhabitants' collective physiognomy and demeanor. The word *Norsk* (Norwegian) appears on many storefronts. Many a sweater follows a traditional Norwegian pattern, and houses often contain examples of *rosemaling* (painted or carved decorations in traditional patterns of flowers, for example). Local identity is underlined, too: people speak the dialect of their community, and are accustomed to interpreting the dialects of other Norwegians. And a few nights each year, many of the inhabitants of our typical country hamlet dance to local folk music played on fiddles (with a few other instruments, probably including accordions and guitar and a bass). An annual fiddle contest in this or a nearby town draws musicians and audiences from a great distance. The folk music community is remarkably strong, and has continued to produce solid performances and to attract new recruits easily through the decades. The vigor of this side of Norwegian life feeds on central aspects of Norwegian character, which has been shaped by the country's terrain, weather, and history.

Norway is indeed far north: most of the population lives between fifty six and sixty four degrees of latitude, roughly the same as the main body of Alaska. The few villages that reach near the seventy first parallel are the largest gatherings of people that far north in the world. Neither the land nor the weather is especially hospitable, though a tributary of the Gulf Stream keeps the coastline more temperate than one might expect. The jagged coast faces west. Norway is a land of seashores, mountains, and narrow valleys, a natural habitat that its poets, novelists, and dramatists never forget. Norway's geological foundation is still changing: rock and clay slides regularly encroach on farms and interrupt travel on the two-lane highways that cling to mountainsides. Weather is a central topic of conversation, and falling rocks and shifting glaciers are frequently audible. Norwegians simply have had to come to terms with this overwhelming environment. Few of the approximately 125,000 square miles are easily habitable. Jonassen estimates that 3% of the land is now cultivated fields or meadows, 24% forest, and 73% mountains or moors (1983:5). How much of the forest is arable is debatable—as is, for that matter, how much of the area now farmed is practical for that purpose by modern international standards. While there are substantial farming areas around Oslo and Trondheim, agriculture elsewhere has always been marginally successful, at best.

Norway's high standard of living is quite new: rugged conditions and scarcity of resources enforced poverty from the first. Little iron was present in the Iron Age, and little bronze in the Bronze Age. The time of the Vikings (roughly 800–1000) is celebrated today, but we should not forget that these raiders were driven by poverty and a deep hunger for good land. Moves in the direction of the feudal mainstream were scotched in 1349, when the Black Death took much of the population (the sagas say two-thirds). This largely removed any potential support for an upper class—a socioeconomic level never to materialize in most of the country—though survivors of the plague may have had more land than before. A long period of stagnation or decline stretched through the Reformation (Derry 1973:1). A common heir to the thrones of Norway and Denmark, Erik III, became king in 1389, and the modest central administration of Norway went to Denmark. A messy succession followed, resolved in 1450, when Christian I became king of Denmark and Norway. The two countries were supposedly equal, but the so-called Twin Kingdoms were ruled from Copenhagen, whose university shaped Norwegian bureaucrats and clergy. Denmark was increasingly favored by the king as time passed, and Norway was declared a Danish province in 1536. Denmark's neglect of Norway gradually lessened after the Reformation was imposed. Danish clergy spread the new word throughout Norway, thus promoting a measure of literacy and of education in general. Only in the seventeenth century did Norway's long period of decline clearly come to an end. National awareness grew rapidly toward the end of the eighteenth century, although Norway's peasant freeholders, however much they cherished the thought of independence, cannot be said to have responded to the ideals and especially the methods of the French Revolution.

During the course of the Napoleonic Wars, Denmark (and thus Norway) tried to remain neutral: this was profitable and popular. Aggressive and arrogant British behavior alienated the joint country, which, forced to take sides, chose Napoleon, and swiftly faced economic ruin as the result of a British blockade. At the Peace of Kiel, signed on January 14, 1814, Denmark ceded Norway to Sweden, thus compensating Sweden for the loss of Finland, which Russia had annexed. But Norway had been largely on its own for six years, owing to the effectiveness of the blockade, and had savored the feeling of independence. The treaty was not implemented immediately, and Norway tried to go its own way. The regent (a Danish prince) was elected King, a Storting (parliament) met April 10, 1814, and a Norwegian

constitution was signed on May 17, 1814; May 17 remains the patriotic holiday of Norway. The constitution favored rural Norway in the
electoral system, forbade the creation of new noble titles (all would
be abolished in 1821), and formalized the Norwegian system of primogeniture, which emphasizes continuity in farm ownership.

Following a modest amount of bloodshed, the new king was de-
posed, but the constitution remained in place, and Norway kept considerable autonomy. Why this was allowed is something of a muddle,
combining oddities of Bernadotte's psychology (he was the marshal of
France who was now king of Sweden) with the desire of Britain and
Russia to keep Sweden from becoming too strong. Bernadotte expected to be able gradually to overcome the prickly Norwegian desire
for autonomy, but was frustrated. When full independence was finally
declared in 1905, a fair amount of ill will was in the air, but no overt
hostilities ensued.

The new country of Norway remained poor, as it was not yet industrialized (coal and iron still had to be imported). Agriculture remained
behind the times, too. During the first half of the nineteenth century,
primitive internal transportation and communications—along with
the absence of agricultural schools—had left the Norwegian peasant
farmers largely ignorant of new agricultural techniques adopted in
much of the rest of Europe: crop rotation, planting of clover and root
crops, seed selection, and such (Liebermann 1970:59). Since there
never was a significant surplus of any kind, a capitalist mentality
("bigger is better") lacked inspiration. Much of the little arable land
was concentrated in remote valleys. The relative isolation of these
farm communities promoted a strong tradition of mutual help and of
self-sufficiency on the level of the rural neighborhood, or *bygd*.[1] Many
Norwegian peasants were classified as freeholders (a comparatively
large number in the European context), but they remained quite poor,
on average. What vigor the economy displayed issued from exports of
wood and of fish, and from shipping services. As late as 1875, agriculture, forestry, and fishing together employed three times as many
people as did industry (Derry 1973:121).

Toward the end of the century, birth rates went up and mortality
rates down without the economic base's expanding to absorb the dramatic increase in population. Considerable unrest and a stunningly
high rate of emigration resulted, with far-reaching consequences. During the peak year of 1882, over 29,000 Norwegians emigrated, mainly
to the United States. The 1910 American census found 403,858 Norwegian-born and 410,951 American-born of Norwegian-born par-

ents—together, a number roughly equal to one-third the population of Norway (Derry 1973:216). The more prosperous land-holding peasant, the *bonde*, could stay home, but many cottagers *(småbruker)* and laborers with little or no land *(husmenn)* either swelled the population of the cities, especially Oslo, or passed through these cities on their way out of the country. This decreased social unrest by promoting social equality in the rural areas: a noble class had never developed, and much of the underclass that could afford to leave did so. Emigration also slowed down the ongoing fragmentation of farms. Laws and custom with near the force of law had kept primogeniture strong: farms would tend not to shrink in the inland valleys, though the availability of supplementary income on the coasts from fishing and other jobs had made farms more likely to be subdivided, and thus made farming often a part-time job. Lieberman suggests that the nationwide syphoning off of surplus workers indeed strengthened the labor movement, but may also have drained "the more enterprising, the more dynamic, the most impatient and discontented workers" (1970:50).

Norway caught the second wave of the industrial revolution, the surge based on industrial uses of electricity. In the nineteenth century, a few textile mills and saws were powered by water wheels. In the years following independence, hydroelectric power made what had been quite a meager economy grow rapidly. Railroads were never economically significant, and it was only in the 1920s that a good road system allowed ready access to most of the southern part of the country. In the late 1930s, in a population of about 3 million, some 838,000 still worked in agriculture or forestry (Grimley 1937:31). However, economic growth since World War II has been phenomenal. American money helped fuel a postwar boom. The discovery in 1969 of the Ekofisk gas and oil fields constituted an enormous windfall, allowing a comprehensive network of social programs in what had become a soundly constructed welfare state. The oil crisis of 1986, in which prices for North Sea oil fell from about $40 to around $10 per barrel, put considerable strain on the system, but Norway's standard of living remains among the world's highest.

The remarkable speed of Norway's transformation from poverty-stricken backwater to prosperous modern state has left few visual traces, since industrial development, expansion of roadways and communication networks, and addition of housing have for the most part been carefully planned and tastefully effected. The population has grown little compared with most places that have undergone similarly rapid modernization. Of some 4 million citizens, half a million now reside in Oslo, Norway's only city that seems as much a part of Europe as of Norway, and less than 200,000 each in the metropolitan areas centered in Trondheim and Bergen. Three-fourths of Norwegians live within ten miles of the sea; roughly half of the population resides in communities of less than 10,000. Even though modern communications have eased all kinds of travel, Norway still looks like a country of small towns and villages nestled in a spectacular, idyllic landscape, the beauty of which impresses even more than its barrenness. But the impact of this century's wrenching changes on national psychology has been profound. On the one hand, Coca Cola, pizza, and other trappings of international consumerism have been comfortably assimilated into daily life, and computer expertise has become a principal export. On the other hand, traditional ways of thought and feeling remain powerful.

Many factors have contributed to and continue to reinforce a heartfelt and pervasive egalitarianism intertwined with remarkable compactness of culture. That feudalism, the Renaissance, and early stages of the industrial revolution all passed Norway by kept it a country without an upper class for most of history. Then, turn-of-the-century emigration did much to lop off both the most- and least-productive sectors of society. Today, laws (including tax rates that send some business moguls fleeing) and attitudes continue to hamper the emergence of an elite. Some of these attitudes are negative inheritances of a claustrophobic village mentality. Many citizens still equate conspicuous high achievement with conceit—no individual ought to raise his or her head above another's, conventional rural wisdom holds. Modesty is among the values that religion has favored, too. Evangelical movements of the eighteenth and nineteenth centuries still cast a net over Norway's "Bible Belt," which extends from Kristiansand in the south through the especially rugged and historically poorest areas of the southwest up to Ålesund. Competing against one's peers is still considered immodest and unattractive by many Norwegians. Modern Norwegians enjoy performing well at sports, but, in the words of Jonassen, they "avoid personal head-to-head competition and the invidiousness and loss of self-esteem that such victories and defeats would involve . . . they race against the impersonal clock" (1983:84).

In addition, an underclass has not been allowed to form. It is a cultural requirement to be self-reliant, to do one's part satisfactorily. To fall short in the not-so-old days of subsistence agriculture in unforgiving narrow valleys would have not merely provoked abstract censure, but caused starvation. Thus, at the same time that excelling is discouraged, stubborn persistence is highly valued. Since education is much respected, and since national finances have become healthy—owing to a happy combination of industriousness and respect for education with the successive windfalls of herring shoals, postwar U.S. aid, and oil discoveries—social leveling has meant leveling up, not down. Almost no one is allowed to fall through the cracks of the educational and welfare systems. The result is a country with a paradoxical identity. Outsiders tend to find Norwegians to be very conformist, whereas most Norwegians think of themselves as individualists. Both points of view contain much truth.

It comes as no surprise that Norwegians are very nationalistic, as much as Americans and more than most Europeans. One occasion of Norwegian prickliness will serve to illustrate the special nature of Norwegian nationalism. In 1972, the Norwegians shocked their government by voting against joining the European Economic Community. This attempt to get Norway into some sort of customs union, one in quite a series of attempts, had near-unanimous support in the government and the media (yet another attempt would fail in 1995). The advantages of EEC membership were obvious: the cost of living would doubtless plummet, particularly through savings on food and on any goods that were labor intensive to produce. However, the referendum failed by a narrow margin. Polls were immediately commissioned to find out which fractions of the population had voted against the union. Gallup and its Norwegian cognate turned up most farmers (just a tiny fraction of the population today), many teetotalers and people living in the far North, and other groups. I found the folk music community to be solidly against joining the EEC. Gallup summarized that the general population voted against union from a "'feeling,' between unease and fear, of the possibility that the pursuit of the obvious economic advantages of the EEC would lead to a subversion of Norway's economic and political independence" (Miljan 1977:196). Folk musicians I talked to focused on an issue conjoining culture and economics, often saying in some form: "Why should we give up our farms so that people in the cities can eat more cheaply?"

For many, perhaps most, Norwegians, being Norwegian is associated more with a home and its immediate surroundings than with the country as a whole, thus assigning enormous value to what to them are the intimately linked concepts of family and place. For many, the essence of Norway is what they see from the windows of their homes or cabins, or perhaps their parents' places: *their* mountains, *their* fjord or river, and the handful of tiny farms they can see, farms long associated with the same families by custom and law.

In older Norse law the right to continuity of family ownership of a farm was absolute. A farmer could not sell his farm to whomever he wished; his ownership was temporary, part of his family's history. In the form of *odelsrett* preserved in the constitution of 1814, if a farmer sold to someone outside the family, a relative could buy the farm back within five years at "fair market value" (Derry 1973:7). In addition, the eldest son had the right to buy out his siblings (after 1962, the eldest child of either sex would be specified). This was less to maintain the integrity of large estates than to keep farms already modest in size from becoming too small to support a family. In the late 1930s, 90% of the roughly 265,000 Norwegian farms (these were 94% owner occupied) encompassed twenty five acres or less (Grimley 1937:32). Some consolidation has since taken place, though custom still keeps most farms tiny, and in families; oldest sons still obey the moral force of *odelsrett*. According to Popperwell, these traditions of land ownership, collectively known as *odelsbonde,* "carried with [them] the conviction that Norwegians had nothing to envy in, or to adopt from, the social systems of other countries" (1972:32). In the nineteenth century, this conviction ignored the plight of the large class of underprivileged tenant cottars *(husmenn).* But much of that class emigrated around the turn of the century, and no underclass of significant size exists today. Moreover, Norwegians now have considerable justification for their continued belief that their way of life is as good as that anywhere else, and quite a bit better than that possible in many places.

As nationalism burgeoned in the nineteenth century, farmers came to be considered the "true inheritors of Norway's ancient power . . . the living link with Norway's ancient glory" (Jonassen 1983:85). Much of that feeling remains even though farmers constitute a progressively smaller fraction of the population; in the 1960s, the percentage of the work force that farmed, fished, or worked in the lumber industry was down to 13% (Derry 1973:430). Now farmers make up less than 6% of the population. Farms remain tiny by American standards, and despite the hard work of those who run them, and the help of whatever modern methods can be employed in their modest borders, must be extremely heavily subsidized to survive. They exist today only partly to produce high-quality food: they are concrete symbols of the past. Less than a third of farmers are full-time today, and many farms are leased by their owners to neighbors, who then can employ some simple economies of scale. Although this undercuts the traditional working of the farms, their symbolic value remains.

Norwegians cannot indulge a feeling for their national history through the high arts, since millenia of poverty and the absence of a court and a noble class meant that these were little practiced before this century. A national sense of tradition-oriented aesthetics, developed over many centuries and reinforced by a younger but ardent nationalism, is reflected in affection for the folk arts that were cultivated, tradition emphasizes, during long winters in ancient farms in isolated valleys. This is most easily seen in woodworking. Thirty-two stave churches of an original seven to eight hundred still stand. These were built using methods of joining borrowed from Viking shipbuilding. A handful of ancient farmsteads are public museums, while many others, just as old, are in active use. Old buildings generally have unfinished wooden interior walls (Plates 4 and 11); so do many modern homes (Plates 1 and 10). Both crude and fine traditional woodworking is found in a great many homes (Plates 1, 4, and 10), as is the array of regional decorative painting styles collectively known as *rosemaling* (see the rack of plates in Plate 3). And national costumes—regional clothing *(bunads)* derived from the Sunday bests of prosperous rural families of the eighteenth and nineteenth centuries—are worn for a variety of formal ceremonial occasions, from weddings to the events at the center of this book—folk music contests, dances, and concerts (see Plates 15, 17, and 18).

These various folk arts have partly survived, but to a greater degree have been revived. Part of the motivation for the revival of cultural traits and crafts is to recall a time when life was simpler and presumably better, a time that may never have existed but that people nevertheless yearn for. Leo Marx has termed this the "pastoral ideal," "an urge to withdraw from civilization's growing power and complexity" to an unspoiled rural environment (1964:9), an ideal made concrete in Norway's skein of subsidized farms. "Improving" any country's past elevates its current status. We will see that the revival of folk music in Norway easily fits Kartomi's definition of a "nativistic music revival," an effort to revitalize a body of music perceived as threatened, for a mixture of "nationalistic, racial prestige, historical, nostalgic, touristic and artistic reasons" (1981:237–38). The amazing strength of the revival partly mirrors the urgency of Norwegian nationalism, employing folk materials as national symbols in Norway. The revival has also benefited from the combination of the longevity of Norwegians (including many fiddlers) and the speed of change from old-fashioned rural to prosperous modern state.

Music in Oral Tradition in Early Norway

The first evidence concerning music in the land that would become Norway comes from archaeology, iconography, and medieval sagas. Among the elaborate carvings adorning the stave churches are stylized depictions of harps and *lur*s (straight trumpets, in recent centuries made of wood and used for signaling and herding). Old Norse literature mentions two bowed stringed instruments, *fidla* (fiddle) and *gigja* (perhaps rebec), whose precise identity remains uncertain, though the terms are coupled often enough to suggest strongly that these were two different instruments. One saga describes frenzied dancing, drinking, and carousing accompanied by a harp, the most common instrument in these epics (and which remained in use as a dance instrument in a few places into the 1800s). The general attitude expressed in this ancient literature toward instrumentalists was and remains a common one in many parts of the world: the profession was needed, but its practitioners were of low status (Grinde 1991:10).

Quite a few other instruments either antedate the violin or arrived in Norway at about the same time. The goat's horn *(bukkehorn)*, perhaps with a few fingerholes, has an obvious pastoral connection. Other instruments whose primary use seems to have been passing time for herders in mountain pastures include the jaw harp, bone flutes (ancient), fairy flute *(tussefløyte,* one of several recorder relatives; in Norway from the 1600s), regional analogs of the clarinet and, of special interest, the willow bark flute *(seljefløyte).* In the spring, when the sap was rising, youngsters would gently separate the bark from a small branch, insert a carved handle just far enough to go under half of the only hole piercing the bark, then use this overblown tube until the bark dried out. This instrument survived as a toy, then became progressively rarer as whittling became a less-common hobby (Ledang 1990:116). Since this temporary instrument is neither mentioned much in literature nor depicted in iconography, we do not know how old or common it was.

Another widespread early instrument, the *langeleik,* a rectangular plucked dulcimer roughly a century older than the violin in Norway, has one melody string and six or seven others used as drones. It was formerly an important dance instrument. Its once-extensive geographical range has shrunk to the central valley of Valdres and surroundings, but now the *langeleik* is popular among urban folk-music enthusiasts.

Most of these instruments were intimately connected with farm and *seter* (mountain pasture) life of the past. Their various functions in that context no longer exist. Today, they occupy a particularly esoteric corner of the folk music revival and, in the larger contests, share a bracket (i.e., contest subdivision) entitled "older folk music instruments." Other, rarer folk instruments neither withstood the test of time nor aroused the interest of revivalists; these are listed in Aksdal's thesis (1982). Of course, several instruments that we associate primarily with art music were used to some extent in oral tradition; notable is the clarinet, which was common in the nineteenth century in many parts of rural Norway.

Vocal music in oral tradition once was vigorous, and featured considerable variety, though perhaps less than in many other countries in Europe. Lullabies *(bånsull),* with generally restricted ranges and few musical ideas, were the simplest genre. The younger of two types of *stev* (short, squarely phrased songs) included four lines of poetry in two nearly identical couplets, set to archaic melodies (often pentatonic). Folk ballads survived until recently in Telemark. The commonest vocal genre, religious folk song, reflects strong religious movements that swept Norway during the eighteenth and nineteenth centuries. Much of this genre's vitality results from the extraliturgical use of religious song in the home (Sevåg 1980:324). The most exuberant complex of genres centered on the *lokk,* herding or stock-summoning songs often starting with shouts and continuing with rhythmically free and melodically extravagant melismas. The *huving* was a long-distance call to people, and the *laling* a *huving* featuring the syllable "la," frequently short and antiphonal. There seems always to have been much overlap between vocal and instrumental folk music. Many Hardanger fiddle tunes take a *stev* as their point of departure, and many a fiddle tune intended for listening *(lydarslått)* for either type of fiddle is based on a melody that began life as a religious tune, lullaby, or *lokk.* And dance tunes could be sung using conventional sets of nonsense syllables when instruments were absent; this practice is called *tralling.* Today, the contexts that once nourished most genres of vocal folk music are gone. These genres survive at many contests in another esoteric specialists' competition bracket, that entitled *kveding* (an older term that includes singing and chanting; a *kvede* is a sung poem or lay).

The modern violin entered Norway during the later 1600s, and was enormously popular in rural areas by the early 1700s (Aksdal 1982:46–47). The Hardanger fiddle, generally believed today to be a Norwegian development of the violin employing sympathetic strings, may be of similar age in Norway, though solid evidence reaches back only into the 1750s (Aksdal 1982:53–58). Our knowledge of fiddlers and the music they played is slender, but provocative, for centuries before our own.

In the absence of a substantial art music establishment, the official town musician *(stadsmusikant)* and church organist (possibly the same person) plied his composite trade at the cultivated end of musical life from the seventeenth well into the nineteenth century (most "serious" music was in one way or another connected with the church). The town musician had the duty and the right to provide instrumental music for public and private festivities of all kinds in and around town. The population was small, and distances large and frequently hard to traverse. In order to begin to patch together an income, the musician would have to play for anyone who lived within a reasonable distance from his base in a town. However, he earned much of his income away from home, through licensing local fiddlers that he might have helped train and certainly would have chosen carefully. According to Sevåg and Sæta, the town musician needed to locate and recruit fiddlers who had solid technique and who commanded both a general modern functional repertoire and local favorite tunes (1992:36). The licensing system reached into even remote mountain valleys by the middle of the eighteenth century. Then, in 1800, a royal decree disallowed the creation of new official musicians in rural areas, so that the institution died out in the countryside along with its practitioners. Only a very few of the later licensed fiddlers were sufficiently important to local traditions for their names to be remembered today in tune titles. Sevåg and Sæta mention two fiddlers from the Gudbrandsdal, Åslag Holen (1749–1838, known as "Gamel-Holin," meaning "Old Holin"), probably an official musician, and Ola Sjugurdsson Skaar (1773–1863, known as "Gamel-Skårin"), who must have been among the last fiddlers licensed (1992:38).

The licensing system provided a channel from cities that had some connection to the Continent to transmit music and violin technique to the most remote areas. We cannot know how efficiently this worked overall or how the strength of these channels varied from one place to another or over time. A licensed fiddler in a thinly populated area cannot have been a full-time musician, and the demands of farming, smithing, or another profession must frequently have kept him from playing for events in his musical fiefdom. Also, plenty of fiddling went on that was not for pay, and thus was not subject to regulation. Finally, certain venues were difficult or impossible to keep under official control; the regional markets, for example, were among the main places where fiddlers met and exchanged tunes. It is probable that the institution of licensing brought some art music performance techniques from town to countryside, offered musicians exposure to local styles other than their own, and encouraged the spread of tunes. Perhaps most important, this system must have contributed to the establishment of cadres of skilled musicians in rural areas and to standards for their performance and behavior, even though these musicians almost always remained semiprofessional and part-time.

Nineteenth- and Early Twentieth-Century Fiddling and Fiddlers

The richest period in the development of Norwegian instrumental folk music began in the late eighteenth century and extended through the middle of the nineteenth century. (The twentieth century is primarily one of revival and consolidation, though growth continues in certain ways.) Surviving evidence from past centuries—especially the nineteenth century—is fairly plentiful, but often disjunct, imprecise, or for other reasons difficult to evaluate. Important fiddlers, often with direct lines of transmission to today's best players, are cited in local records and in stories which freely mix fact and legend. Also, while music from this period is preserved in over two dozen handwritten notebooks, almost none of these were by fiddlers who are now considered historically important (exceptions discussed below). The notebooks have been ignored by most scholars because they seem to belong to neither the world of art music nor that of folk music. But that situation is instructive too: it illustrates a time when these domains of music were less separate than they are today.

The oldest surviving music notebook, kept by Peter Bang of Christiania (as Oslo was called for centuries), was begun in 1679, though two-thirds of the book belongs to the eighteenth century. It is in a tablature that suggests use for lute or guitar, whereas most later notebooks are clearly for violin. Authors of most notebooks from the 1700s lived in the "big" cities of Trondheim and Christiania, and so emphasize fashionable and figure-oriented urban dances. In the early 1800s, the number of notebooks increases; most of these continue to center on figure dances. Around the middle of the nineteenth century, we witness two important, linked developments. Some of the notebooks are now by fiddlers in smaller towns (most from Sør-Trøndelag, the province stretching south from Trondheim), and the number of genres and even specific tunes still in oral tradition today goes up swiftly. Charts classifying the musical contents of twenty seven of these collections by genre, compiled by the scholar who has worked the most with these compilations, Bjørn Aksdal (1988:53–54), illustrate those trends in detail. Dance tune genres which Aksdal joins under the rubric *mote* (eighteenth-century fashionable)—minuet, polonaise, and gavotte—become rare after around 1820. Another set of genres, including the *feier* (in duple time), *engelsk* or *englis* (English, in triple time), and certain other figure dances (e.g., quadrille and reel) flourish from the late 1700s to mid-1800s.

Three of the four genres that are the core of those that today constitute *gammaldans* (old dance) entered this manuscript repertoire during the nineteenth century. The *reinlender* (Rhineländer) and mazurka appear regularly in Norwegian music notebooks starting in the 1860s. The case of the polka is more involved. A number of musically compatible duple-time genres are considered together today as polka variants; they arrived separately, but are close to interchangeable today. These include the gallop (originally and in these notebooks *gallopade*, arriving in the 1830s), *hamborgar* (also quite early), polka (a little later), and schottische (*skotsk*, latest in this group). Over time, each major geographical—and stylistic—area settled on one of the titles, so that the *skotsk* is danced in the Gudbrandsdal, the *hamborgar* in the West, and the gallop in the Røros area, although the dance steps are very similar and tune travel between areas (and thus between genre designations) is frequent (see the discussion of *gammaldans* in Chapter 7). Borrowing tunes between genres is common. A melody called a *reinlender* in one book may appear as a polka elsewhere. And this process can allow a good tune to outlive a dated dance genre: many *engelsk* tunes were reincarnated as waltzes.

The waltz is both the oldest and among the younger *gammaldans* genres. Waltzes were first danced in Norway in the late 1700s, and quickly became popular and frequently anthologized in music notebooks. The genre lost some of its popularity to other *gammaldans* genres during the nineteenth century. It changed gradually; the original type, by century's end called the *gammalvals,* is very different from the Strauss-type waltz, now the most common type, which arrived in the 1870s and 1880s. The later waltz is less rhythmically dense, has longer strains, and was frequently "texted" (given a text, sometimes temporarily).

The production of manuscript books waned around the turn of the twentieth century. One cause of this was the inexpensive printing methods, another the discouraging of fiddling during religious upheavals, particularly in the 1880s, a time when many fiddlers laid down their instruments.

The evidence concerning when certain genres arrived in rural Norway is generally straightforward and reliable, because these were originally fashionable pan-European social dances, likely to be copied when first encountered. Also, many of these dances were probably learned from notes, so that the written page conveys much about what was heard. Certain caveats follow naturally from the nature of the evidence. The few dozen notebooks that survive constitute only a small statistical base, and their geographic distribution is uneven. Many music notebooks are from Sør-Trøndelag, none is from the Gudbrandsdal, and just one, from about 1900, is from the West. As a result, our dating for the first area is far more reliable than for elsewhere. Patterns of commerce and communication were especially good in the area that produced most of the music notebooks, which leaves open the possibility that given genres of music may have entered general use somewhat or even very much later in other parts of rural Norway.

The notebooks are of less help in tracing genres and tunes that originated in Norway. A fiddler's notebook(s) may have complemented parts of his repertoire that were in local oral tradition and did not need to be written down. The Trøndelag form of the triple-time genre that now dominates *folkemusikk*, the *pols* (*polsdans* or *polskdands* in these compilations), entered manuscript notebooks in strength only in the 1830s, but must have flourished vigorously in oral tradition much earlier. It is, or course, quite valuable to be able to extend the history of many of today's tunes back as far as the first notebook in which they were anthologized, even if we are left wondering how long a tune existed prior to that initial notation. *Pols* and other genres that today are classified as *folkemusikk* are freely mixed with *gammaldans* and earlier genres in these books, underlining the fact that these classifications are twentieth-century constructs. It is also interesting to see a *halling* or two in notebooks from an area where that dance no longer is regularly performed (see discussion of the genre below in Chapter 7).

The aid these notebooks offer in documenting idiolects (individuals' repertoires and styles), performance practices, and the general history of style is also limited. Was a given notebook the performer's only one, or just the only one of his that survived? Some transcriptions may be descriptive, the inclusive type of tune representation that scholars like to produce. But more were probably prescriptive, giving the performer enough to go on, but not cluttering the page with elements of style that permeated his repertoire, elements that he could take for granted. Articulation marks, ornaments, and double stops are uncommon in the manuscripts I have seen. Some tunes include bowings, but more do not. Staccato markings, the commonest articulation given in these books, are not part of modern fiddle styles, except when *hallings* are played in certain districts. Ornaments marked are generally limited to some grace notes (spread fairly evenly through post-1850 genres) and far fewer markings of "tr.," certainly sometimes meaning trill, but perhaps on other occasions referring instead to mordents or more complex turns. All of today's styles are much more heavily ornamented than were tunes in these eighteenth- and nineteenth-century manuscripts. Were earlier styles simply less ornate? I suspect this is true—at least for the schooled fiddlers who kept notebooks—but not to the degree that the manuscript evidence suggests. Multiple stops are also very different in these books from today. While modern practice in most areas emphasizes either drones (very rare in the manuscripts) or occasional double stops constructed on drone principles (see anthology of examples for this book), the rare double stops in nineteenth-century sources that I have examined are nearly all convenient harmonic enhancements.[2]

Much has been written about nineteenth- and early twentieth-century Norwegian fiddlers, since to be interested in Norwegian fiddle tunes has long meant to trace paths of transmission, that is, likely lines of descent of players' tunes and styles. Indeed, well over half of Norwegian fiddle tunes are referred to in a verbal formula with this shape: (name of) genre, in the manner of (name of a prestigious fiddler of the past). Mention of that fiddler's name plugs a tune into a pedigree of local fiddlers, and thus celebrates local identity. For example, "Springleik etter Erling Kjøk" is named for the father of Knut Kjøk, one of the top currently active fiddlers and one of my principal consultants. Father and son live in Lom, a small community in the North Gudbrandsdal that has produced an astonishingly large number of highly skilled performers. Erling Kjøk learned from, among others, Ola Gjerdet (1871–1952) and Ola Moløkken (1871–1957). Gjerdet learned from Else-Lars (Lars Kjørren, 1824–94) and Per Spelmann (Per Kringelhaugen, 1830–1907). (Many of the most famous fiddlers were known by nicknames. The names in parentheses were their legal names.) Per Spelmann was the principal musical heir of Fel-Jakup (1821–76), whose enormous talent and extensive travels made him the most famous player of the fiddle from his day to ours. Fel-Jakup first learned from Gamel-Sjugurd (1810–89), who was the son of Lars Hjeltartrædet, who played widely, without a license, near the end of the era of the town musician. Since Gamel-Sjugurd lived long enough to teach Ola Moløkken, Kjøk's fiddling reaches back along at least two potent lines of tradition within Lom (and neighboring Skjåk, legally part of Lom through 1863). Today's young champions from the Gudbrandsdal exhibit a large influence of Knut Kjøk, thus of Erling Kjøk, and thus of a stellar network of past fiddlers whose collective biography at once limns and enhances the history of this community.

Contemporary scholars have devoted much energy to tracing such lineages of transmission. Their work has been fueled by a wealth of evidence and anecdote collected by amateur historians—all enthusiastic, and many careful—from within the folk music milieu. In fact, there is no clear dividing line between scholar and amateur or between researcher and performer in the world of Norwegian folk music. The sample lineage in the previous paragraph draws on (and simplifies) work done at different times and with varying levels of expertise. One source is recent: folk music historian Olav Sæta's elegant and meticulous description of the history of fiddling in Oppland, the province containing the Gudbrandsdal (Sevåg and Sæta 1992:12–25). The other, composite source is older: dozens of short articles recounting facts and legends concerning this community's fiddlers published over decades in *Spelemannsbladet,* the journal published by the National Fiddlers' Association. I cannot reproduce all such information. That would require several books, which ought indeed to be written, but by Norwegians.

Biographies of fiddlers have also appeared in a profusion of semischolarly local publications. These come in all shapes and sizes, generally in modest press runs (or photocopies, these days) and with limited distribution. Most copies end up on local bookshelves, and are occasionally consulted, but they are more important as testimony, as physical demonstration that a given local tradition is sufficiently old, complex, and substantial to inspire scholarship. One work of this kind is Tor Wigenstad's *Spellmenn og Folkemusikk i Dovre* ([after 1983]) a locally printed seventy-page pamphlet. Dovre, at a high elevation in the province of Oppland, is in a transitional folk music area, sharing genres and tunes with both the greater Gudbrandsdal and the far more distant Røros area, with which Dovre shares culture because of travel by people employed in mining in both areas. Wigenstad, a farmer *(bonde)* born in 1911, began playing the fiddle at age twelve, and taught himself to read music. His activities spanned both cultivated town music—he played violin in a string trio, string quartet, and a salon orchestra, and tuba in a brass band—and folk music, in which he was active as a solo fiddler and in the Dovre *Spelmannslag.* He composed the melody to Dovre's patriotic song, and transcribed some 600 tunes from local oral tradition.

Spellmenn og Folkemusikk i Dovre includes seventy of Wigenstad's skeletal transcriptions of tunes, the Dovre song, photographs, drawings, a poem dedicated to Wigenstad, and a variety of prose items. These range from miscellanea, including reproduced newspaper articles, a handful of legends, advice to beginners, and a page on folk music terminology, to the two most substantial sections, eight pages giving short biographies of twenty eight local fiddlers and seven pages on fiddlers from elsewhere who had visited and influenced Dovre's folk music community. Wigenstad devoted several paragraphs to the twelve oldest fiddlers, but just one to more recent figures. For instance, about a prominent fiddler his own age, he wrote:

> 24. *Pål E. Andgard born 1901*
> Brother of #23 [and #25]. He was a cottager [*småbruker*]. Pål played first violin in the Andgards Quartet. Pål was the best fiddler in Dovre when he was at the height of his abilities [*på topp*]. He had a large repertoire and a sure ear. His technique was quite good; he imparted much life to his fiddle and performance. Many of his tunes are transcribed. Pål played in the Dovre fiddle club for many years. He was a good and pious man with many friends.[3]

Just a decade later to appear, but very different in approach, is Frøydis Bjørnsmoen's *"'Puss-Jo,' en Bygdespellmans Liv og Musikk"* (1993). Bjørnsmoen wrote this while a high school student. She is an aspiring fiddler from the Rendal valley, in the north Østerdal, roughly three-fourths of the way from Oslo to Røros. This is in the broad district where *pols* types are played, but outside the immediate orbit of Røros. Frøydis is the daughter of Stein Bjørnsmoen, who fiddles in the A class (see Chap. 2 for description of classes), the only player from his area ever to rank that high (like Dovre, the Rendal is not a high-status fiddle area). Her essay is a laser-printed typescript; I obtained a copy of it while talking with her family at the 1993 National Fiddle Contest in Lillehammer.

However young its author, this small biography is a very fine example of modern scholarship. Bjørnsmoen's sources include local histories, archived field recordings, new interviews, and a classic regional folk music study, O. M. Sandvik's *Østerdalsmusikken* (1943). She supplements her prose with six photographs, one new transcription and a handful of photocopied ones (from Sandvik), and a cassette of tunes associated with Puss-Jo performed by her father (with her, in a few instances). The Bjørnmoens are indirect descendents of Puss-Jo (real name, Jon Simensen Søstu Mømb, 1851–1921; *puss* means "joker"). He was a shoemaker—and, in lean times, general hand-worker, as well as a guide for both cartographers and tourists—with nine children, five of whom emigrated to the United States. In this essay, we learn details of his work, character, and musical activities, which seem to have been typical of a solo fiddler. Apart from his notably puckish personality, the oddest thing about him was that he customarily borrowed, rather than brought, a fiddle to weddings and other jobs.

Histories of all Norwegian local fiddle traditions of any strength have been traced with enthusiasm by fiddlers and their fans.[4] The two sample studies cited treat local styles out of the mainstream, which is the triumvirate of styles from the Gudbrandsdal, the Røros area, and the West. Early figures in the development of these three styles, especially the first, are discussed in many miscellaneous sources, but especially thoroughly in widely scattered paragraphs in the *Spelemanns-blad*. The more famous the figure, the more extensive the body of oral-tradition anecdotes and the more energetically scholars and amateurs have pursued the historical facts. By making a composite of the many biographical sketches, it is possible to come up with a profile of a typical nineteenth- or early twentieth-century Norwegian player of the fiddle.

Nearly all of these fiddlers were male. Now and then one encounters a woman fiddler's name, notably Blind-Marit of North Sel in the Gudbrandsdal; because of her disability, she may have been allowed to pursue fiddling. I was told repeatedly that women didn't fiddle in the nineteenth century, or well into the twentieth, not so much because they were forbidden to as that they followed tradition and seldom could escape the demands of sex-linked patterns of labor. Men worked mightily, mostly outdoors, but seasonal weather patterns and other factors on farms and at sea determined that much work would be in great bursts of energy, all-out efforts that were short (such an effort is characteristic enough to have earned its own name: *skippertak*.) After such strenuous work there was leisure to recover—and perhaps to fiddle. Women, on the other hand, worked steadily in the home for long hours, and couldn't get away for the weekend here and there that was so important for fiddlers to remain in contact with one another. Men traveled to regional markets, common through the middle of the nineteenth century, where fiddling was central to entertainment. And there were very few role models for a woman fiddler. A few consultants added that fiddling's earlier connection with carousing helped keep it a male activity. However, women were often part of lines of transmission, because they sometimes would *trall* dance tunes, that is, sing them employing certain conventional patterns of nonlexical syllables.

Many fiddlers came from families in which fiddlers were already present. This was not a deeding of occupation as in medieval guilds, but rather was connected with the circumstance that there was a fiddle in the house, that this activity was not frowned upon in that family (as it was in many), and that talent might be inherited and was apt to flower in a musically active household. Most of the top fiddlers started early, unsurprisingly. Many began to fiddle using homemade instruments, often of their own construction. For example, Lom's Ola Moløkken made a fiddle at age eight, then got his first "real one" when he was fifteen (*Spelemannsbladet* 1957 [1–2]: 6). Many fiddlers could read music, but many could not; neither alternative seems to have been considered better. To read was to be educated; not to read, yet to be accomplished, was impressive, too. Most fiddlers composed, though a few did this rarely or not at all. Many, many had huge repertoires: several could "go all night without repeating."

Many, perhaps most, fiddlers were small farmers (farming did not become the part-time occupation that it generally is today all at once). For instance, a farmer and important fiddler in the West, Anders Reed of Nordfjord (1849–1924), was said to have one horse, three cows, six sows, fifty to sixty fruit trees, and the income from playing over 300 weddings, each four or five days long (*Spelemannsbladet* 1960 [11–12]: 8–12). Fiddlers performed, generally solo, at dances at summer pastures, at other festivities, at markets, and especially at weddings. The vast majority were as broadly based in music as there was an opportunity to be in their community. They did not set out to be specialists in *folk* fiddling; rather they were the violin players in communities where some classical or band music might be played (and they probably participated in this), but in which oral tradition music constituted most of what was available and performed. A fair number of fiddlers played some kind of horn too; military music helped in the development of marches for weddings, and in some communities left fiddle tunes in keys such as B♭ that were awkward for the violin. Some fiddlers, like Fel-Jakup, showed the influence of art music through their affection for virtuosic command of upper positions, though most must have stayed in first position, as most do today.

Most of the best-known fiddlers traveled a great deal through much of the fiddle area. That Lars Tomasgård (1865–1946) of the Hornindal (in the West) stayed home was considered exceptional. He was known for his hospitality, and fiddlers from elsewhere visited often (Håkon Gausemel, in *Spelemannsbladet* 1955 [1–2]: 11–12). Fiddlers routinely learned tunes from friends living in other parts of the country. We cannot know just how much a learned tune was recast by its new performer, but some style transfer must have taken place as tunes were passed around. New genres of dance music arrived regularly, and were embraced swiftly. In general, it seems that these fiddlers, who had little access to musical variety in their daily lives, were eager to experiment, to seek out new repertoire and new influences, and in every way possible to expand their musical experience. Such an attitude today would result in stylistic incoherence, indeed in sensory overload, but in the much more compact musical world of nineteenth-century rural Norway, embracing variety and novelty was necessary to ensure vitality. I should note also that some Hardanger fiddle players concertized in the United States, and some players of both types of fiddle who moved to America came back to Norway, either for good or to visit.

There were always good fiddlers and better ones, and a competitive attitude was far from rare. This seems rather un-Norwegian, especially for the time, but these fiddlers were unusual individuals to start with. As instrumentalists, they were specialists. When fiddlers were together, comparison was inevitable, especially if an audience were present. Indeed, some form of competition helped prospective employers decide whom to hire to play at a wedding, for example. Two common ways to say that a fiddler was very skilled were that "no one could beat him" and that other champion fiddlers refused to play when he was around (see, e.g., *Spelemannsbladet* 1952 [6]: 9). The first formulation suggests an informal contest, the second the avoidance of one. Many of the prominent fiddlers whose activities spanned the turn of the century would participate quite willingly in the earliest formal folk music contests. In fact, we shall see that one of the central problems of the modern folk music world is how to conduct contests which minimize comparing individuals directly.

The great fiddlers could do amazing things. Some feats came with

the job, like remembering enormous repertoires and physically holding up through the several days of a wedding. But romantic accounts
supplemented these accomplishments with additional improbable,
even magical feats. These illustrate the power of music and of fiddlers,
and honor those fiddlers. For instance, it is said that the the violin of
Magne Maurset (1824–1915, from the West) fell into a river on his
way to a wedding. He fished it out, quickly got it into shape, and
played anyway (*Spelemannsbladet* 1954 [5–6]: 21–22). Fel-Jakup,
perhaps the most traveled of nineteenth-century fiddlers—he regularly
toured in the Gudbrandsdal, North Østerdal, Trøndelag, Møre og
Romsdal, and Nordfjord for some forty years (Sevåg and Sæta
1992:40)—attracted the most legends. During one visit to the autumn
market in Romsdal, a fiddler challenged him. This upstart was good,
but had no hope against the (apparently superhuman) abilities of Fel-
Jakup. Once a jealous fiddler wished to sabotage Fel-Jakup, and hid
his fiddle. Fel-Jakup then went into the kitchen and improvised a
fiddle from parts of a cod. In another tale, the son of religious parents
became a fan of Fel-Jakup, and wished to invite him to play at their
home. The boy's parents swore that there would not be one bow-
stroke in their house. But Fel-Jakup came anyway, and "with mild,
stirring tones pierced their murky, pietistic hearts" (Turtenøygard
1973:8–9).

    This last story concerns the conflict of fiddling (and associated
dancing and possible other carousing) and the vigorous religious
movements of the 1880s and 1890s: "To be a fiddler in the worst
period of the pietistic movement was not very pleasant. Fiddles
and fiddlers were looked down on. They often had to play in secret,
for fiddling was extremely sinful in the eyes of many gloomy
people" (Bjørndal 1949:13). It was believed by many that the fiddle
was indeed "satanic, and that fiddlers were destined for the fiery fur-
nace" (*"heiteste heite"*; *Spelemannsbladet* 1950 [1]: 4). Some fiddles
were burned, and many more retired, particularly by older fiddlers. It
is also said that in turn-of-the-century Nordmøre, fiddles were sometimes hung in doors to ward off traveling preachers. But the overall
effect of the religious movement was to discourage secular folk music
and folk dancing, an effect particularly strong in the mountains of the
Southwest. With many fiddles silent, and others busy with the "new"
dances of the nineteenth century, *folkemusikk* was imperiled, though
less so in the fiddle area than where the Hardanger fiddle was played.
This sets the stage for a folk revival centered initially on the Hardanger fiddle.

CHAPTER TWO

Reviving *Folkemusikk*

Early Folk Music Contests

The "normal" fiddle was a late and very gradual entry into the contest system that sustains it so well today. The very first formal folk music contest in Norway, organized in 1881 by the Norwegian Tourist Board and the Norwegian Youth Organization *(Noregs Ungdomslag),* was for the *lur,* a wooden brass instrument with roots in the Bronze Age or earlier, and other folk music instruments that had fallen almost entirely out of use. The next contests would instead assemble a few dozen players of the Hardanger fiddle, and arouse sufficient interest among participants and listeners to become regularly recurring events. These first fiddle contests were held in the mountainous province of Telemark, then and now the physical and spiritual center of Hardanger fiddle territory, and an area in which older secular music in oral tradition was very much threatened both by natural turnover of repertoire (and of genres) and by religion. One or two players of the fiddle would attend early twentieth-century contests now and again and would be granted a competition bracket, but there could be no doubt that these were Hardanger fiddle events. Contests continued at the rate of one or a few a year but did not grow significantly larger until after World War II. The National Fiddlers' Association would crystallize around these contests in 1923. The first section of this chapter concerns the early fiddle contests, which, although explicitly for the Hardanger fiddle, had an incalculable effect on the subsequent history of all Norwegian folk music.

The very first contest, organized over a hundred years ago and centered on the lur, may be dismissed fairly quickly. It was organized by interests one of which—likely the initiator of the event—was outside the folk music milieu. The Norwegian Tourist Board was eager to add traditional culture to the nature-based attractions of fishing for salmon, boating through fjords, and skiing. The board staged the contest at a upland summer pasture *(sæter)* near the border between Hallingdal and Valdres. Citizens of both valleys supplemented the tourists in the audience, and were intrigued. The older instruments employed doubtless presented enough variety to keep the audience's attention for a few hours, but this event must have been more a display of antique exotica than a true contest, though the judges took their task seriously *(Spelemannsbladet* 1960 [11–12]: 13). To hold a contest at all would seem to run counter to a central value of Norwegian culture, egalitarianism, and the complementary village shunning of pride, of thinking oneself one iota better than others for any reason. But attitudes were loosening, glacially but steadily. Contests for marksmanship and for ski-jumping were held at about this same time. When fiddlers began to compete, they may have had as inspiration or partial justification for their participation the long history of fiddle contests in the United States. Many fiddlers had emigrated, and some had come back, either to stay or for visits. A fair number of Hardanger fiddle players born in Norway competed extensively in contests in their adopted country, and brought news of these events home (see, e.g., *Spelemannsbladet* 1952 [6]: 6).

The first folk music contest conceived in a rural area on the local level was held at 2 P.M. on July 8, 1888, in Grivi, Bø, Telemark. A series of brief articles in the *Spelemannsblad* called it "the first [folk music] contest in the land," "something entirely new" (Nordbø 1952:7, 1955:24, 1963:27). The idea of holding this contest is said to have arisen in casual conversation between two prominent citizens of Bø, according to the son of one of them: "We have so many fiddlers in the village [*bygda*] and each wants to be the best. Shouldn't we hold a contest to see who's the best?" (Nordbø 1952:7). Whether or not arranging the contest was partly inspired by the lur-centered event mentioned above, or by the popularity of fiddle contests in the United States, or by any other events outside Bø, Nordbø's formulation associates this contest with his own home. A flyer dated June 5 was addressed to those who wished to "compete for the championship on Hardanger fiddle." Contestants were asked to register by the end of June, just a week before the contest took place. Such a short span of time between advertisement and event, at a date when communications were much less swift than today, underlines that this Hardanger fiddle contest was conceived as a local event.

There were eight fiddlers at the contest, and fourteen at one held in the same place the following year. Most contestants and judges were from Bø or its immediate environs, though one judge at each contest and a fiddler or two came from Lunde (sixteen kilometers south of Bø) and from Seljord (twenty kilometers west); no participant came from farther than thirty-five kilometers. In each of these early contests in Bø, competition fit into a single afternoon. Festivities followed, including a dance; this supplement to these and later contests would always be as important to both fiddlers and audience as the formal events that took place earlier in the day. During the contest itself, each fiddler played five tunes, one of which had to be "Nordfjorden." Five was the number of the day: there were five judges, and five prizes. The judging was far from unanimous. Two judges had one fiddler at the top, two other judges voted for someone else, and the fifth judge had his own favorite. And members of the audience didn't agree with the judges or with one another: a discussion after the results were announced was so heated that friendships were imperiled (Nordbø 1952:7). The high level of controversy must have resulted from several factors, including differing personal taste, networks of personal loyalties, and the probability that the fiddlers played in several not entirely comparable local styles. A few dozen kilometers may not seem like a great distance, but in Norway it is enough to signal the possibility of distinctly different fiddle styles, especially in the Hardanger fiddle area.

The next folk music contest in Norway was sponsored by a local fiddle club, the Vestmanalaget in Bergen, the day before and in connection with celebrating Constitution Day, the 17th of May, in 1896. The fiddle club sent out a call to country folk *(landsfolk)* who played Hardanger fiddle; twenty signed up. This big-city event focusing on rural culture juxtaposed rustic types in homespun, carrying lunch baskets decorated with *rosemaling,* with ladies wearing hats in the latest Paris fashion (Jerdal 1965:3). According to one Professor Hannaas, who was among the many urban intellectuals attending this contest, "The first contest in Vestmannalaget marked the beginning of a new era for national fiddling. In many villages the [Hardanger] fiddle had mostly gone out of use, replaced by the accordion. But now the musicians will redeem their [Hardanger] fiddles from the neglect into which they had fallen. And the young will sit at the feet of the old, and begin to absorb their ancestors' tunes" (Jerdal 1965:4). This mixture of fact and romantic enthusiasm accurately reflects the tone that the swiftly burgeoning revival would assume.

The winner of this contest in Bergen was Sjur Helgeland, from Vossestranden, over a hundred kilometers away. Bergen was both a cosmopolitan center and a intermediate point for emigration. It was the home of urban citizens for whom *folkemusikk* had a romantic association, and also housed many recently rural individuals who had grown up with music in oral tradition. It was a transportation hub and a destination with a profusion of attractions to supplement those of a fiddle contest, and was the home of a good solid core of folk music performers and enthusiasts. This contest was held annually through 1914. The field of competitors, although just twenty the first year, was forty-eight the next time, and kept growing. The third meeting, in 1898, added fourteen competitors dancing the *halling,* a male solo display dance, and the Hardanger fiddle–district forms of the oldest vital triple-time dance genre, there named the *springar,* gained its own bracket in 1908. Jerdal cites these famous Hardanger fiddle players as participating over the years: "Ola Mosafinn from Voss, Olav Mo from Valdres, Eivind Aakhus from Setesdal, Arne Bjørndal from Hosanger . . . Torkjell Haugerud from Telemark, Sjur Eldegard from Sogn, Lorents Hop from Fana, Kjetil Flatin from Telemark, Olav Okshovd from Valdres, Halldor Heland from Hardanger, Torfinn Litlere from Sunnfjord, Gunnulf Borgen from Telemark, Jon Roseldi [Rosenlid] from Nordfjord, Henrik Gjellesvik from Haus, Sevat Sataøen from Hallingdal, Per Berge from Voss, and Anders Olsson Viki from Sunnfjord," with all but three men in this distinguished list present at the first event in 1896 (1965:4). The wide geographic and stylistic range represented at the 1897 contest made it plausible in Jerdal's eyes to call the event a "National Fiddle Contest," though this was a characterization rather than an actual title (1965:4). The term "National Fiddle Contest" at first represented an ideal and goal. It would gradually become more accurate in a literal sense, even though the "normal" fiddle—and thus over half of Norway—was either unrepresented or extremely underrepresented for over half of the century.

Contests developed in two directions during the 1890s–early 1920s, neither of which was systematically planned or tidy in result. One was to hold more and more local contests, the other to aim at one central annual event that would represent the fiddling of the whole country, a true National Fiddle Contest. Nearly all of this activity was in the Hardanger fiddle areas, and, when the two fiddle types met, the Hardanger fiddle was in control. That is not the least bit surprising, and it inevitably caused some tension—even acrimony. One Knut Vemøy spoke for the fiddle constituency in complaints after a 1902 contest in Ålesund, on the northwest coast, in the broad area in which both Hardanger fiddle and fiddle are played. The idea behind the contest was to give older *national* music "new stimulation," but, according to Vemøy, the judges "couldn't play much themselves, and knew even less about our old national music on normal fiddle" [than they knew about the portion of this music proper to the Hardanger fiddle] (Vemøy 1991:194). He continued airing his dissatisfaction after the next contest in Ålesund, in 1903: "It was obvious, especially in light of the judges' written comments, that the Hardanger fiddle and art performance, as that style has been developed in recent times," [was favored to the detriment of others] (Aarset and Flem 1991b:208). Knut Stafset (mentioned above for his manuscript collection) also complained about "modern art style" triumphing in contests in Ålesund (Aarset and Flem 1991b:209).

What was the "art style" provoking this swirl of controversy? Two meanings are available: art style on the normal fiddle (i.e., bearing significant classical violin influence), and art style on the Hardanger fiddle. In the middle of the nineteenth century, certain Hardanger fiddle players, with the legendary Myllarguten ("The Miller Boy," Torgeir Augundson, 1801–72) in the vanguard, moved their performance venue away from dances (and possible association with sin) into the concert hall. Other fiddlers continued to perform in more traditional settings, maintaining functional links with dance and other festivities. When in the 1880s and 1890s especially harsh religious movements attacked fiddling—with particular success in large parts of what happened to be Hardanger fiddle territory—these fiddlers responded in several very different ways. More than a few came genuinely to believe that fiddling was wrong, and either put their instruments in storage or, in more than a few cases, destroyed them. Others must have knuckled under to community pressure and quit too, whatever their own convictions. But another very talented group joined with Myllarguten and other concert players, and drew the teeth of fanatical critics by changing the function of their playing. Separating their music from dancing removed much of the stigma that had been attached to fiddling, but it also had an effect on musical style. Fiddling for attentive listeners invites, indeed demands more formal musical complexity than is appropriate at a dance, when listeners must devote a portion of their attention to their own physical activities. And aesthetic considerations reinforced the move toward complexity caused by this change in function. Much Hardanger fiddle music is built in two-measure units that vary incrementally (see #102 in the Tune Anthology for a sample modern performance). This way of putting a piece together, which certainly predates Myllarguten and "modern art style" Hardanger fiddle performance, equally certainly makes these tunes suitable for artistic elaboration.

We do not have the judges' commentary from the 1902 Ålesund contest that Vemøy said showed a prejudice toward art-oriented and Hardanger fiddle performance. However, the judges' comments for the first contests in Bø were preserved, and do suggest evaluation by an art standard. I will list the adjectives and phrases that translate gracefully. A few comments (both pro and con) could be applied readily in evaluation of either dance tunes or ones meant primarily for listening. These include criticisms such as unenergetic *(for lite drift)*, incoherent rhythm *(meningsløs takt)*, flat or slack *(slapt)*, unsteady *(ustødt)*, unaffected *(ukunstlet)*, and, on the positive side, natural *(naturlig)*, confident *(bestemt)*, and appealing *(tiltalende)*. But many other remarks may be addressed more specifically to art-oriented playing. These include fully worked-out *(fyldig)*, clean *(rent)*, difficult or intricate *(vrien)*, bow too heavy *(for tung bue)*, polished *(færdig)*, naive *(naivt)*, and meager content *(fattig indhold)* (Nordbø 1955:24–25). The winner, Lars Fykerud, earned many of the positive remarks in the latter set, even though he "worried too much over small details" *(gnager for meget på småteri)*. An art focus was indeed in place. However logical the reasons behind this, it would keep prizes from going to any more traditional fiddler, that is, one whose playing had been formed primarily with the needs of dancers in mind.

These conflicts in how one ought to judge fiddling, on aesthetic qualities versus older functional grounds, and the growing tension between Hardanger fiddle and fiddle, are far from the only features of the current Norwegian folk music milieu that in some measure date back to the very earliest contests. Other critical inheritances include the negotiation of local, regional, and national orientations; the association of fiddling with nationalism (and with romanticism); the privileging of some districts (such as Telemark) rather than an egalitarian approach to regional styles; the decision whether especially threatened folk music styles were therefore particularly valuable or worthy of institutional support; the inclusion of both music and dance in contests; the balance between competition during the day and tradition-oriented entertainment (including dancing) in the evening; and many other details of how contests are put together and how judging ought to be performed. Even the lur and other passé instruments would be back, though not for a while, and in a very limited role. As early as 1896, the stage was set for the formation of a coherent, centralized folk music organization and a true national contest.

The Hardanger Fiddle, National Romanticism, and the Young National Fiddlers' Association

Contests for the Hardanger fiddle continued to proliferate. As early as 1902 there were at least three, the one in Ålesund already mentioned, which was exceptional in that it had a few participants on the fiddle, and contests in Ål and in Oslo, which was in its last years of bearing the Danish name of Christiania. Oslo is physically in fiddle territory, but was (and to a great extent remains) a city of migrants from elsewhere in Norway. In the early part of the century, it was a Hardanger fiddle outpost hosting Hardanger fiddle contests.

As contests continued to be successful in both cities and villages, a handful of prominent and well-educated fiddlers came to believe that it would be worthwhile to create a national fiddlers' organization. A prospectus for such an umbrella organization, sent out in 1922, proposed three central goals: (1) to create better economic circumstances for fiddlers, that is, to work for better payment for village fiddlers working in their home districts, (2) to secure consistent regulations for judging and awarding prizes, and (3) "to make fiddle tunes [*slåtte-musikken*] better known among the general public in various ways" (Mæland 1973:32). These suggestions would be incorporated into the bylaws of the National Fiddlers' Association, which crystallized around these contests in 1923. The three goals work on graduated levels, the fiddler, the fiddle-based event celebrating folk music, and outreach, that is, bringing folk music to the general public. Improving the fiddler's income would prove to be impractical; folk fiddling as even a part-time profession became less and less tenable. But the two other goals—keeping contests and other fiddle events fair and attractive to participants, and fostering public interest in folk music—would remain at the center of the mission of the National Fiddler's Association.

This new national organization was at first quite fragile. Help from an older national organization was sought initially. Between the world wars, the National Fiddlers' Association was affiliated with the venerable Norwegian Youth Organization (Norsk Ungdomslag), which served the interests of young Norwegians, particularly those with rural backgrounds. This affiliation was not sought again when the National Fiddlers' Association was reconstituted after a hiatus caused by World War II. Finances in the early years were precarious, so much so that years passed without any sponsored activities. The youth and tenuous status of the National Fiddlers' Association encouraged a kind of unsystematic, open attitude. For instance, at the 1924 National Fiddle Contest, held in Molde, a prize for ensemble *(samspel)* playing went to a Hardanger fiddle and clarinet duet. The orchestral clarinet would soon join the accordion, guitar, and other relatively modern instruments (modern in folk music terms) in being banned from these events. These instruments certainly had been used in oral tradition extensively and for some time, but they partook of other traditions, too, and their existence was not in peril. But at the 1924 National Fiddle Contest, either the organizers were letting the participants decide what folk music included, or a tainted duet was considered better than none at all. And, in the years before the war, those who organized contests were welcomed into and encouraged to publicize through the National Fiddlers' Association. After the war, a more secure standing allowed a heavier hand to emerge: members were now forbidden to participate in unapproved events (Mæland 1973:33). In its early years, the National Fiddlers' Association was far too vulnerable to be restrictive in that way, but it served a need, and survived.

Arne Bjørndal, the president of the new organization, gave a speech in its first year to introduce the 1923 incarnation of what was now formally entitled the National Fiddle Contest. He presented folk music (by which he meant traditional fiddling) as threatened by foreign instruments and by mechanical, mongrelized music, and sorely in need of revitalization. He invoked tradition, nationalism, connections with other folk arts, the rural smallholder or cotter, and Norway's harsh but beautiful landscape, and asserted that "the tunes of the Hardanger fiddle are part of Norwegian history" (Mæland [1973]: 24–25).

We can't know how many of the few fiddlers in this nascent folk revival would have expressed themselves similarly. Bjørndal was self-educated along German lines, and his speech does seem to issue near-directly from Herder and Grimm, perhaps via Ludwig Lindeman, an early collector of Norwegian folk music (see Lindeman [1963]: 1–3, and Sandvik 1950:9–11 and 73–75).[1] Bjørndal was a scholar as well as a prominent Hardanger fiddle player: he served on the editorial board of early volumes of the largest collection of Norwegian folk music that has been produced, a multivolume set of transcriptions of

Hardanger fiddle tunes (Gurvin et al. 1958+). His opinions, whether or not widely held originally, were potent simply because he was influential.

Having a journal attached to the National Fiddlers' Association was envisioned as early as 1933. Two issues of the *Spelemannsblad* finally came out in 1941, and production resumed when the National Fiddlers' Association was reconstituted in 1946. The *Spelemannsblad* grew from a few mimeographed pages to thick issues printed regularly by 1950. Most of the space in each issue was filled with news of events—mostly contests—and profiles of respected performers. However, there is also evidence of attitudes which echo, elaborate, or harden those expressed decades earlier by Bjørndal.

The link between this folk music revival and national romanticism is illustrated especially clearly in poems printed in the *Spelemannsblad*. Several appeared in each issue through the mid-1950s; then they became progressively rarer. In the course of heaping praise on a fiddler or on a contest, these poems invariably conjoin fiddling with rural life and untamed nature. I will excerpt two poems that announce events. The first, "Prologue to the National Fiddle Contest in Oslo 27/10/1946," begins, "The boy with his little fiddle, at the foot of the wild waterfall," thus evoking a familiar folk figure, the *fossegrim*, the spirit that fiddles in its dwelling behind the waterfall. The author goes on repeatedly to connect Norwegian nature and Norwegian folk music (asserted to be Norwegian in content, rhythm, and sound), in fact using *norsk, nordmann,* or *Noreg* a total of eight times in a few dozen lines (Lilleaas 1947). Another, "Prologue to the Fiddlers' Meeting of 1948," includes these phrases: "From mysterious depths tones take form and life . . . Mountain and valley, deep blue waters, waterfall, creek and rivulet. . . . And the fiddler's soul holds in its embrace his home village's familiar *lur* and his homeland's name." Along the way, the author invokes the names of famous nineteenth-century Hardanger fiddle players such as Myllarguten and Mosafinn, and tosses in Ole Bull and Grieg for good measure (Hald 1950).

A series of articles printed in the *Spelemannsblad* during the early 1950s and bearing the collective title "What These Individuals Say about Folk Music Today" endorsed bits of Bjørndal's message. This comes as no surprise, since the opinions expressed belonged to art composers and other prominent individuals. The prevailing trend was constantly to praise the Hardanger fiddle, considered the most authentic folk instrument, to ignore or patronize the fiddle, and routinely to vilify the accordion. This last instrument was, after all, the one most strongly associated with the music that had largely supplanted *folkemusikk,* that is, *gammaldans* music. This struggle was fresh in the memory of many fiddlers. Also, although *gammaldans* has flourished throughout Norway, it has been especially vigorous where the fiddle is played.[2] This type of fiddle, despite its position as the main folk music instrument for half of Norway, was doubly tarred. It was not exclusively Norwegian, and it was perceived as an accomplice in the attack by the accordion and *gammaldans* on the Hardanger fiddle and *folkemusikk.*

The Hardanger fiddle–centric opinions of the leaders of the National Fiddlers' Association were shared by less-prominent members. A letter from one Johannes Skarprud entitled "Norwegian Folk Music," printed in the *Spelemannsblad* in 1951, conveniently gathers attitudes expressed piecemeal in the hundreds of pages surrounding it. (Skarprud [1874–1962] was a teacher and a booster of local culture in his home province of Telemark. He wrote a few books and poems, among these a song praising Telemark that remains in use).[3]

> Folk music is a true sapling of the Norwegian folk character. It is Norwegian nature in its changing moods, with its mountainous country and sheltered valleys, wild waterfalls and still, dreamy fjords. It is the whisper of wind through leaves and cowbells ringing in mountain meadows and in home pastures that give melody to folk music.
>
> Such a music can't flourish in the city or on the plains. Echos can't ring there, or waterfalls exult. And the spirits that fiddle beneath the waterfalls can't teach young lads there.
>
> The *flatfela* [flat fiddle, i.e., violin] lacks sympathetic strings, which themselves have tonal value. Folk music can't find enough room on it. It's only the Myllargut-fiddle [remember, Myllarguten was the most famous nineteenth-century player of the Hardanger fiddle] that can do the job. It has the Norwegian resonance. . . .
>
> The Hardanger fiddle has more and subtler tones than any other instrument if one has the gift to play it correctly. A Myllargut, Gibøen, Flatland, Helgeland, Løndal, Haugerud, Ørpen, Fykerud, Borgen, and several contemporary players such as Roheim, Haugen, Manheim and others can interpret our rich and large body of tunes, a repertoire so rich that our greatest composers, such as Grieg and Halvorsen and others, drew on these Norwegian sources and thereby made names for themselves well outside Norway. . . .
>
> I wouldn't recommend giving up this folk music: the day we relinquish our Norwegian language and Norwegian tones, it's over for us as a people.

But luckily we're not to that point. The old tunes are winning more and more respect. The fiddle [he refers only to the Hardanger fiddle, of course] is no longer stigmatized through ignorance and narrowmindedness. Even people in cities and in the flatlands are harking to the fiddle's rich tones.

You can dance to an accordion or German fiddle; they have rhythm in them, but lack Norwegian feelings and beauty. They lack tradition; they're not ours.

It is the Hardanger fiddle that is Norway." (*Spelemannsbladet* 1951 (6): 8–9)

It should not come as a surprise that folk music enthusiasts writing in the 1940s–1950s were ardent romantic nationalists. Many of them grew up during the time when Norway was in the last stages of its struggle for independence from Sweden, finally achieved in 1905. And it also was perfectly natural for the Hardanger fiddle to remain at the center of institutionalized folk music for some time. After all, it was proponents and performers of this instrument that began this folk revival and, almost alone, sustained it in its early years. Nevertheless, opinions like that of Skarprud, if still espoused by a few today, do not pass without vigorous challenge. The last section of this chapter will explore the emerging position of the fiddle, and the fifth chapter the quite recent emergence into partial respectability of the music for *gammaldans.*

While Skarprud's definition of Norwegian folk music, like that expressed a quarter of a century earlier by Bjørndal, comes out of pastorally grounded national romanticism, it has a few notable twists. It is essentially a content-based definition, focused on one instrument and its "rich and large" repertoire of "old tunes." And, by disdaining the fiddle (after lauding the passing of narrowminded attitudes toward the Hardanger fiddle!), the definition is geographically bound, since the Hardanger fiddle, however distinctive its appearance and wonderful its music, has a limited territory. The elitism of choosing just the Hardanger fiddle to represent all of Norway is emphasized in several ways, by saying that instrument has "more and subtler tones," which one should exploit "if one has the gift to play it correctly," and by listing virtuosos past and contemporary. I have noted that many famous nineteenth-century fiddlers presented formal concerts, in part to find an alternative performance forum to that of accompanying dancing, which came under fire during the religious paroxysms that convulsed Norway—and were particularly strong in what would come to be the central Hardanger fiddle areas of Telemark and Setesdal—during that century. Such virtuosos came to represent a kind of climax of tradition, in which the best "folk" musicians were evaluated by an "art" standard. This topic will be explored below, in the section on judging.

Growth of the National Fiddle Contest and of Norway's Institutionalized Folk Music Milieu

After World War II, the National Fiddlers' Association gained stability and began to grow, gathering considerable momentum during the early 1950s. Even then, certain problems of the future were apparent in small ways. For instance, when Skarprud and others expressed pleasure that more people were becoming attracted to *"folkemusikk,"* including city folk, they were unknowingly forecasting what has become a general problem in folk music revivals—gigantism. I will give some statistics on the changing size of the general membership, of the National Fiddlers' Association' constituent local fiddle clubs (spelemannslags), and of the annual round of contests and other events that were officially sponsored. The National Fiddlers' Association had 353 members in 1951, 82 of whom had joined that year (*Spelemannsbladet* 1951 [4]: 4). There were about 400 members in 1954, then slow growth through the early 1970s. The year 1973 saw a membership of about 600, and a discouraged mood. There were few young members, and recruiting was not going well. But a surge was on the way: by 1985, membership exceeded 3,000 (*Spelemannsbladet* 1954 [7]: 12, 1973 [6]: 5–6, and 1985 [13]: 30).

The number of fiddle clubs increased proportionally. At first, most were for Hardanger fiddle, then ones for fiddle appeared slowly. In 1951, nine clubs registered with the National Fiddlers' Association were all for Hardanger fiddle, and included one ensemble in Oslo, which would remain the home of clubs that gathered emigrants from rural areas. In 1952, thirteen clubs included two from the fiddle area, Spelemannslaget Jakup Lom from Lom, in the North Gudbrandsdal, and Spelemannslaget Fel-Jakup, from Skjåk, a few miles away. Both were named after the most famous nineteenth-century player of the normal fiddle, but residents of Skjåk, where he lived, were less fond of having "Lom" in his name, although Skjåk legally had been part of Lom when he was alive. (Actually, the address of Spelemannslaget Jakup Lom was in Garmo, another community carved out of Lom.) In 1952, Spelemannslaget Jakup Lom had eleven members, met nine times, and played at two festive evenings, all in all a much smaller group and far less ambitious annual program than most fiddle clubs have today. In 1955, the Vågå Spelemannslag joined, and 1963 saw the addition of clubs in Oppdal and in Lalm. Nearly all of these clubs were in the North Gudbrandsdal; that in Lalm had been part of the one based in Vågåmo. By 1973, there were sixty local clubs registered with the National Fiddlers' Association, but numbers such as this should be regarded as approximations. Some clubs existed long before they affiliated with the National Fiddlers' Association—the venerable Brekken Spelemannslag, a club for fiddle based between Røros and the border with Sweden, got around to joining only in 1980. More than balancing the number of unaffiliated clubs have been those that are registered but do not participate in National Fiddlers' Association–sanctioned activities, or that have become altogether inactive. Of 111 clubs listed in 1985, just forty sent representatives to the annual administrative meeting of the National Fiddlers' Association (*Spelemannsbladet* 1951[2]: 12, 1952 [2]: 10 and 16, 1954 [3–4]: 22, 1955 [11–12]: 11, 1973 [6]: 5–6, and 1985 [13]: 3).

The last decade has seen expansion slow but not stop. There were 121 groups by 1987, ten more than just two years earlier. By April of 1994, a full 143 local fiddle clubs and ten county or regional umbrella clubs were registered (*Spelemannsbladet* 1994 [4]: 22–24). Of the 143 local clubs listed, some twenty-seven did not have any member compete in any bracket of a National Fiddle Contest during 1990–93. A few of these groups may be exclusively local in their activities, or may be ideologically opposed to competition. But most of the twenty-seven are simply inactive, retaining at least one member who hopes to see the club revive someday, that is, the contact person listed in the *Spelemannsblad*.

The locations of the 116 clubs with members who competed in the National Fiddle Contest during the early 1990s are plotted in Figure 2. On this map, "V" indicates a club for fiddle (the "V" is for *vanleg*, meaning normal), "H" one for Hardanger fiddle, and "M" a club including players of both instruments (most of these are in the West or in southern coastal areas, where some fiddlers own and play both types of fiddle). A lower-case letter indicates that a group includes no member who has competed as a soloist during the period in question, but that the name of club appears in the dance or fiddle ensemble brackets. An upper-case letter indicates participation in one or more of the solo fiddle brackets. If an upper-case letter is underlined, the club includes members of the A class, adult fiddlers who have won a first prize in a previous National Fiddle Contest. The map makes clear

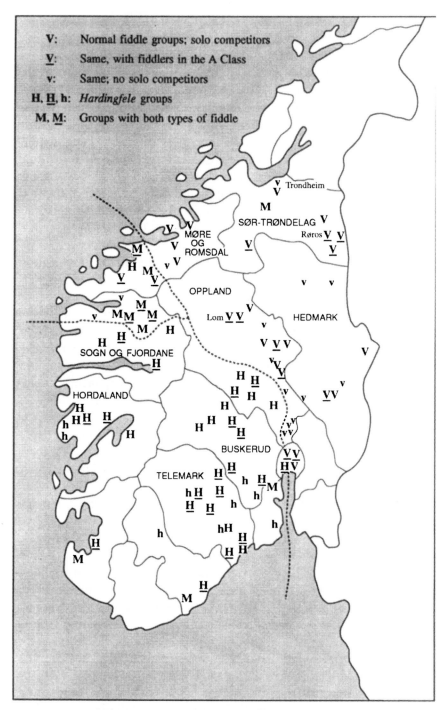

Figure 2. Fiddle clubs represented at the National Fiddle Contest, 1900–93, classified as consisting of normal fiddles (*vanleg fele*), Hardanger fiddles (*hardingfele*), or both

that some parts of Norway have much more active folk music communities than have other regions. Parts of the East, the Southwest, and especially the North are weak, while other areas have nurtured fiddling effectively. Within the fiddle area, it is easy to see the three strongest areas, the Gudbrandsdal (a diagonal within the county of Oppland), the Røros area (in eastern Sør-Trøndelag), and the southern part of the "mixed" area, which is the northern portion of the county of Sogn og Fjordane. Plenty of fiddling also goes on in Møre og Romsdal, and in areas near Oslo. Oslo itself is a special type of "mixed" area. Most of its ten or so clubs represent specific parts of the fiddle or Hardanger fiddle districts. That many of their members are not permanent residents detracts from the clubs' stability.

As the membership of the National Fiddlers' Association has increased, and as fiddle clubs have proliferated, more and larger contests have become progressively more complex. The central annual contest, the National Fiddle Contest, emerged as a truly national event over a period of decades. Figure 3 lists where the National Fiddle Contest has been held each year, along with winners for both types of fiddle, and Figure 4 plots contest locations on a map of southern Norway. The National Fiddle Contest was held regularly only after World War II, and ventured into territory exclusive for the fiddle only in 1954. Over half of these national contests have been staged in three critical Hardanger fiddle counties, Telemark, Buskerud, and Hordaland. The winners' list for Hardanger fiddle also concentrates on these counties, especially Telemark. Of the minority of contests held in the fiddle area, over half have been in the Gudbrandsdal, in the county of Oppland. And the winners' lists are even more skewed geographically for fiddle than for Hardanger fiddle. Nearly every winner is from the northern Gudbrandsdal. The village of Lom once included what are now the separate administrative units of Skjåk, just west, and Garmo, just east. I give a fiddler's affiliation as it was listed in the *Spelemanns-blad* the year he or she won—sometimes by home, sometimes by the title of the fiddle club to which the winner belongs. Several fiddlers listed as in Garmo one year are in Lom the next; they didn't move, but they were classified differently. Vågåmo is not very far east of Garmo. When all of this geographical detail is added up, we see that nearly every winner of the fiddle competition at the National Fiddle Contest comes from a thin strip of land stretching from Skjåk through Lom and Garmo to Vågåmo, a total distance of just forty six kilometers.

With the passage of time, the number of competitors and of separate competition brackets at the National Fiddle Contest has risen

Figure 3. National Fiddle Contest Locations and Winners

	City		Winner/Home	
Year	H-fiddle area	Fiddle area	Fiddle	H-fiddle
1923	Bergen			
1924		Molde	Olav Moløkken, [Lom]	Olav Heggland, Setesdal
1925	Stavanger			
1926	Hønefoss		Olav Moløkken, [Lom]	Gunnulf Borgen
1928	Bergen			
1932		Oslo	Olav Moløkken, [Lom]	
1933	Nesbyen			
1936	Notodden			
1941	Nesbyen		Hans Brimi, Lom	Amund Roheim, Telemark
1946		Oslo	Pål Skogum, Vågå	T. Bolstad, [Valdres/Oslo]
1947	Voss		Alfred Bismo, Lom	
1948		Oslo	Kristen Vang, Skjåk	Eivind Mo, Seljord
1949	Bø			
1950	Nesbyen		Hans Brimi, Lom	G. Haugen, Telemark
1951	Kristiansand		Hans Brimi, Lom	Sigbjørn Osa, Voss
1952	Bergen		Petter Eide, Vågå	G. Haugen, Telemark
1953		Oslo	Hans Brimi, Lom	G. Haugen, Telemark
1954		Lom	Hans Brimi, Lom	Einar Løndal, Telemark
1955	Nesbyen		Hans Brimi, Lom	A. Kjerland, Hardanger
1956	Kongsberg		Pål Skogum, Vågå	Kjetil Løndal, Tuddal
1957	Valdres		Hans Brimi, Lom	T. Bolstad, Valdres (Oslo)
1958	Notodden		Hans Brimi, Lom	K. Løndal, Tuddal (Oslo)
1959		Otta	Hans Brimi, Lom	K. Løndal, Tuddal (Oslo)
1960	Voss		Einar Galaaen, Røros[a]	Odd Bakkerud, Nesbyen
1961	Nesbyen		Petter Eide, Vågå	Jens Amundsen, Bø
1962	Odda		Einar Galaaen, Røros[a]	Hauk Buen, Jondalen
1963	Notodden		Bjørn Odde, Lom	Jens Amundsen, Bø
1964		Vågåmo	Bjørn Odde, Lom	Bakkerud, Nesbyen (Oslo)
1965	Bergen		Hans Brimi, Lom	Bakkerud, Nesbyen (Oslo)
1966		Molde	Amund Bjørgen, Lom	K. Løndal, Tuddal (Oslo)
1967	Porsgrunn		A. Bjørgen, Garmo [Lom]	Bakkerud, Nesbyen (Oslo)
1968		Lillehammer	Hans Brimi, Lom	Bakkerud, Nesbyen (Oslo)
1969	Geilo		Hans Brimi, Lom	Ola Bø, Oslo
1970		Røros	Magne Bø, Dombas	Torleiv Bolstad, Valdres
1971	Sogndal		Bjørn Odde, Garmo	Torleiv Bolstad, Valdres
1972	Gol		Amund Bjørgen, Garmo	Lars Skjervheim
1973	Bergen		Hans Brimi, Garmo	Knut Myrann, Nesbyen
1974		Oppdal	Hans Holen, Vågå	Knut Hamre, Hardanger
1975	Bø		Knut Kjøk, Lom (Oslo)	Bjårne Herrefoss, Telemark
1976	Voss		Amund Bjørgen, Lom	Knut Myrann, Nes
1977		Lillehammer	R. Skjelkvåle, Skjåk (Oslo)	Leif Rygg, Voss
1978	Fagernes		R. Skjelkvåle, Skjåk (Oslo)	Knut Hamre, Hardanger
1979	Førde		Skjelkvåle/Odde/Holen tie	Bjarne Herrefoss, Telemark
1980	Kristiansand		Ivar Schjølberg, [Vågå][b]	Leif Rygg, Voss
1981		Oslo	Bjørn Odde, Lom	Knut Hamre, Hardanger
1982		Hamar	Knut Kjøk, Lom	Hallvard Bjørgum, Setesdal

Figure 3. *continued*

Year	City		Winner/Home	
	H-fiddle area	Fiddle area	Fiddle	H-fiddle
1983	Kongsberg		Ivar Schjølberg, Vågå[b]	Knut Buen, Tuddal
1984	Odda		Bjørn Odde, Lom	Knut Hamre, Hardanger
1985		Otta	Amund Bjørgen, Lom	Knut Hamre, Hardanger
1986	Geilo		Amund Bjørgen, Lom	Knut Buen, Tuddal
1987		Sogndal	Knut Kjøk, Lom	Knut Hamre, Hardanger
1988	Bø		Knut Kjøk, Lom	Hallvard Bjørgum, Setesdal
1989		Trysil	Arne Sølvberg, Stryn[c]	Håkon Høgemo, Sogn
1990		Nordfjordeid	Knut Kjøk, Lom	J. Sundsvalen, Telemark
1991	Voss		Kristen Odde, Lom	B. Herrefoss, Sullarguten
1992	Fagernes		Mari Eggen, Sør-Fron[d]	Alf Tveit, Sullarguten
1993		Lillehammer	Amund Bjørgen, Lom	Øyvind Brabant, Gol
1994	Rauland		Leif-Inge Schjølberg, Vågå	Leif Rygg, Voss
1995	Førde		Leif-Inge Schjølberg, Vågå	Håkon Høgemo, Sogn
1996		Vågåmo	Leif-Inge Schjølberg, Vågå	Leif Rygg, Voss

Note: Missing years indicate those when contest was not held. Under "City," a centered name indicates a mixed fiddle area. Under "Winner, home," a city in square brackets was not listed in the *Spelemannsblad;* Oslo in parentheses indicates where winners lived at the time of the contest, but they still played in their home styles.

[a]Galaaen, the first player from the Røros area to attend the National Fiddle Contest regularly, plays in a cultivated, salon-influenced style quite different from that prevailing in the area today.

[b]Ivar Schjølberg, raised and trained as a fiddler in Ålen, in the Røros area, lives in Vågåmo, in the Gudbrandsdal. He is the only fiddler playing in a Røros-area style to win the National Fiddle Contest in modern times.

[c]Arne M. Sølvberg is the only fiddler from the West ever to win the National Fiddle Contest.

[d]Mari Eggen is the only woman fiddler (on either fiddle type) ever to win the National Fiddle Contest.

rapidly. In 1950 there were four brackets for solo fiddlers, that is, older and younger players of the Hardanger fiddle and of the fiddle, plus two classes for dancers. By 1954, each fiddle type had three competition brackets defined by age—B: most players; C: youths under eighteen; and D: players over sixty—plus a champions' category, the A class. By 1963, there were additional classes for community fiddlers' clubs playing as orchestras (each a *spelemannslag*); for vocal folk music; for older, rarer folk instruments such as the lur and the langeleik; and even for new compositions in the old genres *(nyskaping)*.

The late 1960s, early 1970s saw Norway consider joining the European Economic Community, a prospect which appalled farmers, fishermen, and others especially concerned with continuity in Norwegian

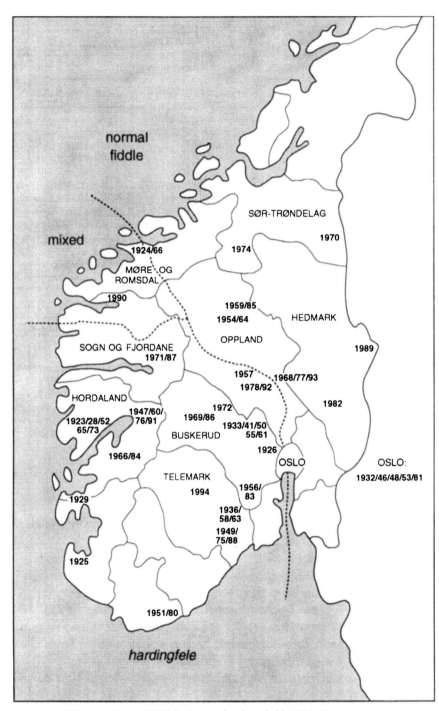

Figure 4. Where the National Fiddle Contest has been held, 1923–93

culture, including nearly everyone in the National Fiddlers' Association. At the same time, the influx of foreign material culture and the impact of outside events, including the war in Vietnam, provoked modest political and social ferment. One eventual response to this complex of pressures on Norwegian sovereignty, tranquility, and cultural distinctiveness was that recruiting for the National Fiddlers' Association increased exponentially. While many of the new recruits reflected the steady extension of the National Fiddlers' Association umbrella into the fiddle area, other new members were politically inspired urbanites, somewhat parallel in background and in ideology to the coffeehouse singers so important in the earlier American folk boom.

Indeed, this was a juncture at which Norway's folk revival might have changed character radically and more closely corresponded to the majority of other folk revivals. The mainstream of the American revival, and of revivals most strongly affected by it, "appealed primarily to individuals who celebrated traditions not their own" (Jackson 1993:73). And, according to Cantwell, the American "folk revival has its meaning in the psychosocial and economic setting of postwar America," in which many young people believed "that the world had been gravely mismanaged by the parent generation" (1991:45, 49). Star folksingers in this and subsidiary revivals did resurrect old styles, but often expressed their alienation by expending more energy writing new songs with personal or political texts. Norway experienced a parallel urban-based revival, based on its own forms of the counterculture. But, for a variety of reasons, this remained less important than the ongoing nativistic revival centered on the National Fiddlers' Association. In one respect, since one of the parents' generation's primary sins was in absorbing too much American culture, aping the American revival would not have been appropriate. Urban-nurtured folk music enthusiasts remained a minority in Norway's healthy nativistic revival. And this minority concentrated much less on writing new songs on protest and confessional topics—most Norwegians suspect public emotion and disdain glibness—than on innovative approaches to performing folk music, often virtuosically. The nativistic revival was enriched by the Norwegian response to the American folk boom, and in the end painlessly absorbed that response. Once again, the insider's path was chosen.

Nineteen seventy-seven was a watershed year for the National Fiddle Contest: the competition was now surrounded by concerts large and small, some by rural traditional artists, others issuing from the modest urban-centered folk movement. Recruits from the urban intellectual community had little interest in *gammaldans* music, which retained its important, but low-status, position in contest weekends, that of music to relax and dance to late at night. Back in the early 1950s, fewer than fifty fiddlers would entertain audiences of a few hundred. Today over 500 musicians and dancers perform for thousands. And the fiddle has progressed from minority status to near parity with the Hardanger fiddle. These developments are summarized in Figure 5.

The folkies have neither gone away nor become much more important in the folk revival. Many recordings of folk music feature them, but they have not entered the National Fiddlers' Association leadership, or penetrated the contest system beyond their public-pleasing role in a few of the concerts during evenings at the National Fiddle Contest. Nor have they been needed to discover and manage traditional performers, a function important in the United States: those performers were already members of or at least known to local affiliate clubs of the association. I agree with Rosenberg's characterization of the American folk revival as unusual in its diversity (1993:2). I would propose that this is an important way that the Norwegian revival contrasts with ours. Since, in Norway's more compact society, most revival activists belonged to one group, grass-roots tradition bearers, the revival remained quite unified—until recently.

As the National Fiddle Contest grew, smaller local contests continued to proliferate. Beginning in the 1950s, contests under the aegis of the National Fiddlers' Association were listed in the *Spelemannsblad*. Of ten such events listed in 1951 and in 1954, one was in Lom. 1955 also saw contests in Romsdal and in Vågåmo. During this early period, some contests were not under association sponsorship. An article from 1954 complained that fiddle clubs that were not in the association arranged flawed contests. The area of Nordfjord, home of today's strongest players of the fiddle in the mixed area of the West, was singled out for criticism: "They among other things use an accordion [*trekkspel*], and such instruments have nothing to do with folk music" (*Spelemannsbladet* 1954 [7–8]: 16). Here a compromise was gradually struck. Nearly all contests, including those in the West, are now under the National Fiddlers' Association umbrella, but local contests are granted some flexibility from the rules that prevail at the national contest. The constellation of contests centered on the National Fiddle Contest continued to grow, until today there are folk music events nearly every weekend during the summer, and more than

Figure 5. Growth of the National Fiddle Contest

Event	1950	1955	1960	1965	1970	1975	1980	1985	1990
Small Fiddle Ensembles									
New Compositions				5 pieces	7 pieces	16 pieces	8 pieces		4
Singing (*Kveding*)			4 singers		7 singers		18 singers		25
Older Folk Instruments			gradual increase		stable number of participants				
Fiddle Clubs (*Lagspel*)									
Normal Fiddle			1 club	4 clubs	7 clubs	11 clubs		18 clubs	22
Hardanger Fiddle			1 club	3 clubs	7 clubs	11 clubs		15 clubs	25
Solo Fiddlers									
Normal Fiddle		soon 4 classes; total of: 9 fiddlers			38 fiddlers		43 players		61
Hardanger Fiddle		soon 4 classes; total of: 37 fiddlers			49 fiddlers		54 players		89
Dance									
Couples, to Fiddle			1 class	4 classes, joint		4 classes			
Couples, to Hardanger Fiddle	1 class	4 classes		joint		4 classes			
Solo Men (*Halling*)	1 class			3 classes					

(Events, listed at right, became part of the National Folk Music Contest the year that the horizontal column begins. Information within a column describes how a given event has changed in how it has been subdivided or in numbers of participants) a handful in the flanking months. Of about thirty annual events, seventeen are locally oriented affairs in Hardanger fiddle areas, two are contests in mixed areas (the county contests for Møre og Romsdal and for Sogn og Fjordane), four are events in fiddle areas (one contest and three festivals), and the rest are events of general interest. The biggest events are three contests, the National Fiddle Contest (centered on folk music), the National Festival for *Gammaldans* Music, and the District Contest for fiddle. The large size of this last-named event goes a long way toward balancing the many small, local Hardanger fiddle contests. Also, the *gammaldans* festival, a young event, has turned out to be mostly for residents of the fiddle area.

Today, there are at least as many players of the fiddle as of the Hardanger fiddle, and National Fiddlers' Association activities seem balanced between those favored by proponents of the two instruments. I will take a close look at a number of these activities in later chapters of this book. The growth of the status of the fiddle has not been without considerable controversy, some of the history of which will be related at the end of this chapter. Before doing that, I will flesh out the statistics of the growth of the National Fiddlers' Association and the contest system by analyzing a factor critical in shaping this growth, the judging of fiddlers at National Fiddlers' Association–sponsored events.

Artistry and Tradition: The History of Judging Contests

The vigor of local folk music traditions in Norway today depends to a great extent on how well local activities are fostered by the national institutional folk music milieu, which, despite ongoing attempts to broaden activities, is still largely focused on contests. While participation in contests is intrinsically enjoyable, doing well in these events is, of course, much more satisfying. The contest judges inherit assumptions coloring their task, rules governing it, and techniques of judging from over a century of work. The first judges of fiddling, at the first Hardanger fiddle contests in Telemark, Bergen, Ålesund, and elsewhere, were often not fiddlers themselves. They were men with prestige in the community, often either in government service or trained in art music. They might or might not be knowledgeable about local folk music or about other regional styles represented by competitors. Among the first missions of the young National Fiddlers' Association was ensuring that judges were truly qualified. The National Fiddle

Contest judges were themselves prominent Hardanger fiddle performers, and local contests under association sponsorship were asked to follow that example. In order to assess how these judges helped shape this folk music revival, I will explore three related questions. First, what were the rules for judging; what were the judges supposed to do? Second, what did the judges want to hear; what can we learn about their actual preferences from their commentary? Third, how well did and do contest-winner lists match fiddler and folk community expectations? Which aspects of the judging system have succeeded, and which remain controversial?

Before World War II, there was no standard judging scheme, no tool ensuring uniformity of assumptions or methods. Nevertheless, the men who judged at the National Fiddle Contest during that period were experts and were also friends. Since they were much the same group from contest to contest, they were able to shape a coherent approach to assessing performance quality. After a given afternoon or evening of competition, the judges sat down together, worked their way to a consensus, set up a prize list, and wrote out comments meant to help players improve. Jostein Mæland (1973:86), who wrote the official history of the National Fiddlers' Association, studied the commentary that these early judges had penned over the years, and found that certain terms recurred regularly. He listed them in this order: *tradisjon, takt* (pulse), *rytme, bogeføring* (use of the bow), *tonereinleik* (intonation), *dåm* (impossible to translate, but something like overall impression or feel), *friskleik* (liveliness), *tempo/fart* (speed), *stødleik* (consistency), *sermerkt* (distinctive), and *hugtakande* (charming). I have reproduced these in the left-hand column of Figure 6, reordered for ease of comparison with two later, official sets of judging rubrics.

After the war, when the National Fiddlers' Association was reconstituted, the steering committee found it appropriate to make up a standard judging form. Its principal architects were a young Hardanger fiddle star, Kjetil Løndal, and experienced judge Henrik Gjellesvik. On the form, a player received one to ten points for each of ten qualities. The first of these was *slåtteform* (form/version of the tune performed). The broad heading of *musikalsk framföring* (musical presentation) included *takt, rytme,* and *tonekvalitet* (tone quality), which itself had three subcategories, *reinleik* (intonation), *styrke* (volume), and that difficult term *dåm,* as well as *musikalsk givnad* (talent). Last, under *teknik,* were *fingertame* (fingering), *bogeføring,* and *framferd* (general success, with intimations of level of difficulty). These rubrics appear in the central column of Figure 6. Comparing these with the

Figure 6. Judging Rubrics

Terms Judges Regularly Used before World War II (according to Mæland [1973])	Official Rubrics, Just after World War II	Official Rubrics, Beginning in 1955
Tradition	*Slåtteform* (form/version of the tunes performed)	*Slåtteform* (today: *slåtteform/tradisjon*)
Pulse Rhythm Tempo	Musical presentation pulse rhythm	Pulse and rhythm
Intonation (*tonereinleik*)	Tone quality intonation volume	Intonation
Feel (*dåm*) Liveliness (*friskleik*) Consistency (*stødleik*) Distinctiveness (*sermerkt*) Charm (*hugtakande*)	feel (*dåm*) talent (*musikalsk givnad*)	Feel/expression (*dåm og drag*)
Bowing	Technique fingering bowing success (*framferd*)	Technique

list of terms used before the war shows that the new regulations followed previous, less-systematic practice rather closely.

The postwar judging scheme proved unwieldy, and was simplified in 1955, the same year that the total of points awarded to players was first published. Ten rubrics became five: *slåtteform,* pulse and rhythm, tone quality, *dåm og drag* (approximately translated as "feel and expression"), and technique, these joining the previous arrays of terms in Figure 6. This set of rubrics still holds, though *slåtteform* has been revised to read *slåtteform/tradisjon,* thus wedding prewar custom with postwar rules. Criticism of the system has been regular and eloquent. The rubrics overlap, they reflect evolution from an unsystematic aggregate of terms rather than clear analytical thinking, and the system contains ideological snares (Groven 1964:4–6). Indeed, what to one judge seems to be good "tradition" may appear blasphemous to an adherent of a different school of playing in the same town. Numerous alternatives to this judging system have been proposed. Their discussion has provoked profitable reflection concerning what the rubrics ought to mean, but these haven't been changed.

Both postwar judging schemes were meant to be employed from the bottom up, that is, by assigning points under each rubric for the performance of a given tune, then totaling the points. Certain thresholds of total scores yield a first or second prize; there are as many first prizes as fiddlers with sufficient total points, with the winner being the fiddler with the top score. Some—perhaps many—judges actually worked in the other direction, first representing their intuitive initial impression of a performance with a total score, then parceling those points out into the boxes beneath the rubrics (*Spelemannsbladet* 1971 [3]: 23). Today, this seems to be how most judges operate (and, incidentally, how some American fiddle contest judges ply their craft). I asked a half-dozen judges of fiddle performance who were active in the early 1990s how they worked. Just one said he wrote down the small scores first, then adds them up, while all of the others admitted starting with the total score, then working backward, occasionally revising the total after looking at the individual rubrics. This suggests that a formal scheme might have been and might remain superfluous. So believed Arne Bjørndal, first head of the National Fiddlers' Association, and who, along with Henrik Gjellesvik (who helped shape the first postwar judging scheme), judged at the National Fiddle Contest regularly before the war. Bjørndal asserted during a 1953 National Fiddlers' Association reconsideration of the judging system that "a judge who knows what he's doing can do just as well" without the scheme (Mæland [1973]: 89). Nevertheless, having a standard form symbolizes objectivity and fairness, and offers a simple and concise way for each judge to tell a fiddler what aspects of his or her playing need to be improved. The judging forms do have a space for comments, but this space generally is left blank.

For several years after the war, judges at the contest both followed the new standardized rules, thus filling out official forms with set rubrics, and continued prewar practice by composing prose evaluations of each performance. This was a lot of work, and would have to be given up as the number of contestants rose. Old-style evaluations of performances at the National Fiddle Contest during the years 1950–55 were published in the *Spelemannsblad;* comments useful to the contestants under evaluation might well help readers improve their playing, too. These comments help flesh out the picture of desirable style that is merely sketched in the judging rubrics, and also illustrate some change in judging during these few years.

The most general impression offered by these comments is that the upper tier of Hardanger fiddle players were trying to support what they saw as the high value of their tradition through fostering "better" playing throughout that listening-based forum, the contest. In other words, what had been a veneer of art atop a folk tradition back in "the good old days" was intended to permeate the entire tradition. That standards were both art oriented and rising is indisputable. Positive comments following the 1950 National Fiddle Contest included "clean and supple," "nice tone," "subtle nuances," and "refined and dependable technique," while criticisms included "must practice to hold the bow more loosely," "subdued," "lacked a lively rhythm," and, ending over half of the evaluations, something to the effect of: "needs more practice and good guidance" (*Spelemannsbladet* 1950 [4]: 5, 7). The aim of this dominant constituency in organized folk music was to fill contests with polished, artistic performances of complex versions of traditional tunes.

Judges' evaluations of performances at the 1950 National Fiddle Contest averaged five lines of prose, that is, about forty words per player. The path of least resistance was often followed, that being to simply translate the numbers on the official form into prose. In addition, problems in bowing seemed central. Two relatively short evaluations will serve as samples: "Einar Løndal [Hardanger fiddle], Tuddal [in Telemark], played 'Sandsdalen,' *springar*, and 'Førnesbrunen' [*gangar*, but elaborately recast as a listening piece; see tune #102] with good pulse and rhythm, in tune and with good tone, good technique, but not as fresh and full of life as one has often heard him play before." "Erling Kjøk, Lom [famous fiddle town in the Gudbrandsdal], fiddle, played 'Skålhalling' and 'Springar after Rolv Gaupar,' good pulse and rhythm, sympathetic tone, but somewhat anemic [*bleikt*]. The fiddler needs to practice the bow hand and pursue more animated [*livfullt*] performance" (*Spelemannsbladet* 1950 [4]: 6–7). These two sets of comments are representative of the measured praise awarded the majority of Hardanger fiddle players and of the less-sympathetic reception for those employing fiddle. It is hard to imagine that Kjøk, a legendary player of the fiddle, really deserved a rating so much harsher than that awarded the skilled Hardanger fiddle player, Løndal. Two related factors may be at work here. One is that Hardanger fiddle players were more accustomed to contests, had been playing in them more often, been practicing more, and really were in better shape than contest newcomers from the fiddle area.[4] But we may also be seeing Hardanger fiddle–playing judges (these comments were signed by Gjellesvik) evaluating fiddlers accustomed to playing for dances on the art scale attached to Hardanger fiddle performance.

Claiming that Kjøk's bow hand needed work, and that his playing was unanimated (probably meaning not using contrasting dynamics) would square with use of dance-oriented short, vigorous, uniformly rather loud bow strokes.

The published evaluations from the 1952 National Fiddle Contest feature the characterization *"bunden* [limited] *teknikk"* repeatedly. Criticisms of performances on fiddle are very short, less than a fourth the length of those for Hardanger fiddle players, and make no mention of technique. Perennial champion Hans Brimi of Lom, who won the fiddle side of the National Fiddle Contest nearly every time he entered, was dismissed with "pure tone and nice feel" (*Spelemannsbladet* 1952 [5]: 21). Are these brief reports evidence of lack of interest, of not feeling confident enough about the fiddle to say more, or both? To address the problem of a judge not well-enough informed about styles not his own, judging courses proliferated in the 1950s (and remain common today). In any case, pressure increased at least to try to balance panels of judges between Hardanger fiddle and fiddle experts. It was felt that there should be at least one judge from the fiddle area; perhaps two of three judges should be from the half of the country where a given National Fiddle Contest was held. Many plans were suggested, and quite a few tried. The fairest solution, to have a separate panel of judges for fiddle, was at first simply too expensive. Over a decade would pass before this could be afforded on a regular basis, but the folk music community continued to grow, and an ever-increasing fraction of this growth came from the fiddle area. Separate judging teams were tried, abandoned, then permanently adopted.

Today we still have one panel of three judges for Hardanger fiddle, and a complementary panel of three judges for fiddle. But this arrangement was far in the future during the last two years in which judges' commentary appeared in the *Spelemannsbladet*. The 1954 contest was in Lom, in the Gudbrandsdal. There were two judges each from the Hardanger fiddle and fiddle areas. In 1955, the contest was back in a Hardanger fiddle stronghold, Nesbyen. Here were four judges, just one of whom, Sven Nyhus, was a fiddle player. The idea of two overlapping panels of three judges was attempted: For Hardanger fiddle, the panel included Geirr Tveit, head (a composer who knew much about Hardanger fiddle music), Rikard Gøytil, of Rauland (in Telemark), and K. Kleven of Nesbyen. The panel for fiddle dropped Gøytil and added Nyhus.

Bowing received more and more detailed attention in the judges' commentary from both years. Almost all fiddle players (including the top players) and the less-skilled among the Hardanger fiddle entrants in the 1954 contest were told to "practice" *(øve inn)* or "develop" *(utvikle)* better bowing technique. One player needed "a better grip," another to "practice holding the bow perpendicular to the strings"; others were admonished not to slip *(skleik)*, wheeze *(kvesing)*, twist the bow, or be either sloppy *(slurva)* or stiff *(Spelemannsbladet 1955 [1–2]: 23)*. Sven Nyhus, today one of the most influential and certainly the most controversial figure in the world of the fiddle, was already in 1955 a tenacious and eloquent advocate of his instruments. As scion of the most prominent folk music family in the Røros area, he was trained both on fiddle and on orchestral viola, and as a result had precisely the combination of fiddle expertise and art orientation calculated to catch the ears of the Hardanger fiddle–playing judges. While he advocated adoption of violin-derived technique, he also invoked the "tradition" of specific locations in the fiddle district many times.

The heart of Nyhus's message may not have been spelled out, but it was impossible to ignore. He certainly didn't dispute the Hardanger fiddle judges' collective opinion that fiddle playing ought to be more cultivated, but cumulatively his comments insisted that his instrument should not be judged using precisely the same criteria as were employed in evaluating Hardanger fiddle performance. Geirr Tveitt could not let this pass unchallenged. He was, perhaps because of his profession, the most art-oriented of the judges of this era. He noted, while evaluating Hardanger fiddle players, that one commanded *"eit herleg* [a lovely] pianissimo" and that another's bow was *"for mykje sul ponticello"* (too close to the bridge). He was so displeased with Nyhus's commentary about fiddle performance that he insisted on printing a dissenting view, in which he asserted that fiddlers ought to vary dynamics more and vary tone more *(Spelemannsbladet 1956 [5–6]: 15–18)*, that is, be more like the best Hardanger fiddle players.

Indeed, although the spirit of art music would dominate more and more, its letter was resisted now and again, even by such strong proponents of delicately nuanced Hardanger fiddle performance as Tveitt. One Hardanger fiddle player featured on the weekly radio show "The Folk Music Half Hour," the same Torfinn Litlere mentioned by Ludvig Jerdal as among the performers adding luster to the early contests in Bergen, attracted the ire of Henrik Gjellesvik:

> "[What was] especially unsuccessful was that [Litlere] adopted violin technique in his own musical creations *[tonestykkje]* and inserted Paganini harness-racing up and down the fingerboard—and

presented this as Norwegian folk music for the Hardanger fiddle. In my opinion this is as bad as style can get. . . . If Torfinn Litlere had employed normal fiddle for this, in a program not labeled folk music, then he could have played his own compositions with all the technical resources that he desired . . . as an artist *[unstnar]* he is responsible for this presentation." (Gjellesvik 1956:2)

The "Paganini harness-racing" must have meant going out of first position, which is not part of traditional Hardanger fiddle technique.

Jens Synnes, a player of the fiddle, provoked a similar response at the 1955 National Fiddle Contest with his "virtuosic technique applied to fiddle tunes" *(bravurmessig teknikk i slåttemusikken)*. The panel wondered "how far one can take violin technique into playing fiddle tunes, and have these remain folk music." Even Tveitt, who found Synnes quite musical, remarked that "it [was] rather dangerous for a country fiddler to succumb to *[freista seg på]* international technique" *(Spelmannsbladet* 1956 [5–6]: 17–18). Artistic, listening-oriented performance of folk music was desirable, but not when overdone, not when fluent technique began to overwhelm the small pieces making up folk repertoires. This is a fine distinction that still is negotiated today, and will be discussed further in later chapters.

A second problem that swiftly arose and still nags today issued naturally from the contest format. The largest number of pieces a given player has been asked to perform during a day's competition has been five, at the first Hardanger fiddle contests in Bø, Telemark. After that, three was a common number for a while; then two became and has remained the norm. This is all that time permits in the large contests of today; two tunes remain the minimum to present a reasonably broad picture of a performer's ability. As early as 1956, Erling Kjøk noted that some players seemed undercommitted to their local repertoires, leading to the same tunes being played at contest after contest. He felt that this led to the "good old tunes" being far too seldom performed *(Spelemannsbladet* 1956 [11–12]: 4–5). This problem was remarked on repeatedly in the years that followed, and today takes two forms. One is that just aired, that a player will polish a very few tunes, then use them over and over again at contests. A complementary problem is the emergence of a contest canon, a smallish number of tunes that seem, owing to a felicitous combination of level of complexity, general attractiveness, and (temporarily) sufficient rarity, to be used by player after player in contests. This subrepertoire of tunes rotates a bit, because tunes become overused, but the general problem seems destined to persist.

A more critical problem in judging has been fidelity to one's home tradition, quite a serious matter in a country with a highly developed sense of place. Fiddlers were and are penalized for reaching outside their traditions. Not only has this been considered inauthentic and disloyal, but it has also been believed that "a fiddler can fully command only his own village's style *[bygdespel]*; it is exceedingful difficult to learn those from elsewhere" (*Spelemannsbladet* 1969 [1]: 10–11). One fiddler at the 1950 National Fiddle Contest was condemned for playing "a blended form from Valdres, Hallingdal, and Telemark" (*Spelemannsbladet* 1950 [4]: 5), another at the 1955 contest for abandoning his home style, that of the Hallindal, for a quasi-Telemark performance (*Spelemannsbladet* 1956 [5–6]: 15). But the alternative for some was being doomed to performing in a local style that was considered inferior: Hans Brimi, the legendary fiddle player from what would later become a high-status district (for the fiddle, that is), played in the 1951 contest a *halling* (music for a solo male display dance in duple time) that "didn't sound much like one" to the judges, owing to its "insignificant musical content" and "inauthentic form" (*Spelemannsbladet* 1951 [4]: 7). Trouble was brewing here.[5] The revival of Norwegian folk music had long been the responsibility of Hardanger fiddle players, who therefore certainly deserved to be allowed to determine the shape of that revival. Even if they knew little about styles proper to the fiddle, they were musical men, Hans Brimi told me in 1989, and they were obviously sincere in their assessment of what high-quality fiddling ought to be like. But Norway is a remarkably egalitarian society, and damning fiddle players for fidelity to local style and identity would not be unchallenged for long.

The "Normal" Fiddle in the National Fiddlers' Association

Through the early 1950s, the revival of Norwegian music was a fragile, albeit stubbornly vital, movement based almost exclusively on the Hardanger fiddle. The price of healthy growth in later decades, and of becoming truly national, was the inclusion of other instruments, especially the fiddle. Change, abetted by the passage of time and concomitant changes in Norwegian society, could not help accompanying growth, regardless of how wedded to a given vision of Norwegian folk music the original constituencies of the National Fiddlers' Association have been. At first the changes involved few new musical genres and a minimum of newly articulated theory, but, since many of the recruits were from hitherto underrepresented areas of

Norway, the inherited assumptions worked less well. Much change was linked in one way or another with the gradually rising status of the fiddle. This change was at first very slow. Knut Vemøy's complaints after early contests in Ålesund may or may not have reflected wider dissatisfaction—after all, most organized folk music activity was in pure Hardanger fiddle areas. The first player of the "normal" fiddle to attend the National Fiddle Contest regularly was Hans Brimi of Lom. His style was and is as lyrical and artistic as playing on the fiddle could be, but at first, he was given low scores. But he is not a firebrand. He simply came back year after year, played well, and inspired other fiddlers to come to these events, particularly fiddlers from his home area.

One seemingly simple change, important for symbolic reasons, was to standardize the name of the fiddle that looks like a violin, the *vanlig fele,* the "normal" fiddle. As early as 1953, the head of the National Fiddlers' Association, Ludvig Jerdal, noted that "we often hear the terms German fiddle *[tyskfele]* or flat fiddle *[flatfele;* both of these terms appeared in Johannes Skarprud's scathing letter of 1951, quoted earlier in this chapter]. Players who use this type of fiddle have put us on notice that they don't like these terms. There is something 'disparaging' *[nedsetjande]* about them. Let's stick to the term 'normal fiddle' to differentiate it from the Hardanger fiddle, they say. I don't want to take sides; let's consider this issue further, in the *Spelemannsblad"* (1953 (1): 5). A few years later, a prominent fiddler from the Gudbrandsdal, Petter Eide, advocated retaining Jerdal as head of the National Fiddlers' Association because, in addition to having many fine qualities, Jerdal was "neutral in the Hardanger fiddle / normal fiddle issue" *(Spelemannsbladet* 1959 [7–8]: 8). Although *tyskfele* and *dusingfele* (roughly "dime-a-dozen fiddle") saw limited use, *flatfele* remained common for some time in official communications of the association. This term was long used in association bylaws, and the fiddle remained the *flatfele* in the *Spelemannsblad* for decades after it was known that many of its players found this offensive. A letter of protest was printed in 1973, which gave the editor an opportunity to reinforce the status quo. In the letter, Helge Dillen, a player and scholar of the fiddle, asked those who wrote in the *Spelemannsblad* to use the term *vanleg fele,* as respected Norwegian folk music scholar Eivind Groven had suggested. Dillen characterized *flatfele* as "both nasty and discriminatory." The editor replied that *flatfele* was a term drawn from folk tradition *(ei folkeleg nemneform),* and added that he found *vanleg fele* artificial *(konstruert; Spelemannsbladet* 1973 [6]: 20).

The various terms for the fiddle that its players dislike certainly are current in dialects of Hardanger fiddle areas, and these terms do have some historical basis in local usage in and out of Hardanger fiddle territory (see Jenstad 1994:53–54 and 330–31). Although more than one meaning of flat seems to be intended, it is undeniable that the body of the fiddle is perceptibly less arched than that of many a Hardanger fiddle, and is much less arched than many older examplars. And, while each Hardanger fiddle is constructed by hand in Norway, many fiddles are imported. These days, a fair number come from Asia, but in the past, Germany was a common source. Whereas a Hardanger fiddle is generally a carefully made, expensive instrument, fiddles span a wider range of quality, from ones every bit as fine as the best Hardanger fiddle down to the poorest factory models cranked out abroad. They may not be a "dime a dozen," but the humbler specimens are indeed cheap in cost, appearance, and sound. But each of these terms, whatever its grounding in history and in denotation, does connote a low opinion of the instrument to the players of the fiddle. Most of these players—not all, but the overwhelming majority—use none of the derogatory terms, and feel and have successfully insisted that they ought to be able to say what their own instrument should be called, at least in official communications of the National Fiddlers' Association and in a national publication such as the *Spelemannsblad*. *Vanlig* (or *vanleg*) *fele* prevailed in the *Spelemannsblad* in recent years, gradually yielding to simply *fele,* and the alternative names are not heard today in public forums. But *flatfele* is still used by many Hardanger fiddle players from, for example, Telemark, when they are at home. It cannot be expected that *vanlig fele* will replace *flatfele* any time soon in all corners of Norway, any more than all Hardanger fiddle players in the core areas for that instrument will come to believe that the two types of fiddle and the repertoires they play are equal in worth.

The disdain that some Hardanger fiddle adherents have felt for the fiddle goes beyond use of terminology, of course, even though most everyone seems to be striving to be fair. In 1952, these words appeared in the *Spelemannsblad*: "I would like to say a few words to the NRK [Norwegian National Radio]. All folk music is good, but that doesn't mean that all fiddlers are equally good. That's particularly true in those parts of the country where they only know the normal fiddle [*flatfela*]. The playing on normal fiddle on radio is often a bit thin [*spinkelt*]. Isn't that reason to have them play in groups on the radio? On the other hand, this doesn't hold for the Hardanger fiddle" (1952

[3]: 4). These comments have three critical ingredients. They include—indeed begin with—an attempt to be fair: "All folk music is good." Second, the criticism issues from fact. A solo performance on fiddle can seem less full than one on Hardanger fiddle. The fiddle often has been played in ensembles with either other fiddles or other instruments, including that perceived enemy of folk music, the accordion. That the Hardanger fiddle has long been more likely to be performed alone may be entertwined with how tunes are arranged on it, with the many double stops, occasional effect of polyphony, and overall feel of busyness that a solo instrument produces. Perhaps some fiddle playing would be more authentically represented in ensemble, and sound better on radio that way. But—and here is the third element—the author of *these* comments clearly considers that the "thin" sound of the fiddle is not as good as the sound of the Hardanger fiddle.

It was possible to remove certain areas of conflict by avoiding direct comparison between the two types of fiddle. Once the National Fiddle Contest was large enough so that money for two or more panels of judges was available—there have been seven panels in recent years—nearly every competition bracket was divided by affiliation with one or the other type of fiddle. Thus, we do not just have solo brackets for each fiddle type, but separate categories for fiddle clubs *(lagspel)* employing each instrument, for pair dancing to music played by each, and for fiddle construction. The only competition brackets that involve fiddles and not divided by fiddle type are two of the dance events, that for solo *halling (lausdans)* and for dancing by entire clubs *(lagdans)*. During a mixed event such as the National Fiddle Contest, no one in the audience sits through every performance or competition bracket. Spectators tend to seek out events with contestants from their own areas, although this tendency overlaps with an overall greater interest in the high-skill brackets. The fiddle district events are at least as well attended as the Hardanger fiddle district's, on average. Also, most fiddle clubs use just one type of fiddle. The few that don't, all located in the "mixed" area in the West, generally do not combine fiddle and Hardanger fiddle in performance. Moreover, these clubs' mixed instrumentation is matched by catholic thinking about folk music; the polarized views espoused in central Hardanger fiddle and certain fiddle areas are avoided.

Impossible to avoid are interrelated larger issues that are loosely linked to the different fiddle types, and that also provoke controversy between style areas for fiddle, and even between players in an area. The fiddle has lost less of its historical connection with dancing than has the Hardanger fiddle, and its players are less enthusiastic about contests than those of the Hardanger fiddle. I speculated above that players of the fiddle whose performance style was especially dance-oriented seemed to lose points for this during the 1950s. Some time later, objections to the effect of contests and concerts on musical style began to mount. Sverre Halbakken complained in 1972 that "the old pieces have over considerable time in contests become evaluated on a false scale, i.e., from the point of view of one-sided concert use. It's a dangerous development to separate out pieces from a dance reper-toire" (*Spelemannsbladet* 1972 [6]: 18). Shortly thereafter, Ivar Schjølberg asserted that "the contest system is an elite development that we must get away from. . . . All folk music is in principle equally good [but] the "well-developed/expanded" *[godt utbygde]* tunes and dances are favored at contests" (*Spelemannsbladet* 1974 [2–3]: 10). Such comments as these generally appeared singly, and were diplomat-ically phrased. Their impact was indeed felt, but gradually and only somewhat later. What is of greatest significance is that most were from players of the fiddle. At the center of these players' restlessness was a desire to make contests more responsive to folk dance and other folk-ways, even to replace or supplement contests with other types of event. Today, the annual array of events under the aegis of the National Fiddlers' Association consists of many contests and a very few con-certs in the Hardanger fiddle district, but balances contests with con-certs and mixed festivities omitting or minimizing competition in the fiddle area. And the degree to which an art orientation is appropriate in fiddle or Hardanger fiddle performance continues to be controver-sial, especially for the fiddle. In the following chapters, I will examine these topics as folk musicians of today approach them.

1. Ivar Schjølberg, school principal, at home in Vågåmo, 1989. He was raised in Ålen, and continues to play solo in a Røros-area style, although shifting to a Gudbrandsdal style with the Vågå Spel- og Dansarlag for daily playing and ensemble competition. He won the National Fiddle Contest in 1980 and 1983, and led the National Fiddlers' Association during 1984–88.

2. Reidar Skjelkvåle, city official in charge of cleanliness of food and water, at home in Oslo, 1993. The most famous of the fiddle-playing sons of Rikard Skjelkvåle, he was raised in Skjåk in the Gudbrandsdal, but has lived in Oslo for decades, where he led a fiddle club for migrants from the Gudbrandsdal. He won the National Fiddle Contest in 1977 and 1978, and tied with Bjørn Odde and Hans Holen in 1979.

3. Amund Bjørgen, manager of a furniture factory, winner of the National Fiddle Contest in 1966, 1967, 1972, 1976, 1985, 1986, and 1993, at home in Lom, 1991.

4. Knut Kjøk, farmer, winner of the National Fiddle Contest in 1975, 1982, 1987, 1988, and 1990, in front of the Fel-Jakup Prize (a tapestry) in the home he shares with his parents in Lom, 1993. His father, Erling, was one of the most influential fiddlers of the previous generation; his mother and sister are prominent singers. He learned principally from his father but, during his years of university study in Oslo, worked with fellow Gudbrandsdal transplants Reidar Skjelkvåle and Pål Skogum.

5. Knut Kjøk conducting the Lom Spelmannslag during evening dancing at the 1993 National Fiddle Contest in Lillehammer. He also fiddles for an outstanding *gammaldans* ensemble, Bælg og Streing (Bellows and Strings; selections from this group's repertoire dominate the section of the Tune Anthology devoted to *gammaldans* music).

6. Arne M. Sølvberg (right), farmer, of Stryn, observing Helga Norman Møller, student (who intends to teach violin to children), of Trysil (now living in Oslo) in my hotel room in Lillehammer, 1993. Arne won the National Fiddle Contest in 1989, when Håkon Høgemo won the Hardanger fiddle division. They were the first winners to come from the West.

7. Tron Steffen Westberg, student (of environmental studies), in his parents' backyard in Brekken, 1993. He lives in Telemark as of this writing, and often plays Hardanger fiddle.

8. Arild Hoksnes, free-lance radio personality, program creator, *gammaldans* authority, and musician (raised in Aukre), and son, at home outside Trondheim, 1993. He began editing the *Spelemannsblad* in fall of 1994.

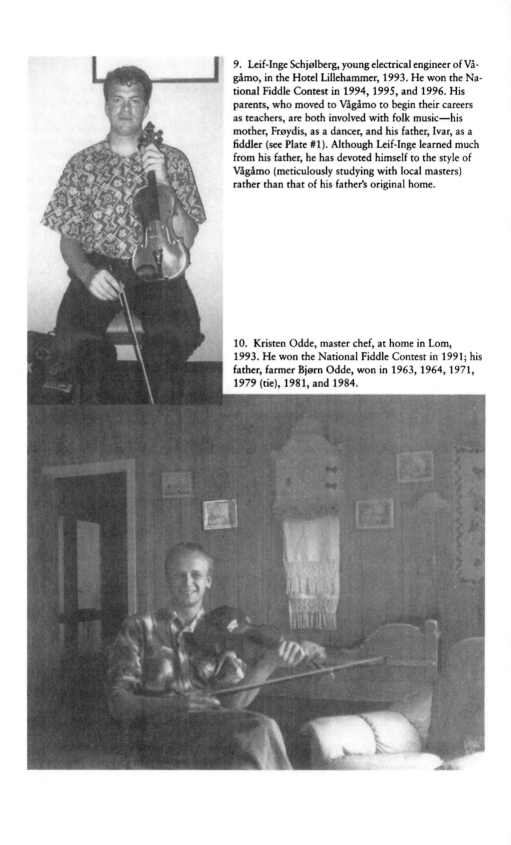

9. Leif-Inge Schjølberg, young electrical engineer of Vågåmo, in the Hotel Lillehammer, 1993. He won the National Fiddle Contest in 1994, 1995, and 1996. His parents, who moved to Vågåmo to begin their careers as teachers, are both involved with folk music—his mother, Frøydis, as a dancer, and his father, Ivar, as a fiddler (see Plate #1). Although Leif-Inge learned much from his father, he has devoted himself to the style of Vågåmo (meticulously studying with local masters) rather than that of his father's original home.

10. Kristen Odde, master chef, at home in Lom, 1993. He won the National Fiddle Contest in 1991; his father, farmer Bjørn Odde, won in 1963, 1964, 1971, 1979 (tie), 1981, and 1984.

11. Mari Eggen (left), of the mid-Gudbrandsdal (but now teaching violin in Røros), with duo partner, Helene Høye, and singer, following a concert at a small museum in Vågåmo, 1991. Eggen learned at first from a neighbor, but later from Knut Kjøk, Pal Skogum, Amund Bjørgen, Hjalmar Fjellhammer, and contemporaries in her home fiddle club; her repertoire is a broad mid-to-north Gudbrandsdal one. She won the National Fiddle Contest in 1992; she was the first woman to capture either solo fiddle division.

12. Marianne Tomasgård (left; raised in Nannesstad, north of Oslo, but playing tunes from her father's former home in the Hornindal, in the West), with her cousin, playing in the chamber division at the 1991 National Festival for *Gammaldans* Music in Vågåmo.

13. Stein Bjørnsmoen (lower left; from near Hamar, but has moved around Norway because of his job in the oil industry) and friends from the Hamar area (with an Austrian and an American), relaxing in the camping area for the 1993 National Fiddle Contest.

14. Sturla E. Sundli (an emerging star, center) and friends, in front of the ski-jump for the 1993 Olympics, playing *gammaldans* music for the crowd pictured in Plate 13.

15. Bente Kvile Buflod, of Trysil, playing for dancers competing in the 1989 National Fiddle Contest in Trysil, the logging heritage of which is celebrated in the photomontage used as a backdrop.

16. Øystein Rudi Ovrum (left) and the other members of Nye Ringnesin, a typical modern folk *gammaldans* group, including members from several towns in the Gudbrandsdal, competing at the 1991 National Festival for *Gammaldans* Music in Vågåmo.

17. The Vågå Spelmannslag, competing in the fiddle club division in the 1993 National Fiddle Contest in Lillehammer.

18. The Lom Juniorlag, competing in the junior fiddle-club division in the 1989 National Fiddle Contest in Trysil. Note that there is not just one regional folk outfit worn.

CHAPTER THREE

Fiddlers and Fiddle Clubs in the Late Twentieth Century

Who Becomes a Fiddler?

The purpose of this chapter is to delve more deeply into the collective background and character of today's fiddlers' and to look closely at the types of fiddle clubs they join. Many of the fiddlers I will mention repeatedly appear in the gallery of photographs. Some of my conversations with fiddlers were fairly free, while others were tightly structured around a set of interview questions. In most interviews, I would intersperse questions with requests for tunes. I would let the conversation flow in directions dictated by its own dynamics, but try to pose some form of basic questions sooner or later. In a few cases, where it was inconvenient to interview in person, I sent willing fiddlers a page of questions, a repertoire sheet, and a blank audio tape. I will begin this summary with groups of the questions on the written form of the interview and the responses elicited.

"Hvor kommer du fra?" "Og foreldrene dine?" "Hvilket yrke har du idag?" "Hvilke yrker har/hadde de?" ["Where are you from?" "And your parents?" "What is your current profession?" "What are/were your parents' profession(s)?"]

Most of the fiddlers in their fifties whom I interviewed were from the same towns or villages as their parents. Exceptions included Ivar Schjølberg, who moved to the Gudbrandsdal for reasons of health, and Reidar Skjelkvåle, whose profession forced a move from the Gudbrandsdal to Oslo. Also, all of the fiddlers who were farmers (of whatever age) were, of course, from the same locations as their parents, since farming is an inherited—and slowly shrinking—profession, one almost never taken up by children of parents in any other line of work. On the other hand, while the older fiddlers have managed to stay home, most of the younger fiddlers I interviewed, that is, those under thirty five, do not now live where they grew up. Many would like to go home, and some will eventually manage to. Kristen Odde, in his early thirties, came back to Lom after his studies and, though now a master chef, seems to be in line to take over the family farm (I would guess that he will combine professions in time, though it is far too early to tell). Knut Kjøk, now in his mid-forties, studied in Oslo, but returned to Lom to work the family farm. Some professions might allow an eventual return home, such as Mari Eggen's teaching of violin to children. She now lives and works in Røros, but a similar job might open up someday in the Espedal or at least nearby, in the main valley of which the Espedal is a tributary, the Gudbrandsdal. But more and more professions will be less portable. For instance, Bente Tomasgård Storbakken's research with emulsifiers will be unlikely to return her to the Horningdal, in the West.

Most Norwegians wish intensely to reside where they grew up, indeed believe deep down that they should and that it ought somehow to be possible. On the other hand, they know intellectually that modern life and the contemporary distribution of professions will inevitably interfere with their desire and inherited duty to stay or return "home." Ideally, a fiddler grows up where his or her parents did, and naturally cultivates the fiddle repertoire and style of that area. But when the parents grow up and play in the style of a place other than where their child is raised and begins to fiddle, the assigning of tradition becomes more complicated. Younger fiddlers then have a choice of where to locate their folk-music "home." This will generally be where they grow up, but can instead be where a fiddling parent (in most cases the father) was raised. Marianne Tomasgård plays music from her father's former home, the Hornindal (in the West), where she has never lived, while Siv-Marit Johnson Nyplass plays in the Røros style, not any associated with Tromsø, the far northern city from which her parents moved just before her birth. How to choose a valid home tradition will only become more complicated as time passes and families relocate more often.

The range of professions among today's top fiddlers is fairly typical for modern Norway, although farmers are somewhat disproportionately represented. Virtually everyone has rural ties; it is hard to find any Norwegian without farmers just a generation or two back.

"Når begynnte du å spille fele?" "Hvem lærte deg?" ["When did you begin to fiddle?" "Who taught you?"]

Most of the top fiddlers began playing between the ages of six and eleven. Few begin earlier, for several reasons. Norwegians are careful to let children be children, and don't attempt to create prodigies of any kind by pushing them into any demanding activity (skiing is not considered one of those; many kids are on short, wide sticks nearly as soon as they can walk). Also, smaller violins (the standard children's quarter, half, and three-quarter models) are not numerous in folk fiddling families. Starting later than an age of eleven or twelve is also uncommon among the better fiddlers. Exceptions to this pattern, such as Jens Nyplass (began at sixteen) and Arild Hoksnes (seventeen), generally have developed dexterity and musicality for many years on other instruments. Many other fiddlers start this late or even later in life, but they aren't really in the running to join the select group of the truly skilled.

Many fiddlers now in their mid-sixties or older began to play on primitive homemade fiddles, a practice dating back centuries. Just one of my consultants in his fifties, Bjørn Odde, did this. All of the younger fiddlers I interviewed started on real violins. It seems that the formerly common practice of starting to play on a protofiddle was a matter of necessity that never became a valued custom.

All other players and many younger fiddlers first learned from either their fathers or other relative or from lodgers in their homes, with supplementary exposure to others who came to the house to visit and fiddle. Some of the younger top fiddlers came up through the fiddle club *(spelemannslag)* system. In brief, a child may have his or her first lessons with the leader of a children's club that serves as a training group for the main local fiddle club, then the youngsters destined to be top fiddlers will "graduate" to work directly with one or more central older fiddlers in the area. The least traditional approach, but one becoming more and more common, is for a fiddler first to learn some violin playing at school, then choose to branch off in the direction of folk fiddling. The most traditional approach was indicated in the words of two fiddlers I interviewed. Young fiddler Ståle Paulsen described himself as initially "self-taught," while older Bjørn Odde said that "no one" taught him. In both cases, the verbal formulation reflects the fact that in the traditional way of learning fiddle, there are no formal lessons, but rather unsystematic observation and imitation, and rote learning of repertoire. Odde's way of saying this is particularly old-fashioned in its modesty. He did not have a teacher, but claimed no role for himself in the learning process either.

The vast majority of the better fiddlers grew up in families that already had fiddlers in them. It is not that older players carefully handed down a hobby or a part-time job, but rather that these houses were ones in which music was welcome, fiddles physically present (instruments that once represented a considerable investment, and still are not something to buy on a whim), and a first teacher or model readily available. This is another pattern that will continue to loosen up, since less of the time relaxing after work on a winter's evening need be inside the home, because travel is so much easier now than in the past, and since more schools have music programs, a modest but increasing number of which now include folk music.

"Hva slags musikk ble spilt og hørt i hjemmet ditt?" "Fortell litt om hvorden musikksmaken did har utviklet seg." "Kan du beskrive samlingen din av grammofonplater og Lydbånd?" ["What kinds of music were played and heard in your home when you were growing up?" "Say a bit about how your own musical taste developed." "Could you describe your collection of records and tapes?"]

Nearly every prominent fiddler was raised on a steady aural diet of *folkemusikk* and *gammaldans* music. Players today associated more with *gammaldans* music than with *folkemusikk,* such as Arild Hoksnes and Sturla E. Sundli, also heard more *gammaldans* music as children. Most all of these fiddlers' mothers belonged to a generation in which women rarely fiddled. If these women were musically active, this took the form of singing, often of hymns but sometimes of folk songs or folk religious songs. The few fiddlers who recalled hearing all sorts of music at home in their youth, particularly Arild Hoksnes and Marianne Tomasgård, are also the well-known fiddlers with the most catholic tastes today. Harald Gullikstad's father was both a teacher and part-time farmer, precisely the professions that Harald combines. In his father's day, teachers had to be models of propriety and couldn't go to dances. His father played church organ and did not interfere with Harald's exposure to the fiddling of the upstairs lodgers.

Nearly all of these fiddlers enjoyed the folk music and *gammaldans* music heard constantly in their homes from as far back as they remember, or at least like to recall that this was the case. Other musical tastes, particularly in recorded popular music, were usually age-bound, arriving and departing in a typical schedule. Today, although some fiddlers claim to like "all kinds" of music, many more supplement their affection for the oral tradition tunes they perform with a taste for classical music or jazz, musics that, like folk music, require careful attention on the part of the listener. Most, but not all, fiddlers own substantial collections of recordings, with some or considerable emphasis on *folkemusikk* and *gammaldans* music. In one exception, Reidar Skjelkvåle has a good-sized collection of recordings, but few are of folk tunes. He prefers to restrict these to the active side of his musical life; he listens to some kinds of music and performs others. Many fiddlers from the Røros area or elsewhere in eastern Norway own quite a few recordings of Swedish fiddlers, sometimes nearly as many as they have of Norwegian traditional music. But few of them play more than a handful of Swedish tunes (Marianne Tomasgård, with her relatively free and confident approach to tradition, is the exception here). The joint collection of Jens Nyplass and Siw-Marit Johnson Nyplass is about 30% jazz recordings, 20% folk music (about a third of that Swedish), 40% rock or pop, and 10% classical (she prefers Bach, he Tchaikovsky). The proportion of folk recordings they own would increase were more available.

"Hvor bor du idag?" "Tror du at du skal bo der alltid?" "Hvordan er du knyttet til området/stedet hvor du vokste opp?" ["Where do you live now?" "Do you expect to remain there for the rest of your life?" "In what ways are you linked to the area where you grew up?"]
    None of the fiddlers anthologized here spent their childhoods in any of Norway's bigger cities, though many have lived in either Oslo or Trondheim during their university years, and a few still begrudgingly remain in those cities. Of the fiddlers over the age of forty whose tunes appear in these pages, nearly all now live near their birthplaces. Exceptions include Ivar Schjølberg, who left Ålen partly for reasons of health, and Reidar Skjelkvåle and Stein Bjørnsmoen, whose professions keep them away from "home." On the other hand, well under half of the fiddlers under forty considered here live (as of this writing) near their birthplaces and the homes of the styles of fiddling they nurture. Kristen Odde's profession of master chef has let him come home to Lom in the Gudbrandsdal, and Jens Nyplass, Siw-Marit Johnson Nyplass, and Magne Haugom have managed to stay in the Røros area, the first two by taking over the Nyplass farm and Haugom by stubbornly patching together a livelihood in the area he loves.
    Each of the fiddlers I talked to who now lives near where he or she

was born expects to stay there, but most who now dwell far away from their original homes expect to move again. Bente Tomasgård said in 1989 that she might have to move to Oslo to get a job in her field; she didn't, in the end, have to go there, but isn't back home in the Hornindal either. Reidar Skjelkvåle came the closest to admitting having moved permanently. He said, "Well, I've lived here [in Oslo] a long time," without enthusiasm. All fiddlers said that they were strongly linked to the places they grew up, and those who were comfortable analyzing that connection described it as being through family and music (the order of these two terms was split fairly evenly).

"Hva slags musikkaktivitater tar du del i idag?" "Hvor mange timer bruker på hver aktivitet i en typisk uke?" ["What sorts of music-related activities do you participate in these days?" "How many hours a week do spend with each during a typical week?"]

Nearly all fiddlers belong to and take part regularly in the various activities of fiddle clubs. Many fiddlers, including most of the top fiddlers I interviewed, also belong to *gammaldans* ensembles. There are a few exceptions. Harald Gullikstad ended ten years in a *gammaldans* group in 1987, and Amund Bjørgen does not belong to such a group. But both men, like all fiddlers belonging to a fiddle club, play quite a bit of *gammaldans* music through their clubs (less often true for Hardanger fiddle players) and both have done some judging at the National Festival for *Gammaldans* Music. Some players are in several clubs, reflecting a simple desire for many hours in the company of other musicians or resulting from a change of residence. A Norwegian nevers truly moves away from where he or she was raised, and so will seize chances to play with groups from "home," but at the same time will keep in playing trim and social health by participating in folk music performances wherever he or she lives. For instance, Bente Tomasgård played with Spelemannslaget i BUL Nidaros while studying in Trondheim in 1988–89, but also with her first home club (the Hornindal Spelemannslag) when travel home or to a big folk event created an opportunity. She also played with another home club made up of young women, a virtuosic ensemble called the Honndalstausene.

Some of these fiddlers also perform in duets or trios. These chamber ensembles may play in concerts, but their main venue is the chamber ensemble bracket *(gruppespel)* in contests. Mari Eggen has won that bracket several times with her duo partner, Helene Høye; Leif-Inge Schjølberg often pairs with Ivar Oddness (a slightly older friend in Vågåmo) or with his father; and Marianne Tomasgård competes in a

duo with a cousin. Tron Westberg and Magne Haugom are among the most polished duets, and are easily the most popular with audiences (though Tron's move west may spell the end of their partnership), whereas Bjørn Odde and his sons Johannes and Kristen occasionally assemble to form the most skilled trio. Many other fiddlers form such alliances—some stable, some not—from time to time.

Several of the better fiddlers are near-professionals or work full-time in music-related activities, although patched-together incomes, far from rare in Norway, remain the rule for those who earn money in connection with folk music. Arne M. Sølvberg is one of a half-dozen folk musicians employed half-time by the county of Sogn og Fjordane. When I spoke with him during the summer of 1993, he wasn't sure that county money would continue to be available for support of this cadre of folk musicians, but he had mixed feelings about this, since he felt his farm needed more attention. Mari Eggen, among the handful of fiddlers who have studied folk music in an academic setting for a year or two, spent a year working in a folk music group in Florida's Disney World, and now teaches children violin in a music school. Arild Hoksnes, for some years folk music consultant for national radio, now successfully freelances in this area, and has just (fall 1994) taken on the half-time position of editing the *Spelemannsblad*. All of these musicians fiddle many hours a week in many settings, playing in some or most of these for little or no pay. Hoksnes, for instance, remains active in Hørkelgådden, a *gammaldans* and *folkemusikk* ensemble with roots in Nordmøre, has a *gammaldans* ensemble in Trondheim called *Nordafjells*, helps out Spelemannslaget i BUL Nidaros now and again, produces records, has had a transcription business, and more. While most fiddlers are folk musicians only in their spare time, these and a few others are on the way to creating a new profession, the full-time folk musician earning a living outside academia.

The majority of fiddlers neither expect nor wish to earn their living in music. Their practice habits often reflect this. The most common pattern of solitary practicing adds just an hour or two a week to the time spent with their fiddle club, which varies from just an hour or two in slack seasons to ten or more hours when preparing for or participating in contests, dances, or other events (true for both fiddle types). Rather than practice systematically, most top fiddlers just work carefully toward specific occasions, and skip those events if generous time to prepare is not available. There is some difference between the approaches of the champions in their fifties and those now in their

late twenties or early thirties. Kristin Odde practices more than his father, Bjørn, and Leif-Inge Schjølberg practices more, and more systematically, than does his father, Ivar. Although the parents have greater and less-flexible responsibilities, this doesn't fully explain the situation. The younger generation grew up with more and more regularly available leisure, and in many cases structured much of this free time around fiddling. Technical standards in contests continue to rise as a result, and the older generation is being passed by during this decade. Whether or not the youngsters are as musical as the previous generation is hotly debated, but that they have overtaken their elders in technical fluency is undeniable.

"Er det noen dansetyper i folkemusikken eller gamaldans du spiller idag som du liker bedre en andre?" *"Kan du skille mellom felemusikk som du spiller pa kappleik og til dans?"* ["Of the genres of folk music and *gammaldans* music that you play today, are there some that you prefer?" "What is the difference between what you play in contests and at dances?"]

However much a champion fiddler enjoys playing *gammaldans* music, he or she likes folk music best, and, among *folkemusikk* genres, almost always prefers that complex triple-time genre whose local variants are called *springleik, springar, pols,* and so forth. While most fiddlers were remarkably patient with all of my questions, and rather skilled at keeping a straight face when I floundered, more than a few jaws dropped when I asked this particular question. Several players would only play examples of their local species of this array of genres for me, however wide their repertoires. They clearly felt that this was the music I should collect and study. There were few addenda or exceptions. Bente Tomasgård mentioned especially liking both *springar* and *bruremarsj* (bridal march), the latter a genre especially strong in her area, and Kristen Odde added *halling* to *springleik*. Arild Hoksnes and Sturla E. Sundli, who come from areas richer in *gammaldans* music than in *folkemusikk*, as a result favor *gammaldans* tunes in older styles.

The more successful a contest fiddler, the more easily he or she answered my question concerning differences between contest and dance music. Knut Kjøk spoke for many in describing contest pieces as harder, more unusual, and rarer. Tron Westberg added "driving rhythm" to these characterizations. Mari Eggen both specified genres played more at contests than elsewhere, (i.e., marches and listening pieces) and mentioned that tempos at dances were faster. Bjørn Odde

demonstrated the subtler and more varied rhythms he and many others employ at contests, and Amund Bjørgen said that he sought a certain purity *(reinleik)* in contest tunes. Other top players, particularly players of *pols* such as Ivar Schjølberg and Jens Nyplass, averred that there was little difference between how they played at dances and at contests, and also stated that theirs was an uncommon, but justifiable, choice. I will examine current approaches to contest playing in more detail in later chapters, but one generalization may be made now. The better players may have different attitudes toward how one ought to choose tunes for contests and how to shape a winning performance, but all have thought long about this issue, and each has developed a heartfelt point of view.

The last question on the structured interview was *"Hva ellers vil du si?"* ["What else would you like to say?"] Sometimes this was phrased differently: "What other questions do you think I should have asked you?"

Most fiddlers were more comfortable playing another tune than continuing to talk, although a few of them decided this would be a good moment to criticize some aspect of the folk music milieu. One older fiddler spoke harshly about the younger generation, most of whom he felt played mechanically and, even if talented, had let an emphasis on technical expertise smother that gift. Several fiddlers criticized the contest system. Others added details that belatedly had come to mind on a topic discussed earlier.

In further, more relaxed conversation, I continued to explore the general topic that several of the previous questions had been intended to lead toward, that is, why these persons had become fiddlers, and what about them besides their fiddling might set them apart from the general population of Norway. Some players were uncomfortable with this line of inquiry; they seemed to wish to obey the old village dictum of not considering themselves special or superior in any way. They tried to keep their replies narrowly restricted to circumstance. They had encountered and been attracted to fiddling in the family or among friends, and owed much to the generosity of one or more mentors or to the nurturing atmosphere of a solid fiddle club. Nevertheless, plenty of other Norwegians with similar opportunities did not become fiddlers. Might members of the folk music milieu have particular character traits? Is fiddling regularly coupled with other activities, or with patterns of taste or of consumption?

Neither the Norwegian folk music community nor the subset with which this book is concerned, players of the fiddle, constitutes a taste public as defined by Gans (1974:71). Members of each generation of this community and of the subdivision in question do indeed match up well in terms of income, educational background, religion, and general character, but in each of these ways and in many others also blend into the general population of Norway (possibly excluding more internationally oriented segments of the population of Oslo, which is Norway's only truly European city). Nor is the more flexible concept of the culture class helpful. This has been defined simply as a group with shared patterns of consumption, not initially assuming the common demographic factors sought in defining a taste public (see Peterson and DiMaggio 1974:504 and Lewis 1975:229). The problem once again is not lack of unity in the concerned population sample, but that the variety in Norwegian life is less in comparison not just with the United States, but with most other countries in Europe, as well. Most of the Norwegian populace (again, perhaps excepting Oslo) is a single culture class and a unified taste public, with statistically significant differences only between generations.

What ties these fiddlers together is, in the end, what one would expect: a strong dedication to the traditional Norwegian skein of local identities and to the Norwegian way of life. It is not an accident that the vast majority in the folk music community opposed joining the European Economic Community in 1972, nor that today's members continue to be wary of closer ties to Europe and of any other hint of a threat to Norwegian sovereignty. Arild Hoksnes suggested to me that fiddlers are especially eager to talk to old people, thereby learning repertoire and at the same time absorbing traditional attitudes. I found that folk musicians are slightly less likely than are other Norwegians to have stark modern furnishings, and correspondingly more likely to own elaborately carved, unfinished antique furniture and anything decorated with *rosemaling* (see the first few plates). They are a bit more likely to wear specifically Norwegian formal garb *(bunader)* on ceremonial occasions, and are even perhaps marginally more stubborn than average Norwegians about employing local spoken dialects. These differences between this community and the general populace are very modest, but I believe valid, and they do add up. Norwegian players of the fiddle are among the those who have chosen to bear some responsibility for Norway's remaining distinctly and persistently Norwegian, though many or most Norwegians believe in this goal to some extent.

The Fiddle Club

Nearly all Norwegian fiddlers belong to a fiddle club, some of them to two. In these groups, experts stand next to musicians of middling or little ability, all joining together to play the tunes of their community. Although much of this book deals with those considered to be the best musicians, most fiddlers are dedicated lovers of music, dancing, and tradition whose enthusiasm outweighs their skill. The fiddle club offers a home for individuals of widely varying levels of both skill and commitment to commune through music, to celebrate local culture, and to learn—and perhaps to rise into the ranks of the master fiddlers. And the top fiddlers need not be reduced to solitary playing, or to none at all, if circumstances limit their practice time. If they are out of playing trim for a while, or if they feel the time has come to retire permanently from solo competition, they simply relax among friends and neighbors in the nurturing, but less demanding, routine of orchestral performance. Most important, the atmosphere and activities of a lively fiddle club are the most powerful recruiting tools that Norwegian folk music possesses.

Ensemble fiddling dates back at least to the eighteenth century in Norway. The earliest records link more than one fiddle playing at a time primarily to weddings. Whether multiple fiddles generally meant just greater volume or whether several distinct parts were played we don't know. In time, both playing in parallel octaves and in simple arrangements dominated by parallel thirds and sixths came into use, but how this compared in frequency with simple unison doubling cannot be known. In any case, ensemble playing before our century was generally the result of happenstance or job related and included, at most, a handful of fiddles. The formal institution of the fiddle club is really rather recent, with the vast majority of clubs formed after World War II. Nevertheless, this institution was immediately tacitly considered authentic and traditional. Though originally controversial, the fiddle club ensemble performance bracket *(lagspel)* has in recent decades become in certain ways the most important part of most contests and concerts, even though much older forms of performance— for example, some *gammaldans* genres—remain either controversial or banned on the grounds of age. Audiences love to hear *and* see a complete club perform for reasons symbolic, social, and aesthetic, and having numerous clubs present swells audience size exponentially. I will describe a sample few of these fiddle clubs, in each case presenting some mix of history, analysis of membership, and inventory of activities.

One of the most successful clubs is the Vågå Spel- og Dansarlag, which has the largest total membership of any club affiliated with the National Fiddlers' Association, about 220 fiddlers, dancers, and other aficionados. The area nurturing the group, in the heart of the north Gudbrandsdal, is rich in traditional music. Ola Ringneset ("Gammel-Ringnesin," 1811–1902) and Iva Bråtå (1827–1916) were far from the earliest well-known fiddlers in the area, but became central influences on local fiddling. Earlier fiddlers remembered in the titles of numerous pieces included Aslak Holen ("Gamel-Holin," 1749–1838) and, among roughly a dozen other performers, one nineteenth-century woman, "Blind-Marit" (Marit Arnesdotter of Sel, a nearby village).

The Vågå Spel- og Dansarlag was founded in 1952 as the Vågå Spelmannslag, with no more than a dozen fiddlers. Musicians from the area had formed ad-hoc ensembles before—Øvsteng makes special mention of a young people's meeting in Lillehammer during June of 1927, at which five fellows from Lalm played together (1992:7; Lalm is a hamlet in the Vågå area just twelve kilometers downstream from the larger village of Vågåmo). Initially, membership of the Vågå Spelmannslag drew about equally from Vågåmo and Lalm, and leadership of the club alternated between the two hamlets annually after 1956. In 1961 the group split for economic reasons into the Vågåmo Spelmannslag and the Lalm Spelmannslag. The latter group lasted as a formal entity just four years; its members, while distinguished, were older, and they had less luck recruiting and in maintaining cohesion than the other club. It is difficult to predict which locales will prove lasting fertile ground for fiddle clubs and where, instead, enthusiasm will flag. In this half-century in the North Gudbrandsdal, formerly vigorous milieus, including Lalm and Skjåk, have declined, while Vågåmo and Lom/Garmo have flourished (Skjåk, the home of Fel-Jakup and later the Skjelkvåle clan, may be about to stage a return).

The Vågåmo Spelmannslag reclaimed the title and territory of the Vågå Spelmannslag in 1980, then in 1990 incorporated the young Vågå Dansarlag (founded in 1981) to become the Vågå Spel- og Dansarlag. Membership stabilized within a few years at around twenty regularly participating fiddlers. Photographs of the group from 1955, 1965, 1978, and 1983 show only men, while a picture thought to be from the later 1950s includes one woman, Borgny Eide, member of an important family of fiddlers from Lalm (Øvsteng 1992:18, 30, 32, 55, and 19). Women were not explicitly forbidden to fiddle in early times, but generally followed tradition and did not. Time was often not available, and the often raucous and bibulous atmosphere enjoyed by many male fiddlers (especially in earlier years, though not entirely gone even in these wholesome days) was not one women generally found attractive. The first club bylaws included a provision procribing intoxicants at practices and other meetings (Øvsteng 1992:18), a provision that took hold gradually. Today there are a handful of young women fiddlers in the Vågå Spel- og Dansarlag proper, and as many girls as boys in the younger groups that feed into the senior club.

This fiddle club has always been linked with contests. The same year that the Vågå Spelmannslag was founded, it organized a contest for the Ottadal, the province including the Gudbrandsdal. The second of the series of contests that would in time be entitled the District Contest for fiddle took place in Vågåmo in 1955. The club sponsored this important contest again in 1962, 1967, 1978, and 1983, as well as the National Fiddle Contest in 1964. This last task was not easy, even though just 135 fiddlers and 143 dancers registered for competition. Hotels then were few, and nearly all competitors and audience members who had traveled a significant distance to the event had to be lodged privately. The group's most ambitious job of sponsoring an event was the 1991 National Festival for *Gammaldans* Music (described in the Chap. 5). Holding it in Vågåmo was made possible by the rapid increase in hotel beds in recent years, the growth of camping as a lodging alternative at all such events, and the construction that year of a new public meeting (and sports) hall, the Vågåhall, where most of the events in the festival would be held.

Each fiddle club has an administrative leader, a position that generally changes hands every few years, and a musical leader, whose tenure can be much longer. Harald Haug (b. 1920) led this club for its first thirty seven years. His first task was to convince a variety of strong-opinioned tradition bearers to submit to "club discipline" *(lagdisiplin),* far from an easy job. Once the group settled into a routine, he would choose repertoire (with feedback from members), craft arrangements of tunes, and lead rehearsals. His approach to many aspects of leading the club was colored by a musical life much more varied than is typical for younger fiddlers today. Haug led or participated in not just the fiddle club but also a salon orchestra, an accordion ensemble, dance bands, a choir, and a *"janitsjar,"* or brass and percussion ensemble. He reads music, and presented his arrangements of tunes in notated form. These arrangements, generally in three parts, emphasized parallel thirds and sixths, with modifications at cadences to yield an effect that is harmonic in a quite conventional way. This worked well for the *gammaldans* tunes, but went a bit less smoothly for melodies in the older genres, and of course was anachronistic for those genres (though the question of authenticity in any area of performance practice is thorny). By the late 1980s, this approach inspired some objections in the club. A few younger members felt that it would be more accurate historically to stick to playing in octaves in the arrangements, and to refer to written music less. Haug retired from the senior club and became one of the instructors for younger players (not an uncommon move for former club leaders). After a brief period of modest turmoil for the group, Kristian Gården (a great-great-grandson of Ola Ringneset) took over as musical leader. Arrangements are now of both old and new types, and pieces of paper somewhat less in evidence than during the Haug years—Gården does not read music himself.

One continued use of notation is in repertoire lists. A *"slåtteoversikt for spelemannslaget 1986,"* that is, a list of the fraction of the repertoire devoted to tunes in *folkemusikk* genres issued that year (and still in use some years later) is two pages long. The first page lists thirty one tunes in three groups, eleven *vals* (i.e., old waltzes), nine *brurmarsj,* and eleven *springleik*s, and the second page adds a group *"på oppstilt bass"* (thus in the tuning A D A E; these include seven *halling*s, a waltz, and four *springleik*s), and a second group *"på oppstilt ters og bass"* (thus in the tuning A E A E, specific to the key of A major; these include six *springleik*s and three waltzes). Seven of the titles on the first page have tune incipits penciled in.

The list for 1991 consists of a page each for *folkemusikk* and *"gamaldans."* The left side of both pages lists twelve tune titles, with the first two or three measures of each tune given on the right (omitting double stops, but including ornaments). Including all of the tune incipits became more important as most of Haug's written arrangements went out of use. The shortest title is "Masurka," the longest "'Vriompeisen,' vals e. J. Hølmo / K. Gården." Enough of the titles are long and distinctive enough so that no title repeats; the list is useful to both music readers and nonreaders. Most of the titles mention a tune as being *"etter"* (in the manner of) someone, and several give more than one name, thus tracing several steps in the transmission and shaping of a tune. The level of attribution detail reflects the need to choose among versions of tunes that various members of the fiddle club knew before those tunes were taken up by the group. Playing precisely the same notes strengthens the feeling of ensemble, may—when different versions of tunes are not the same length—prevent more serious problems, and yields the synchronized effect needed to do well in contests. On the other hand, some critics feel that this practice impoverishes tradition by narrowing the variety of versions of tunes in general use. In fact, this process of selection, employed partly to fulfill contest needs, may be roughly balanced by another regular practice that is also linked with competition—individual fiddlers' seeking out rare versions of tunes for the solo bracket.

This club has from the beginning emphasized performance as a club over solo competition. In recent years, just Ivar and Leif-Inge Schjølberg have represented the group in the solo A class of fiddlers, but the group as a whole has done well in competition all along. They won the club *(lagspel)* bracket at the National Fiddle Contest in 1957 (tied with Lom), 1961, 1971, 1976 (in a three-way tie), 1978 (tied with Lom), and 1982; they have placed in the top three a total of seventeen times (by 1994). They have won the District Contest thirteen times, and almost always take second or third place at the much younger National Festival for *Gammaldans* Music. Overall, their record in club competition is second only to that of the Lom Spelmannslag, their friendly rival based a dozen kilometers up the valley. The Lom Spelmannslag has won (or tied) the club competition at the National Fiddle Contest a full thirteen times, and placed in the top three on eighteen occasions. Winning has become progressively harder in all brackets, of course, as the number of entrants has increased. For instance, the Sør-Fron Spel- og Dansarlag is young both in club age and in that nearly all members are less than thirty years old. This group first placed in the top three at the National Fiddle Contest in 1988, the first of three times it won the club bracket.

The Vågå Spel- og Dansarlag has punctuated its regular activities with both travel abroad and accomplishments outside its normal routine at home. Its first tours were to Sweden in 1965 and Belgium in 1968; it has made return visits to both countries. Other trips include several to Scotland and even to the upper Midwest of the United States in 1970. The group has in return been host to visiting ensembles. Since 1986 they have sponsored an annual weekend of concerts and dances (Folkemusikktreff). This is part of a movement throughout much of fiddle territory to have fewer local contests, replacing these with gatherings with less tension and more direct celebration of local tradition. In 1992, a music school was established in Vågåmo. Although it primarily teaches art music, as do most music schools, it draws on the membership of the Vågå Spel- og Dansarlag for instruction in folk

Figure 7. Musicians Active in the Vågå Spel- og Dansarlag, 1989–93

	Sex/ Approx. age (1989)		Profession/Comments
1.	M	63	truck driver; has played a long time; musical leader in 1993
2.	M	45	farmer, has worked in factory
3.	M	72	painter
4.	M	37	editor; his father led the group for many years, until 1988
5.	F	37	nurse; wife of #4
6.	M	48	foreman in furniture factory; lives in Skjåk (near Vågåmo)
7.	M	28	electrician; his father played
8.	M	49	teacher; plenty of fiddling in family; moved from Ålen (in Røros area)
9.	M	23	apprentice electrician; musical leader in 1989; son of #8
10.	M	43	engineer; member of famous local fiddle family
11.	M	17	student; son of #6
12.	F	17	student; daughter of local veterinarian; from the West
13.	M	68	retired museum curator; formerly prominent in the *LfS*
14.	M	26	carpenter
15.	F	15	student; granddaughter of a longtime member; joined after 1989
16.	M	43	pilot; originally from Møre og Romsdal; joined after 1989

Note: Since 1989, fiddler #3 has stopped participating due to age, and fiddler #9 has moved to near Oslo, though he still participates in many of the group's activities.

music. The Folk Music Archive for the North Gudbrandsdal, founded in Vågåmo in 1993, will doubtless have plenty of input from the fiddle club.

Although the complete membership of the Vågå Spel- og Dansarlag exceeds 200 today, just a fraction of that number are fiddlers who participate regularly. The core group of musicians numbers under twenty, about the same number of fiddlers as have played together since the mid-1950s. Figure 7 lists members by sex, approximate age in 1989, profession, family relationships between group members, and in some cases background in fiddling or original home if not Vågåmo. Several families are represented more than once. Fiddler #4 is Trond-Ole Haug, son of Harald Haug and until recently editor of the *Spelemannsblad*. Fiddlers #8 and #9 are Ivar and Leif-Inge Schjølberg. Other immediate family relationships are noted in the chart, but extended relationships are not, and these are important. Fiddler #1, current musical leader Kristian Gården, is one of many members past and present who are descended from the Ringneset family, and other members have genetic or musical pedigrees that lead back to other prominent early fiddlers in the district. Separating the concepts of "local" from "family" would not only be difficult; it would miss the central point that these concepts are intertwined in the psychology of many Norwegians.

The ranges of professions, educational levels, and ages represented in the club are broad, but in no way surprising. On the other hand, statistical bases this small naturally exhibit a quirk or two. For instance, that this group includes fewer farmers than the Lom Spelmannslag bears no special significance. A few of the members moved to Vågåmo from elsewhere. In addition to Ivar Schjølberg, from Ålen originally, fiddler #6, Trygve Auale, commutes from Skjåk (so near that most of the repertoire is shared); fiddler #5, Rigmor Høye, a nurse married to fiddler #4, is from the Østerdal; and fiddler #13, Leif Løchen, came from Oslo. Both Høye and Løchen married in Vågåmo; this is perhaps as common a reason as professional opportunity to move. Løchen, who plays many instruments, was formerly prominent in the National Fiddlers' Association. He resuscitated the *Spelemannsblad* after World War II, and spent some time as National Fiddlers' Association chair.

Like most clubs its size, the Vågå Spel- og Dansarlag includes a principal senior performing ensemble (the group whose membership is analyzed in Fig. 7), a junior group (a *"rekrutt* [recruit] *lag"*) and a few smaller assemblies of the youngest fiddlers, whose meetings are basically lessons. Today, a typical weekly practice of the senior club takes place in the secondary school cafeteria (this is the school where member Tor Stallvik, a well-known dancer, is principal). A committee of three fiddlers in leadership positions in the club has already selected the repertoire to be practiced. In 1988–89 this team included Kristian Gården, musical leader of the club, Leif-Inge Schjølberg, its administrative leader, and Ivar Oddnes, immediate past administrative leader and a skilled composer of second parts (accompanying lines). The practice schedule designates an evening as either *kappleikøving* (contest practice) or *gamaldansøving*, reflecting that while tunes in the older dance genres are played in contests today, local folk dances are almost completely devoted to *gammaldans*.

To begin a practice session, Leif-Inge plays an *a* for the group to tune to; his tuning is particularly stable since he practices regularly (an unusual trait). The rehearsal is low pressure and full of humor. In the two hours (at most) of the meeting, the group will rehearse five to eight tunes. If a contest is imminent, just two to four tunes are worked on, relatively intensively. Each piece is introduced by the leader precisely as it will be performed publicly, ornaments and all, with fiddlers joining in as they catch on. Musical notation may or may not be present, and is at most a memory or learning aid; the definitive version of the tune is what the leader is playing (perhaps a fifth to a third of the members of many clubs do not read music, and most fiddlers who do read do so laboriously, with a particularly precarious command of the notation of rhythm). This perhaps somewhat inefficient, but traditional, rote method of learning tunes is common to the vast majority of clubs. When a piece is taken up by a club, some players will be learning it for the first time, while others will be getting a version under their fingers that is different from one already in their personal repertoire.

Since few players in any club practice intensive simply to maintain the quality of their performance, it might seem surprising that the overall level of performance in this and many clubs remains high. Fiddlers do want to prepare for special events, to perform respectably and not let their fellow members down, and plenty of such events take place. In addition to a handful of dances that they accompany, and a few one-time local performances, the Vågå Spel- og Dansarlag participates in the regular annual rotation of contests and concerts. Approximately two-dozen folk music events are of general enough interest to appear in the event list in the *Spelemannsblad*. A folk musician will attend perhaps a half-dozen of these, for example, one or two local events and several national events. Whether or not a player is on stage at a given event, the allure of musical fellowship in the evenings or playing together in the parking lot mandates some practicing in advance.

Individual fiddlers in the Vågå Spel- og Dansarlag, as well as the group playing as such, are integral to the success of the event unique to the North Gudbrandsdal, the Gudbrandsdalsstemne, held each spring. This is a busy weekend of concerts and dances (described in the next chapter, along with other events). Both the club and the best musicians belonging to it compete in the National Fiddle Contest, held on or near the summer solstice; the National Festival for *Gammaldans* Music, usually held about three weeks later; and the District Contest for fiddle, normally held in early fall. Then, a few members will attend the annual meeting of the National Fiddlers' Association, or some other locale's special event like the Gudbrandsdalsstemne, or perhaps the Førdefestivalen (which is international, but with strong Norwegian participation).

The history and present activities of the Glåmos Spellmannslag parallel those of the Vågå Spel- og Dansarlag in some ways, and contrast in others. Glåmos is a hamlet twelve kilometers north (upstream) of Røros, the high (and cold) mining community—now, with the mines closed, dependent on tourism—that serves as the center of the *pols* area of eastern Norway. Members of the Glåmos Spellmannslag live along the road from Røros through Orvos (home of Jens and Siw-Marit Johnson Nyplass) to Glåmos. Rehearsals are generally in Røros, and the Glåmos Spellmannslag is now the signature club of the immediate Røros area. This district possesses as rich a folk music heritage as does the Gudbrandsdal, but has faced this century's folk revival with rather different attitudes. Documentation of fiddlers extends back into the eighteenth century, but becomes much richer around the middle of the nineteenth century. Just a few of the most prominent fiddlers are: Jens Smed ("Smed-Jens," 1804–88), Ole Henriksen Sulhus (also a smith in the mines and a small farmer, "Sulhusgubba," 1811–97), Ola Klemmetvold (Klemmet-Ola," b. 1905), Henrik Mølmann (1883–1972), Peder Nyhus (b. 1905), and Einar Galåen (b. 1913). As in Vågå, ensemble playing on an informal or by-the-job basis predated the creation of a fiddlers' club. In Røros, the practice can be dated back well into the nineteenth century. Jens Smed and his student Christian Dahl were known for performing together in octaves, in the *"graint og grovt"* (fine and coarse) style, which remains the basis of part-playing in this area.

Peder Nyhus, whose father came from the Funesdal in Sweden, learned much from both Henrik Mølmann and from Ola Klemmetvold, who was the main custodian of the Sulhus tradition. Nyhus, recently deceased, was the principal tradition bearer for fiddling in the immediate area around Røros. Just as there is a contrast between especially artistic, contest-oriented fiddling and performance focused on vigorous dance accompaniment in the north Gudbrandsdal, physically oriented and clean fiddling have existed side by side for some time in the Røros area. In the oldest surviving generation of fiddlers in the north Gudbrandsdal, Hans Brimi represents elegant, delicately nuanced performance, while Ola Oppheim stands for dance playing, with a driving rhythm. These qualities are certainly not mutually exclusive; Brimi is a fine dance fiddler, and Oppheim's playing presents plenty of subtleties. Nevertheless, the side of performance each emphasizes is audible. Both men have been showered with honors, but Brimi entered the contest system early, and has been much the greater influence in the north Gudbrandsdal. In the environs of Røros, Einar Galåen is the cleanest, most art-oriented folk fiddler in the oldest generation, and was the first and for some time the only player from his area to participate in the contest system on the national level. However, Nyhus (who obviously enjoyed contests—a wall in his home is covered with prizes), a much more dance-oriented fiddler than Galåen, was clearly the more influential player.

While the Vågå Spel- og Dansarlag started as a club based in a small community, which therefore contained several groups of related fiddlers, the Glåmos Spellmannslag began as a family group, then expanded to include more and more members of the local community. The Nyhus family had been playing together for some time when the group was formally established in 1950. Its first members were Peder Nyhus and his son Sven, Oddvar Sandnes, and Lars Bendixvold (brother of Anna Nyhus, wife of Peder and mother of Sven). This remained a family group in 1970, at that time including Peder, Anna (who accompanied the group on a *harpeleik,* a strummed zither), Sven and Olav Nyhus (Sven's younger brother), and also Harald Gullikstad and Kristine Wivelstad (related to Jens Nyplass, current musical leader of the group). Since that time, Sven Nyhus has achieved national prominence. His considerable influence radiates out from his long-time home of Oslo, and when he joins a fiddle club in concert, it is Oslo's polished Østerdølenes Spellmannslag (which will be briefly discussed below as the quintessential "city" club). And many younger fiddlers have joined the Glåmos Spellmannslag in the last two decades, so that its family character has been diluted.

The 1989 membership of the Glåmos Spellmannslag is described in Figure 8a. Like most clubs, it is paralleled by a junior, *"rekrutt"* club. The senior club contains three members of the Nyhus family, before Peder's death, but these may be the last members of that clan to belong to the group. Fiddler #1 was Peder Nyhus (still active in 1994!), fiddler #8 his son Olav, and fiddler #5 Olav's American-born wife, Mary Barthelemy, who is the current (1994) administrative leader of the club. Either Olav or Mary plays the zither on a given occasion; Olav may also sing nonlexical syllables when playing zither. Fiddler #2 is Harald Gullikstad, a prominent local fiddle authority whose participation dates back decades. Fiddlers #4 and #3 are Jens Nyplass, musical leader of the group, and Siw-Marit Johnson Nyplass, his wife, who takes on Jens's duties when Jens is absent.

The professions of members in the *lag* are a fair sample of those practiced in the Røros area (Rørostraktom), particularly if we increase our sample by also looking at the professions of the members of the Brekken Spell- og Danselag (see Fig. 8b; Brekken lies thirty five kilometers east of Røros, easily accessible by roads or along a complex of

Figure 8a. Musicians active in the Glåmos Spellmannslag, 1989

Sex/ Approx. age		Profession/Comments
1.	M 84	farmer; head of main local fiddle family; source of music for this group
2.	M 50	school teacher with small farm; learned folk music from upstairs renters
3.	F 24	cashier in pharmacy; no fiddling in family, but married to #4
4.	M 27	worker in farm-oriented store; gradually taking over family farm; leader of group
5.	F 40	tour guide, and helps with farm; married to #8, who is son of #1; American
6.	F 21	student, gone by 1993, but plays with group when can; from Brekken
7.	M 40	former telephone engineer; now craftsman at local museum; from N. Trøndelag
8.	M 55	worker at textile factory; son of #1; married to #5; solid fiddler but better singer
9.	F 24	driving teacher near Trondheim; born near Røros, returns on weekends

8b. Musicians active in the Brekken Spell- og Danselag, 1989

1.	M 47	teacher; he and wife from Røros; father of #4
2.	M 78	farmer/craftsman; father played; middling fiddler but important tune source
3.	M 22	worker with reindeer; national guard; father from Gudbrandsdal; leader in 1993
4.	M 20	student; son of #1, by 1993 in Telemark and mostly playing *hardingfele*
5.	M 67	retired customs officer at Swedish border; makes fiddles; plays some classical
6.	M 65	former worker in building supplies; now paints/traps ptarmigan; extended family fiddles
7.	M 67	carpenter/builder; another long family tradition of fiddling
8.	M 35	carpenter and worker on uncle's farm; son of #7
9.	M 13	student; in extended family of #7
10.	M 40	various professions tried; plays many instruments; in extended family of #7
11.	F 25	secretary in insurance company; lives with #10
12.	M 40	physical therapist; from nearly Sweden; married into community
13.	M 55	artist/craftsman; fiddling in family
14.	M 33	veterinarian from Trondheim; grandfather had a cabin near Brekken
15.	F 40	same immigrant from U.S. as #5 in 8a; rare to play in two groups

lakes; it is just twelve kilometers farther to the border with Sweden). There has not been much industry in the area since the great copper mines closed two decades ago, but tourism is now strong. Nevertheless, this area loses many ambitious youngsters. Tron Steffen Westberg, fiddler #4 in the listing of members of the Brekken club, was in 1989 enduring his mandatory stint in the army, but was home often enough to play frequently with the Brekken Spell- og Danselag and in a highly successful duet with Magne Haugom, fiddler #3. Westberg, long the only fiddler from Brekken in the A class, no longer lives there, and may be losing some of the folk music-based fraction of his incentive to return, since he has taken up the Hardanger fiddle. But Magne Haugom, like Jens Nyplass in Orvos, has decided that remaining in this tradition-rich area is more important than pursuing any ambition at the high level that his ability merits. Nyplass is taking over the family farm. In the summer of 1993, Haugom was commencing a meagerly remunerated employment as the collector for and curator of a modest folk music archive housed on the grounds of the mining museum in Røros. This is not the first systematic collecting to take place in this area, of course. Sven Nyhus's monumental collections of his father's and a few central Brekken fiddlers' tunes were the first thorough modern studies of any fiddle repertoire (1973 and 1983), and the Glamos Spellmannslag had recorded over 200 tunes for the national radio by 1970. But the small, locally nourished archive reflects a wave of local scholarly activity nationwide—as does the modest archive for the north Gudbrandsdal located in Vågåmo—and, happily, provides a way for Magne Haugom, leader of the Brekken Spell- og Danselag, to remain in the Røros area for a time.

A typical practice session of the Glåmos Spellmannslag takes place in a basement room in an old building in downtown historic Røros (once a week, roughly 6:30 to 8:30 P.M.). Members sit around and smoke for a while, then a few fiddles emerge from their cases. Nyplass gives each fiddler an *a*. The first tune is announced by his playing its first measure or so, quickly and with little heed to rhythm. As a rule, the group plays through each tune without pause, though Nyplass has them work on details now and again briefly. No written music intrudes, although Peder Nyhus was used as a one-man archive to recall a detail or two in a given tune, and Jens or Harald Gullikstad might glance later at the tune as transcribed by Sven, in the copies of Sven's books both have at home. In any case, the ensemble agrees on a single version of a tune, and this version must seem consonant with Peder's version. This seems much more straightforward than it can become. While all agree that Peder Nyhus was the ultimate authority concerning how a tune should go, his repertoire existed in several historical layers: (1) as transcribed in Sven's main book (thus from before its publication date of 1973, in the cases of some tunes much earlier), (2) as learned in a fixed form in more recent times by the leader or complete membership of the Glåmos Spellmannslag, and (3) as Peder played it on a given occasion. *His* conception of the identity of any tune remained somewhat fluid, a fact that could clash with the need for a competitive club to achieve tight ensemble. On many occasions, I saw Nyplass leading the club in a wonderfully synchronized performance of a faithful rendition of Peder's version of a tune . . . with the only bow not with the group being Peder's, as he deviated modestly, and seemingly without conscious intent, from the version that had been so painstakingly learned from him.

The Brekken Spell- og Danselag of 1989 had no fewer than five members over the age of fifty five, four of them venerable individualists who could not conceive of not playing their own versions of tunes regardless of what the club was doing. I liked the effect of ornaments popping up in different spots in the ensemble as a tune progressed. And tradition was well served, as various old versions of tunes were aired and offered to younger players. But the feeling of ensemble could not be very tight, and the group could not do at all well in contests, which indeed arouse even less enthusiasm in this group than in the Glåmos Spellmannslag. But by 1993, several of the older fiddlers in the Brekken Spell- og Danselag were attending less regularly, and the new musical leader was young Magne Haugom. This group may be about to follow the Glåmos Spellmannslag a few steps along the road toward the contest-oriented mainstream.

There is no question that the Glåmos Spellmannslag remains primarily dance oriented. They play regularly for dances both at home and occasionally on the road. During a weekend visit to Trondheim in the spring of 1989, they accompanied one dance at a cabin owned by BUL Nidaros for over three hours, then the next night performed even longer as the guest musicians for Arild Hoksnes's weekly Danskafé (a dance with live music). On both evenings they mixed a large dose of *pols* with a leavening of *gammaldans* tunes in oral tradition in the Rørostraktom.

I also saw a subset of the club backing performing dancers. One afternoon during July of 1993, Peder and Olav Nyhus, Harald Gullikstad and I (an instant convert to zither), accompanied four dance couples in two representative venues. In numerous settings, citizens of Røros earn money catering to tourists, and our first stop was a paying job at an ancient farm that is now an open-air museum. We played a few numbers in the courtyard for the dancers, then continued inside over cider. The second function was at an old-folks home, where we were remunerated in heart-felt applause and fattening refreshments. It is in such small, local settings that this fiddle ensemble is most at home.

Although Peder Nyhus enjoyed contests and the attendant fellowship among folk musicians, and entered the solo brackets for older fiddlers faithfully for decades, and although Siw-Marit Johnson (now Nyplass) has staunchly represented the club for years in the A class, other leaders of the club have long been adamantly opposed to the contest system. Harald Gullikstad, after doing some judging decades ago, concluded that the atmosphere was oppressively inauthentic, and ceased participating. Nevertheless, he lent his powerful playing to the vigorous performance of the club during competition at the 1993 National Fiddle Contest, which the club won for the first time (they had never before placed even in the top three). Jens Nyplass agreed with Gullikstad's objections for some time, although he couldn't ignore contests completely, since he was living with the club's only A-class fiddler. Indeed, even his asserting in 1989 that contests ought to be held in small rooms, with dancers responding to the music, illustrates a kind of engagement with the system; he was thinking about how contests needed to be changed to serve both history and current needs. He has since relented in his opposition to contests but not compromised his principles. He competes in the A class, with considerable success, but plays tunes that are common in dances, and does so in a style no different from how he performs those same tunes in a dance setting.

The Røros area, through its premiere folk music clubs, the Glåmos Spellmannslag and the Brekken Spell- og Danselag, has been host to contests and other events regularly since shortly after World War II. Their participation in events sanctioned by the National Fiddlers' Association parallels that of the top Gudbrandsdal groups closely. All attend the National Fiddle Contest and the younger National Festival for *Gammaldans* Music, which the Glåmos Spellmannslag hosted in 1994. The Vågå Spel- og Dansarlag and the Lom Spelemannslag celebrate and advertise their local styles through the Gudbrandsdalsstemnet, while the groups from the Røros area sponsor a somewhat similar annual weekend of locally focused concerts and dances, Brekkendagan (discussed in the following chapter). The Gudbrandsdalsstemne represents a step away from unrelieved contest orientation for the Gudbrandsdal groups, while the Glåmos Spellmannslag has made a number of small but real concessions in the opposite direction, toward the competition focus of the mainstream. Despite manifold differences in the histories, activities, and functional orientations of the clubs considered here, parallels between them are striking too, and may be increasing as each fiddle club adjusts to changing times.

My home fiddle club when I lived in Trondheim during academic year 1988–89 was the Spelemannslag i BUL Nidaros (BUL abbreviates National Youth Association, literally Union of Rural Youth). Placing Nidaros, the old name for the district, in its title associates the club with Trondheim's distinguished history. The city was founded as the capital of the kingdom of Norway in A.D. 997, and is where Norway's modern kings are crowned. King Harald Hardråde, who fell at Stamford Bridge in 1066, set sail from Trondheim. It became the center of the archbishopric of Nidaros soon afterward, and the site of Nidaroskatedralen, the largest cathedral—or large medieval building of any kind—in Scandinavia. Then, in 1536, the Reformation instantly reduced the town's importance. It no longer had concentrated power of any kind, but remained the provincial farming and fishing center.

While Trondheim remains the outlet for one of Norway's richer agricultural areas, its modern national profile reflects its emergence as a center for education and especially for advanced technological research. The membership of Spelemannslaget i BUL Nidaros reflects that twin focus (see Fig. 9). Half of the group as constituted during 1989–93 was employed in science and technology, in most cases in research, while another third of the members were teachers or students (most of the students were in science or technology, too). All in all, the overlapping fields of science, technology, and education account for the professions of twenty five of the thirty musicians active in the club at any time during 1989–93.

This is a city fiddle club reflecting modern urban demography. Although many or most of the members of the clubs from rural areas live where they were raised and are strongly grounded in their local traditions, a minority of those belonging to Spelemannslaget i BUL Nidaros are traditional musicians from Trondheim. More members are migrants from elsewhere in Norway, or are temporary residents (students and visiting researchers), or, in third place, persons raised locally but in a more modern than traditional setting, thus not in constant touch with their own folk music heritage. The migrants include not just musicians raised in other distinct style areas within the fiddle district but also musicians from Hardanger fiddle areas (musicians #7, #13, #18, #20, #23, and #27, in Fig. 9), as well as from areas where both fiddle and Hardanger fiddle are cultivated (musicians #6, #10, #11, #17, #25, and #26). On occasion a true foreigner joins. Fiddler #22, Joachim Fettig, is from Germany; he has returned home. And not long before the years covered in Figure 9, one of central members of the group was Swedish-born Eva Hogalund. Last, while I did not formally join the club during my year in Trondheim, I was welcomed,

Figure 9. Musicians active in Spelemannslaget i BUL Nidaros, 1989–93

	Sex/ Approx. age (1993)	Profession/Comments	Years in Group	Original Home
1.	F 33	data-processing engineer; accordion	11	Steinkjer (N. of Tr.)
2.	F 35	nurse	13	Trondheim
3.	M 50	teacher; music educated; gave fiddle courses	35	Trondheim
4.	M 43	researcher; in Trondheim 10 years; guitarist	8	Otta (Oppdal)
5.	F 41	secretary	4	Trondheim
6.	M 62	manager; in Trondheim 43 years; dancer	40	Møre
7.	F 37	researcher; in Trondheim 13 years; dancer	8	Ålesund (far west)
8.	F 36	architect; in Trondheim 18 years	4	Vinstra (Oppdal)
9.	M 48	engineer (beer)	15	Trondheim
10.	M 41	researcher; in Trondheim 18 years; double bass	14	Sogn (far west)
11.	M 42	grad. student; 13 years in Trondheim; dancer	9	Breim (far west)
12.	M 50	teacher; in Trondheim 32 years; dancer	30	Ålen (near Røros)
13.	M 39	researcher; in Trondheim 15 years	14	Telemark
14.	M 51	bank director; dancer	30	Trondheim
15.	M 46	researcher; dancer	6	Trondheim
16.	M 38	researcher; dancer	13	Trondheim
17.	F 41	engineer; in Trondheim 20 years; plays H-fiddle too	4	Møre
18.	M 52	architect; in Trondheim 33 years	30	Hardanger
19.	M 62	farmer; plays accordion	9	Trondheim

These 1989 members were gone by 1993:

20.	F 30	driving instructor; also in Glåmos group	3	Røros
21.	M 33	electrician; led group several years, to 1992	10	Ørlandet (near Tr.)
22.	M 40	researcher; in Trondheim 1987–90	2	Germany
23.	M 33	researcher; 8 years in Tr; plays H-fiddle too	5	Hardanger
24.	M 26	student	10	Trondheim
25.	F 24	student; strong fiddler; in Honndalstausene	3	Hornindal (west)

These members of Spelemannslaget i BUL Nidaros joined during 1989–93

20.	M 26	engineer; in Trondheim 2 years; accordion	2	Buskerud
21.	M 25	optician; flute	2	Sel (Oppland)
22.	M 40	student; guitar	2	Trondheim
23.	F 38	teacher; in Trondheim 8 years; flute	2	Levanger (N. of Tr)
24.	F 30	teacher; in Trondheim 10 years	1	Sel (Oppland)
25.	F 23	student; in Trondheim 2 years; flute	2	Toten (Oppland)
26.	M 36	researcher; in Trondheim 4 years	1	Møre
27.	F 23	student; in Trondheim 4 years; flute; dancer	2	Østlandet
28.	M 20	student; now in A class; best in this group	2	Røros
29.	F 19	student; plays H-fiddle too; daughter of #30	3	Trondheim
30.	M 47	musician; new leader of group; father of #29	2	Trondheim

originally as an observing scholar whose tape recording was generously not regarded as a nuisance, and later on as a frequent participant.

Although just a few members of the Spelemannslaget i BUL Nidaros are both fairly local and strong tradition bearers, they account for its musical leadership in recent years. Åsbjørn Eide (uncle of young star Sturla E. Sundli, discussed elsewhere in connection with tune #76), musical leader of the club in 1989, comes from Ørlandet, a mere sixty kilometers or so west-northwest, including a short ferry trip across the Trondheimsfjord. The next musical leader, Knut Olav Aasegg, spent many years in Heimdal, which, even though separately incorporated, serves as a far-southern suburb of Trondheim. Last, Gunn Brøndbo, from Steinkjer (some 120 kilometers northeast of Trondheim) lacks an official leadership role in the club, partly because an accordionist cannot even be on stage during most contests. But she is in my opinion far and away the best musician in this fiddle club, ranking with the top A-class fiddlers that are most represented in this book (musician #19, Trondheim farmer and accordionist Torbjørn Vikhammermo, is also quite strong). Brøndbo helps in many ways with the group's organization, with finding and selecting suitable tunes, and by composing lovely, original, yet unobtrusive second parts.

Just as the leaders of this club come from here and there in the provinces of Sør-Trøndelag and secondarily from Nord-Trøndelag, so do many of the tunes performed. A repertoire list dated January 16, 1989, and labeled *"Aktuelle danseslåtta, våren-89"* (current dance tunes, spring of '89), includes sixty titles under six rubrics. Seventeen tunes were gathered under the genre label *pols,* another seventeen under *reinlender,* thirteen under *vals,* four under *masurka,* six under *polka,* and three under *marsj/halling.* Of the *pols,* quite a few are best known as performed in the central *pols* area, the Rørostraktom. However, tunes such as "Litjhurven" (tune #49), "Steffen Henningsgård" (tune #47), "Snar å ta åt," and many others in this section of the repertoire are hits performed throughout eastern Norway. Including these is a nod in the direction of the Røros area, but not a pledge of fealty. However, other *pols* by their titles and customary geographically limited venues point to specific communities, many but not all spread throughout Sør-Trøndelag. There is an "Eldgammel pols fra Budal" (roughly fifty kilometers due south of Trondheim), a "Brurpols fra Brekken" (over 100 kilometers southeast of Trondheim), and from neighboring Nord-Trøndelag, "Gopolsen hass Hilmar" (i.e., Hilmar Alexandersen of Steinkjer, even farther away to the northeast), and a

"Brudedans i Leksviken" (due north from Trondheim, across the fjord). Also, in the other small *folkemusikk* category of *marsj/halling* we find "Målselvhallingen"; Målselv is in the far north.

No traditional rural fiddle club would play so many tunes whose primary homes were so far from the home of the club. The Lom Spelmannslag and Vågå Spel- og Dansarlag, based just a dozen kilometers apart, share some repertoire, but each emphasizes tunes or versions of tunes not played, or at least not as common, in the neighboring community. The same is true of the repertoires of the Glåmos Spellmannslag and of its companion club, the Brekken Spell- og Danselag. But as a city fiddle club the Spelemannslag i BUL Nidaros needed to evolve a broader-based, more inclusive approach to *folkemusikk,* one that is regional rather than local. The *folkemusikk* portion of the group's repertoire for 1989 illustrates a geographic spread that roughly corresponded to the spread of former homes of members from this province, made some attempt to focus on regional repertoires not otherwise regularly aired in the National Fiddlers' Association (i.e., northern tunes), and, last, paid some heed to the home of the 1989 leader, Åsbjørn Eide, from across the Trondheimsfjord. In 1994, tune choice continues to shift to suit the new leader. Being flexible in order to take advantage of the strengths of a musical leader has limits, of course. When transplanted Swede Eva Hogalund led the group (before Åsbjørn Eide's term), she could not expect it to study her home fiddle style and tunes, but found what she thought would be a rich and sufficiently close style in Røros, where she had studied with Harald Gullikstad. But the difficulties of Røros *pols* exceeded the abilities and inclinations of many fiddlers in Spelemannslaget i BUL Nidaros. This group is certainly interested in tradition, and tried to please this leader, but also insists on having a good, relaxing time, a need incompatible with learning a difficult and, for many members, not very familiar fiddle style.

While the view of tradition evinced in the *folkemusikk* portion of the tune list is geographically liberal in comparison with repertoires of rural clubs, the group cast its net even wider in the *gammaldans* section of that list. *Gammaldans* tunes played in spring of 1989 included a "Masurka etter Halvard Ørsal" (of the county of Møre og Romsdal), a "B-dur vals etter Ivar Bråtå" of the Gudbrandsdal (anthologized here as #30), and a "Hamborgar" from Horningdal, in the far west. Another *hamborger* (not on this list), "Randabygdaran," became one of the tunes that the group played most that year, which the group learned from visiting fiddler Bente Tomasgård (see tune

#120). Each of these major fiddle styles is represented in the 1989 repertoire list by another piece or two. An even broader repertoire appears in the hefty loose-leaf binders of photocopied manuscript music that each player carries to rehearsals. Those notebooks are in a sense a collective music commonplace volume, illustrating several chronological layers of repertoire, tunes learned along with tunes only intended to be picked up, and tunes for a one-time event; such as a wedding. Every category of tune and geographical area cited in the 1989 repertoire list are supplemented in this notebook; none was an isolated case. In addition, types of tunes appear that I never found in the repertoires of other clubs for fiddle. These include a "Gangar" from Setesdal (a Hardanger fiddle tune from one of the central Hardanger fiddle counties), four (!) examples of a Swedish genre, the *gånglåt*, among these the very popular "Gånglåt frän Äppelbo" (given here as tune #101), and American tunes, including "Oh, When the Saints," "Billy Boy," and "Five Foot Two, Eyes of Blue."

In what ways are the repertoire and operation of Spelmannslaget i BUL Nidaros traditional, and how not? These days, most clubs hew much more closely to their own communities' folk music than does this club, but many nineteenth-century fiddlers were as liberal as this group chooses to be. What may be least traditional about the repertoire is not how distant the homelands of many pieces are, but rather how few tunes are specific to the Trondheim area. And although the group uses notation frequently, it is not employed literally. During the first rehearsal of the group that I attended, in February 1989, I picked up a spare fiddle and joined in as the group read from a photocopy of a transcription. I played precisely what was on the page. My pitches were correct, but my rhythms came in and out of focus, and I played too few ornaments. I was confused, and looked up to see Gunn Brøndbo smiling. "All of our tunes are '*etter* Åsbjørn'" [after Åsbjørn Eide, then the musical leader], she stated. After hearing that, I knew to use the notation as a partial mnemonic aid, but to learn the tune as the rest of the group did, largely by listening to the leader (some members do not read music at all). And what of the instrumentation of the club? Groups such as the Vågå Spel- og Dansarlag bring in an accordion or two, a guitar and a string bass for certain uses, but such instruments are absolutely central to the activities of the Spelmannslaget I BUL Nidaros. In fact, without the accordions, the quality of the sound produced diminishes significantly, since the accordionists are the among the best musicians in the group. This makes the group what is sometimes called a *gammaldans* club, but doesn't make it inauthentic. It harks back not to the most recent history of revived Norwegian folk music, but rather to a slightly earlier, less self-conscious time, when the constitution of ensembles was more serendipitous than systematic.

The National Fiddlers' Association was linked with the National Youth Association before World War II; the Trondheim fiddle club retains that connection in its name (BUL), general goal, and in some specific activities. Chapters of the National Youth Association have long functioned as homes away from home for rural people living in larger cities. This fiddle club is a folk music haven for migrants from elsewhere in Norway, in almost every case from much smaller population centers; the transition from rural to urban may wrench less than at the turn of the century, but moving away from home is still no small matter. And this group may be even more focused on accompanying dances than are the main clubs from the Rørostraktom; this city club is at least as ambivalent as those rural groups concerning supplementing dance events with contests. In addition to a rotation of annual and one-time activities parallel to those of the other groups described, each Wednesday (except during the summer), six to ten members of the club play for a dance at the local National Youth Association chapter's downtown headquarters. In this setting, both older dance genres and younger *"turdansar,"* or figure dances, are important. The figure dances, with such names as "Figaro," "Fandango," "Feier frå Sandsvær," "Sekstur frå Namdalen," and "Stakkars Per," differ from both *folkemusikk* and *gammaldans* genres in that they are not couple dances, but rather elaborate sets with more dancers, who then socialize with more than just a partner or two during and after the dance. Most of these genres have just a single tune per dance type. A separate section of sixty-two of these tunes follows the main body of over 250 *folkemusikk* and *gammaldans* tunes in the loose-leaf music notebooks used by the club.

In the biggest city, Oslo, the mixed membership characteristic of Spelmannslaget i BUL Nidaros separates out into several other, very different types of club. In this much larger population, tradition bearers from elsewhere in Norway are sufficiently numerous to form clubs. Musicians from the Hardanger fiddle district can choose from among several clubs that mention a specific region in their title, and players of the fiddle from Oppland gather in the Gudbrandsdølenes Spelmannslag. A resident of Oslo from Skjåk (near Lom), Reidar Skjelkvåle, leads the club, which mixes other residents of Oslo who moved from the Gudbrandsdal with students from there, whose eventual professions may or may not allow a return home later. In regionally based clubs such as these, tune choice can be a delicate matter, but deciding among versions known by individuals from nearby towns is a process not so different from deciding among distinctive versions from within a single town in groups such as the Lom Spelmannslag and Vågå Spel- og Dansarlag.

The largest club for fiddle based in Oslo, the Østerdølenes Spellmannslag, is, like the Gudbrandsdølenes Spelmannslag, meant to explore the *folkemusikk* and *gammaldans* tunes of a region. However, the region is very different, and most members are true denizens of Oslo, thus city dwellers without a traditional folk music background, though many come to the club as fluent classical violinists. And whereas Spelmannslaget i BUL Nidaros occasionally welcomes the individual foreign fiddler, the Østerdølenes Spellmannslag generally has several members from abroad. I attended a practice session during January of 1989 that, save for the music worked on, could as easily have been a chamber music rehearsal. The leader, Marit Larsen, has a background mixing classical training with more traditional elements. Her genial and efficient instruction of the group focuses on technical command of short fragments, and building from there. The resulting ensemble is powerful, unified, and only marginally traditional. This status may not be permanent. Larsen has begun work for the folk-music division of the national radio, and is reducing the bravura violinistic element in her own performance style, a change bound to reflect in her leadership of this urban group.

Why have I devoted so much attention to city fiddle clubs? The future of Norway cannot help becoming increasingly more urban, with more and more people forced to move away from their homes, from their extended families, and from the centers of their folk music traditions. The practice of nurturing folk music will inevitably continue to replace serendipitous continuity with self-conscious mechanisms that preserve and revive in progressively more complex ways. Perhaps more city folk-music clubs will form in the coming decades. Whether or not that occurs, the progressive modernizing of rural life must influence the majority of small-town fiddle clubs either to become more like the city clubs or, more likely, to take special steps to guard against that.

CHAPTER FOUR

Contests and Concerts

The summer calendar of nearly every fiddler and fiddle club revolves around contests and concerts. Whether or not musicians consider these events essential to maintaining folk music in Norway, these events structure the folk music year, inspiring practice, requiring travel, and offering opportunities to display folk traditions publicly. Dances are scheduled around those main events in the annual calendar, and are important in other ways.

Local contests

Folk music competition was at first a local affair, regardless of the aims and claims of contest sponsors. Small contests set the stage and provided a cumulative model for the National Fiddle Contest. Then, that national contest in turn was mirrored in miniature in more recent local and regional affairs. Today there is an annual National Fiddle Contest and many smaller annual contests which gather traditions of broad regions (several from within the Hardanger fiddle area, as well as the single District Contest for fiddle). Much of the fiddle area has turned, for most local demonstrations of folk music, from contests to concerts. But annual local contests are still held every year where the fiddle and Hardanger fiddle areas overlap in the far West, in the counties of Sogn og Fjordane and of Møre og Romsdal. The West has long insisted on a degree of independence troublesome to the National Fiddlers' Association. Today, aspects of folk music activity that once marked this vital area as annoyingly restive have been adopted nationwide.

I visited a small annual contest in 1989, the County Contest for

Sogn og Fjordane, held that year in the hamlet of Jostedal and sponsored by the Jostedal Spel- og Dansarlag, which happens to be a Hardanger fiddle club in this mixed-fiddle area. This club was first formalized as the tiny Jostedal Spelemannslag in 1954. That its first leader
lived in and somehow led the club from Oslo was one symptom of
fragility, and it was forced to suspend activities several times. It was
reconstituted as the Jostedal Spel- og Dansarlag in 1979, and includes
a senior musical group, many dancers, and now a flourishing recruit
club to nurture apprentice fiddlers. The umbrella county organization,
the Sogn og Fjordane Folkemusikklag, created in 1981, includes some
twenty local member clubs, a dozen of which provide most participants to events such as the County Contest and is quite active. It sponsors courses on the county, regional, and local levels in instrument
building, contest judging, singing, dancing, and above all in playing,
including pioneering instruction on guitar and bass, instruments considered peripheral to or unsuitable for folk music in some parts of
Norway. In addition, the group helped found a county folk music archive in 1983, supports a part-time six-person folk-music ensemble,
helps publish folk tunes both in transcription and on audio recordings, and, starting in November of 1988, has issued a monthly
journal called the *Spelarstikka* describing local folk music history and
current events. It is an understatement to note that this organization
and its member clubs are vigorous and growing.

No one will end up in the remote Jostedal by chance. My way there
was tortuous. The journey began, before the Trondheim city buses
started running, with a walk to downtown, then a shuttle to the air-
port and a flight to Bergen, on the west coast. The next flight, to Sogndal, was on a commuter plane that could seat twenty at most. This
plane descended from the clouds and perched on a narrow spit of land
jutting into—yet dramatically high above—a tributary of the Sogne-
fjord, at this point well over a hundred kilometers from the open sea.
A twenty-minute shuttle-bus ride into the hamlet of Sogndal ex-
hausted public transportation. I walked and hitched several rides on
slender roads through a half-dozen tunnels into ever-narrower valleys,
until arriving at Jostedal, a handful of buildings three of which made
up the school at which the contest would be held. On April 7 the snow
remained over a foot deep. The valley's watercourse was still mostly
iced over, since the high mountains flanking the valley kept the stream
in cool shadow for much of the day.

Jostedal is one of three hamlets now gathered administratively as
the municipality of Luster, which houses just over 5,000 people in

its 2,670 square kilometers (two-thirds of which is mountains with permanent snow or ice). Settlement is thin, despite being compressed into a few valleys, and there was no lodging in the center of Jostedal. Visitors slept in locations up and down the valley as much as a dozen kilometers from the school, in little hotels and campgrounds that usually catered to visitors to Jostedalsbreen, Norway's largest glacier. Sometimes I could catch a ride part way to my hotel, sometimes I walked this wild and lovely trace between slowly melting snowbanks. Why do I make so much of the setting? Both the sense of remoteness and the spectacular natural features were woven into the fabric of this and similar events. People on stage always wore their own regional costume *(bunad),* reminding us of local history through the beautiful items that encased them, while the physical setting did much the same thing to us all, on a grander scale, each time we ventured outside during breaks as well as during our travels to and from the contest.

All events took place in the combination gym and assembly room of the school, the only large room in the immediate vicinity. Local people attending the contest had been there many times before for a variety of school functions, sports, and other community events. Most small towns have such an all-purpose room, a place that may have been just an enclosed space when built, and which remains physically unprepossessing, but that soon echoes with events—routine, or exhilirating, or solemn—that draw members of the community together. This particular hall accommodated about 270; nearly all seats would be filled at climactic points, and a fair number throughout the event.

Any contest needs judges. Some early contests—including the National Fiddle Contest—were marred by controversy over judging, specifically, whether judges from the Hardanger fiddle area could evaluate performance on the fiddle fairly and with authority. As time passed the National Fiddle Contest grew sufficiently large and financially sound enough to afford separate panels of judges for the two fiddle types, as well as for dance from each of the two broad areas. Modern local contests such as the County Contest for Sogn og Fjordane, although larger than the earliest national contests, nevertheless can make do with two panels of three judges, one panel for all instrumental performance, and another for all dancing. There are brackets for both fiddle and Hardanger fiddle in this and other local contests in this part of Norway, but this does not present a problem of fairness in judging, since judges generally play both instruments. In 1989, the panel included two men in their late fifties and Torunn Raftevold, a woman then in her mid-twenties. She is a skilled performer in the A class on both Hardanger fiddle and fiddle, and belongs to the Honn-dalstausene, a small ensemble of young virtuoso women fiddlers. But judges are usually more seasoned. To find a woman for the panel of instrumentalists necessitates looking to the younger generation, since this is the first in which there are substantial numbers of female fiddlers.

Judges generally sit together near the performers. When dancing is evaluated, "near" usually means on the stage, so that competitors can be observed from head to toe. When fiddlers are competing, the first row in the audience is close enough. In American fiddle contests, judges are often encouraged—even required—to sit apart from one another and not communicate; final results are tabulated by someone else. I suppose we are trying to ensure objectivity by guarding against the possibility of undue influence between judges. The more-trusting Norwegian folk music community benefits from judges being allowed to pool their expertise. After the first few performances in a contest, the judges retire briefly to compare scores, making sure these are sufficiently congruent to allow later comparison to go smoothly. The final results emerge from a conference during which the judges negotiate to establish a single list of scores.

The A class for fiddle at this contest initially had just two competitors. To enlarge it, Torunn Raftevold was asked to change hats for a few minutes and compete in this bracket. This was clearly a last-minute adjustment—she mounted the stage wearing street clothes rather than a *bunad*. It was expected that the judging could work around her changing of functions, and still be fair. In the intimate world of high-level competition, it is far from rare for a judge to leave the panel to avoid the appearance of impropriety. For instance, at the 1989 National Fiddle Contest, Ivar Schjølberg excused himself from judging while his son Leif-Inge competed.

Every contest begins with speeches to welcome all present and to honor those who put the event together. All listen respectfully; the audience will remain quiet and attentive throughout the competition. Sound-amplifying equipment is good and generally unobtrusive. Here the six microphones (there would be fewer later), two small amplifiers, and modest rank of speakers were joined on stage by a pair of large urns of flowers, and on a slanted wall behind, a hand-knit rug and a four-inch brass bell. The room itself was rather plain, so that those few elements and the regional costumes of those on stage stood out visually. After about a half-hour of speeches, the local semiprofessional folk music group supported by the county of Sogn og Fjordane performed a half-dozen pieces, some involving the whole ensemble, others a few members. This introduced the topic of local folk music in a concert setting, which is done at one or several points in every contest. Then the short concert competition proper began. Each player or ensemble played two pieces, whereas the dancers performed one longer dance (up to about four minutes compared with a minute and a half to two minutes for each competition fiddle tune). In no case did performers speak; a master of ceremonies quietly announced them and the pieces they would play. A joke or two leavened two of the introductory speeches, but that was the only planned humor during the weekend. The mood of the competition would remain warm but businesslike, with the audience paying careful attention throughout.

Evenings were more relaxed, of course. Ensembles playing for hour-long stints for dancing (one might be a *gammaldans* group, the next a fiddle club in town primarily to compete during the day) would be miked just a bit louder than the day's competitors, so that the people dancing or socializing could hear the music while chatting above it, but would not need to shout. The day's music is mostly *folkemusikk* at any such event, while the night's dances are almost all drawn from the younger genres that make up *gammaldans*. Dances from the four main genres of *gammaldans*—the waltz, mazurka, *reinlender,* and local dance genre in a polka rhythm (here the *hamborger*)—dominate the evening, with a *springar* or two added for variety. Also, this relatively liberal district enjoys some of the modern additions to *gammaldans,* genres one is not apt to hear outside coastal areas (in the course of two dance evenings in Jostedal I heard three western swing tunes and one tango).

This contest featured a remarkable number of separate brackets of competition for two reasons. Although this was a local contest, the delimited geographic area upon which it drew is home to both fiddle types, both represented by competitors in each age group and in the common ensemble types. Also, this is a very progressive district in what is allowed within the definition of oral tradition music, therefore permitting categories of competition not considered sufficiently authentic elsewhere. The more customary brackets are these: (1) A classes for fiddle and for Hardanger fiddle, containing participants who had won a first prize while competing in a B class at the National Fiddle Contest (no lesser contest will do), (2) C classes for each fiddle type, with performers under eighteen years old, (3) D classes for each fiddle type, for performers over sixty years old, (4) B classes for all other fiddlers, those aged eighteen through sixty who hadn't yet won a first prize at the National Fiddle Contest, (5) *Gruppespel,* ensembles of two to four fiddlers in various categories; here there would be only a single entry in one category, "Gruppespel vanleg fele klasse C," (6) *lagspel* (fiddle club) brackets for Hardanger fiddle, fiddle, and, here, a single class for *lagspel* junior rather than the usual two classes, (7) classes for singing *(kveding)* and for players of older folk music instruments (none entered this time), and (8) dance classes divided much as are the fiddle classes, though at this contest dancing to the two fiddle types was not separated, and a normally separate category of *lausdans* (i.e., *halling*) was collapsed into other brackets. There also were various categories that one would not encounter at the National Fiddle Contest, including brackets for *torader* senior, junior, and ensemble (the *torader* is a two-row button accordion), for *gammaldans* ensembles, and for a fiddle club in its *gammaldans* incarnation, with accordion(s), guitar, and bass. Apart from the caveats mentioned above, this local contest was typical, which makes it worthwhile to lay it out in detail. The schedule of this event was as follows:

Friday, April 7, beginning at 8 P.M.:
Torader junior (four registered; three competed)
Torader senior (three accordionists)
Gruppespel Gammaldansmusikk (eleven groups registered;
    1 dropped, another added)
Torader lag (two groups)
Vanleg fele klasse A (none registered; three competed)
[Recreational dancing followed until after 1 A.M. Saturday.]

Saturday, April 8, beginning at 10 A.M.:
Dans klasse B (twenty couples registered, an additional three
    competed)
Vanleg fele klasse D (two fiddlers)
Hardingfele klasse D (one fiddler, who also competed in above
    class)
Kveding (two singers)
Vanleg fele klasse B (four registered; two competed)
Dans klasse D (two couples registered; one competed)
Dans klasse C (eleven couples)
Hardingfele klasse B (seven registered; one dropped but one added)
Gjesteklasse ("guest class," one *hardingfele* player from Ålesund,
    outside the county)
Vanleg fele klasse C (eight registered; seven competed)
Hardingfele klasse C (four fiddlers)
Gruppespel vanleg fele klasse C (one duet)
Dans klasse A (seven couples; also one solo dancer to a *halling*)
Hardingfele klasse A (four fiddlers)

Lagdans junior (two groups of children)

Lagdans (three groups, one entered three times with different dance
   genres)

Lagspel hardingfele (five clubs)

Lagspel vanleg fele m/komp. (with accordion(s), guitar, and bass;
   two clubs)

*Lagspel hardingfele m/*komp. (three clubs)

Lagspel vanleg fele (four clubs)

[Recreational dancing followed until about 2 A.M. Sunday.]

Sunday, starting at 11 A.M.:

Folkemusikkgudsteneste (religious service with many folk-music
   interpolations)

Meisterkonsert (winners' concert; each player, dancer, or group
   with one number)

The order of competition and the number of competitors in some
brackets reflected national trends. In all Norwegian folk music contests, the brackets considered to be of least interest appear first, and
the climactic categories come late on Saturday. In this contest the
fiddle A class was not listed in the printed program, and popped up
out of the usual sequence. My impression is that fiddlers belonging to
that bracket had not planned to compete, and did not register, but
were present with their local fiddle clubs, had their arms twisted at
the last moment, and were put on stage before they could reconsider.
If the placement of this category is neglected, the remaining order is
typical. *Lagspel* and *lagdans* capture the most attention from the audience owing to visual display, greatest number of participants, and thus
most dramatic embodiment of local identity, and so competed last on
the program. Next most important are the various A classes, where
performance is the most skillful. After that—reading backward
through the schedule—come the C classes, the children, whose skills
vary but whose charm and promise for the future entrance audiences.
Then, nearer the opening of the event, come—in no particular order—brackets eliciting narrower interest, such as *kveding,* and performers of middling skill, those in the B and D brackets. In this contest, the less- "authentic" categories, those involving accordions in
any way, were placed on the first day. In big contests, the first day
is Wednesday or Thursday, and categories presented on that day are
definitely of lesser interest. This small contest's short schedule left this
less clear, since for many audience members, Friday evening would be
a "better" position than early on Saturday, when many people would
be getting a slow start after a long night of socializing and *gammaldans.* The number of participants tells several tales. There are

roughly as many fiddle and Hardanger fiddle competitors; in fact, more than a few fiddlers compete on both instruments, and one complete fiddle club did that too—Fjelljom, led by fiddler Arne M. Sølvberg, who is in the A class for each fiddle type. But in the C class, children taking up the fiddle outnumber those on Hardanger fiddle, reflecting a national trend. Last, it is significant that the D class was so small, despite there being plenty of older fiddlers around and active, and that just two of the four fiddlers registered in the B class actually competed (a small sample, but I saw this happen many times). Unfortunately, the contest system has fewer rewards for those who are not, are no longer, or have little prospect of becoming stars, even in egalitarian Norway.

My first visit to a folk music event in Norway was to the 1988 District Contest, which took place in Røros on September 2–4. This annual contest, the largest of the contests specifically for the fiddle area, has a character between that of a local contest like that just described and the National Fiddle Contest. It takes place early each fall in locations intended cumulatively to represent the whole fiddle district, though the sites at first alternated between just the Gudbrandsdal and the Røros areas, the two small areas that first represented the fiddle most vigorously within the formal folk music revival. The first in the series of contests that would coalesce into this massive event, which took place in Røros on June 24–25, 1950, was also the first folk music contest to be held in that community. An article in the *Spelemanns-blad* bemoaned the fact that "unfortunately, the National Fiddlers' Association has had little interaction with our country's *[flatfelespel-emennene]*" (fiddle players, but using the pejorative *flatfele* for fiddle) and praised the fact that the association was sponsoring this event, since the association should be an organization for all who cultivated Norwegian folk music (1950 [2]: 16). In those days, travel was much more difficult than today, and so many more contestants came from nearby, making for an event more local than regional. Of the twenty one fiddlers listed as winning prizes, sixteen came from within fifty kilometers of Røros (eleven of those from the Røros/Glåmos/Brekken axis), just three from the Gudbrandsdal, and one each from further north in the Trøndelag and from the far West. More of a balance at least between the two main areas was sought in subsequent contests. In 1956, the "Fele" contest "mellom [between] Gudbrandsdalen og Østerdalen i Glåmos" (Glåmos is just a few kilometers from Røros) was served by three buses carrying 108 people in from the Gudbrandsdal. A total of seven clubs and forty eight fiddlers competed, while that same year, forty five fiddlers (forty three of whom played Hardanger fiddle) participated in the National Fiddle Contest (*Spelemannsbladet* 1956 [7–8]: 13, 27).

This 1950 contest (like the next few) attracted a daytime audience of about 500, increasing during the dance evenings to over 600. The only female fiddler, Kristine Wivelstad of Glåmos, was greeted with an ovation. At the opening of the event, Magne Manheim, head of the National Fiddlers' Association and one of the judges for the contest, played a *springar* and a *halling* on Hardanger fiddle (at a time when the reverse—introducing a Hardanger fiddle contest with performance on fiddle—would not have been conceivable). And another critical tension within the system appeared, that between listening- and dance-oriented performance. At the prize ceremony, O. M. Sandvik, then the most prominent scholar of Norwegian folk music, recommended that fiddlers pay more attention to bowing. *Pols* were played too loud then, he felt, which tended to obscure the most delicate and lovely details of a tune. The judges seemed to agree: Hans Brimi, elegant representative of the Gudbrandsdal, won, with second prize awarded to the most art-oriented fiddler from Røros, Einar Galåen. But the public—mostly from the Røros area—disagreed with the judges, preferring fast, lively *(kvikke)* tunes (*Spelemannsbladet* 1950 [2]: 16).

Of the more than 700 fiddlers and dancers who competed at the 1988 District Contest, over a hundred of them were under eighteen, augeuring well for the future of traditional music and dance in the fiddle area. Audiences numbered in the thousands. A hamlet like Jostedal could not be host to such an event anymore than could have 1950s Røros. As towns have grown and the economy improved in recent decades, many areas have been able to afford to build a community center *(samfunnshus)*. In Røros, the center lies just a short walk from the historic district and the railroad station, at which I arrived at the end of a two-hour trip south from Trondheim. At the center one large building houses two good-sized meeting rooms, one doubling as a gym and the other called the Røroshall. In order for this event to fit into three days (Friday from 4 P.M., all of Saturday, and Sunday through late afternoon), both big rooms were in near-continuous use. Almost all playing and dance accompaniment was by fiddle. On Friday, the E class (fiddlers over seventy, six players), D class (five fiddlers), and C class (thirty one fiddlers, five of whom were under thirteen years old) competed. A long Saturday started at 9 A.M. with *nyskaping* (new compositions, eleven entrants) followed by *eldre fol-kemusikkinstrument* (one on *tussefløyte,* two each on *bukkehorn* and *trefløyte*) and *kveding* (just two singers). Then came the fiddlers in the B class (sixteen entrants), a single Hardanger fiddler in a "guest" class, and the star fiddlers of the A class (seventeen entrants). The day of competition ended with *gruppespel* junior and senior (respectively three and eighteen chamber-sized ensembles) followed by *lagspel* junior (eight kids' clubs). *Lagspel* senior, the most popular bracket (there were twenty four clubs and a packed audience) began at noon on Sunday, after the folk music service at the old Røros church and preceding the prize ceremony.

The size and scope of this event automatically make it different from local contests such as that described from Jostedal. Whereas the Sogn of Fjordane County Contest could be sponsored by a single fiddle club, this District Contest was arranged by some 170 members of three clubs, the Glåmos Spellmannslag, the Brekken Spell- og Danselag and the Røros Folkedanslag, with major responsibilities parceled out carefully among representatives of the three clubs. Costs were substantial but manageable, and as a result so were entrance fees, even though these remained less than half those at the biggest festivals, the National Fiddle Contest and the National Festival for *Gammaldans* Music. 1988 District Contest tickets cost about $8 per day of competition, $10 per dance evening; a combined ticket for all three days and both evenings cost Kr.200, about $30.

The three judges for such events customarily represent the three biggest fiddle style areas, Oppdal (concentrating on the Gudbrandsdal), the East (emphasizing the Røros area), and the mixed fiddle area of the West. On this occasion, they included Hans H. Holen, from Vagåmo in the Gudbrandsdal, Magnar Sundt, originally from the Røros area (then residing in Oslo), and Arild Hoksnes, originally from Aukra in the county of Møre og Romsdal (then residing in Trondheim). The careful attention to geographic spread is meant to promote fairness by making sure someone on the panel is knowledgeable about each fiddle style. Three judges are not enough, of course, if every style has proponents at a contest. None of these three gentlemen knew much about fiddling in the far north, and each judge would know more about his own local tradition than he would about neighboring styles. Having a judge from a fiddler's own community might be thought to be an advantage, but this may instead turn out to be a liability. In a given community, more than one school of fiddling may flourish. Two of the judges from this contest had harsh words—

and probably low scores—for the specific versions of tunes chosen by fiddlers or groups from their own home.

Concerts

Although contests seem likely to remain the commonest and largest folk music events in Norway, concert-based festivals have emerged as an alternative in recent decades. Most of these are local events. The basic flavor of an event and shape of the weekend are those set by contests, which already contain one or two short concerts with a local theme. For instance, at the county contest for Sogn og Fjordane, part of the first session was an hour or so of local folk music performed by the county-employed folk music ensemble, and, at the longer District Contest in 1988 in Røros, several hours one evening were devoted to a "Røros evening" featuring a series of local stars. In a local concert-oriented festival, the locally flavored concert, already present for a few hours at any contest, expands to take up the time occupied by competition at contests. I will briefly mention some of the activities at two concert-based weekend festivals, the Gudbrandsdalsstemne and Brekkendagan.

The Gudbrandsdalsstemne for 1989 took place in Lom. On Friday evening, May 5, a *gammaldans* festival took place in the Lom community house. It was set to begin at 8:00 P.M., though when we arrived an hour after that, just a few couples were on the floor. Eventually the room filled, largely with teenagers dancing to a series of local *gammaldans* ensembles. The third group, Bælg og Streing (with fiddler Knut Kjøk) was remarkable, both for listening and for dancing; I transcribed the melodies they played for the final section of this book's anthology of tunes. Saturday's activities started at 1 P.M. in an open area in downtown Lom, with an outdoor concert lasting about forty minutes by a part of the Lom Spelemannslag. Then that fiddle club and many of us in the audience broke into small groups with various destinations. The general goal was to inundate Lom with folk music. The group I followed, four fiddlers belonging to the Vågå Spel- og Dansarlag, went to an old folks' home. We stopped in two open areas within the home, and the four fiddlers played a total of nine hits, mostly from *folkemusikk* genres. Some of the residents ignored us, but many gathered around. At our second stop in the building, three very old ladies sat quietly off in a corner on a couch. They neither conversed nor seemed to notice their surroundings at all. But when the fiddlers struck up a *springleik,* their large-buckled, shiny black shoes began to tap on the first and third beats of the measure, in unison with all of the other feet. After our visit to the rest home, it was time for the "Spelemannsmiddag," a late lunch for festival participants in a large restaurant. Conversation turned to the *gammaldans* controversy (discussed in the next chapter). Two fiddlers each played a few tunes at the meal's close.

The most formal event of this Gudbrandsdalsstemne began at about 6 P.M., back in the community house. Short speeches alternated with a tune or two played by a variety of local fiddlers and ensembles. This went on until early evening, when the chairs were cleared and the scene yielded to more *gammaldans* into the early morning. But at the same time that the dancing was starting, a short but remarkable concert took place about a block away, in the gym of the elementary school. The Fel-Jakup Pris, a *vandrepokal*—cumulative traveling prize, a common type of prize in Norwegian folk music, had been in the hands of five fiddlers, all from this area. The prize, a beautiful tapestry of a fiddler gazing skyward (see Plate 4), was established in response to an earlier one for the "best" contemporary player of the Hardanger fiddle, the Myllargut Pris. Each year, the Fel-Jakup prize went to stay in the home of the winner of the A class for fiddle at the National Fiddle Contest, then eventually came to rest in the home of the first fiddler to win it a total of four times, and then the prize was permanently his. The performers in this concert in the Lom gym, the Fel-Jakup Konsert, were the five fiddlers who had topped the A class during that time and had temporarily possessed the tapestry—Reidar Skjelkvåle, Bjørn Odde, Ivar Schjølberg, Amund Bjørgen—and the permanent winner of the prize, Knut Kjøk (each represented many times in the tune anthology). They each played four pieces, introducing each carefully. In contests, the performers don't talk; this concert was a unique occasion for these gifted performers to demonstrate their historical awareness in words as well as sound. The tunes included many a *springleik* and *halling,* a quirky waltz, a mazurka (!), and several exquisite listening pieces (those performances I anthologized were "Gurileiken," "Lomsvogga," and "Per Bergom"—tunes #96, #34, and #126).

The high point of the 1989 Gudbrandsdalsstemne, the Fel-Jakup Konsert, assembled the fiddlers who, by the standards set over time at the National Fiddle Contest, constitute the best in Norway. It is remarkable that this gathering of national champions could be an intimate local affair in the north Gudbrandsdal. At the same time, it is important to note that the pieces that these gentlemen chose to present in a concert were the very sorts of tunes and versions with which they attained their high status in the contest system.

While there was no shortage of fellowship and dancing at the Gudbrandsdalsstemne, the other concert-based local festival I will describe, Brekkendagan, emphasizes those aspects even more. This is because fiddling in the Røros area focuses less on contest playing, thus less on "excellence," than on effectiveness for the dance. I attended this largest of the local festivals in the Røros area on June 9–11, 1989. Although nearly all participants and audience members at the Gudbrandsdalsstemne slept at home—apart from me, visitors from far away were, like Reidar Skjelkvåle of Oslo but from Skjåk, originally from the area—many who performed at Brekkendagan were not local. My home fiddle club in Trondheim, Spelemannslaget i BUL Nidaros, rented a *hytte,* in this case meaning a sort of rustic dormitory, that was part of a camping complex adjacent to Brekken's open-air museum, Henningsgården, where many of the activities making up Brekkendagen took place. The *hytte* had a common eating area, and a series of side rooms each sleeping four to six. Staying there meant that we could practice informally at the drop at a hat, and in general were thrown together more and more intimately than at home in Trondheim. Any large folk music event promotes this sort of fellowship.

Brekkendagan comes by its subtitle of "Svensk-Norsk spell-og dansetreff" (Swedish-Norwegian meeting of fiddling and dancing) naturally, since Brekken is just a dozen kilometers from the Swedish border, and the festival featured participants from Sweden. The main events, concerts on Friday and Saturday afternoons, included, along with various Norwegian individual performers and fiddle clubs from throughout the counties of Sør-Trøndelag and Østerdal, Arne Moden, a flashy Swedish *einrader* player (the *einrader* is a one-row—and two-chord—button accordion), Swedish fiddle duos from Malvang and Rättvik, and a Swedish fiddle club from Rättvik, which would also take its turn playing for the evening dances. The general tone was inclusive and welcomed music from outside the area. Sturla E. Sundli, from near Trondheim, chose to play Scottish tunes. And, when it was discovered that an American fiddler, Dick Price, was in the audience, he and I were asked to present a few American pieces. I got out my guitar (brought along because I was on duty as accompanist for Spelemannslaget i BUL Nidaros), Price and I rehearsed for twenty minutes, and then we performed three tunes for a very charitable audience.

The main concerts during Brekkendagan took place in Brekken's

Bjørkly ungdomshus, a multipurpose community hall used especially by local youth. About half of the main room is a renovated old building; the other half is a new addition. The room, which contained one hundred seventy six chairs, was comfortably full on Friday, then packed on Saturday. Not everyone was in a chair: children ran freely, as part of a more relaxed atmosphere than I witnessed at any other Norwegian folk music event.

Certain ingredients of the weekend are common to all Norwegian folk festivals. Each fiddle club that had played a few tunes during the day's concerts put in an hour accompanying dancing each evening in one of several dance venues. And, as usual, there was a combined church service and concert on Sunday. Two other presentations added to the local flavor of the event. Saturday night, prominent local musicians from several generations offered an intimate concert of solo fiddling from Brekken and Røros. Also, early Saturday afternoon, members of the Brekken Spell- og Danselag presented the "Brekkspellet," a pastiche of skits and tunes celebrating local history. This was done outdoors at the Henningsgård, where many of us were camped.

The National Fiddle Contest Today

The National Fiddle Contest (Landskappleik) is the biggest, longest, and most conservative Norwegian folk music festival, the contest that remains the center of the year for most Norwegian folk musicians, dancers, and fans. I will contrast the 1989 contest held in Trysil, a small town in southeast Norway near the Swedish border, with the 1993 contest in Lillehammer, which was billed as a pre-Olympic event.

A festival this size usually draws on the energies of at least three local fiddle clubs. Each event lasts four days, Thursday through Sunday in late June or early July, although the mammoth Lillehammer contest actually extended Wednesday through Sunday and began offering concerts two days earlier. Providing housing is a massive challenge: I stayed in a school dormitory in Trysil, then in a hotel built to serve the Olympics in Lillehammer (in a bathless room so small that the television hung from the ceiling). These days the National Fiddlers' Association provides seven full panels of judges, one each for solo Hardanger fiddle, solo fiddle, dance to Hardanger fiddle, dance to fiddle, *kveding,* older folk music instruments, and fiddle construction (all panels with three judges except for the last, which has two for each fiddle type). There are so many contest brackets—most well subscribed—and so many concerts flanking these that two venues do not suffice. In Trysil, a small town with typical amenities, events went on simultaneously in the movie theater and the community house, with some others in a hotel and in a church. In winter sports–oriented Lillehammer, events took place in Kristins Hall (the first public use of this new Olympic building), in the main auditorium at Maihaugen (a major open-air museum), elsewhere in Maihaugen, and in a church. Parking, busing from remote lodgings, and child care all demanded careful planning and staffing.

Events were ordered in each National Fiddle Contest as at most contests, with D classes (for those over sixty), B classes, and brackets for exotica such as older instruments scheduled early, followed by the C classes (for the charming—and perhaps promising—youth), and then, in the most prominent time slots, fiddle-club competition and the A classes for the star solo fiddlers. The fiddle brackets and those for Hardanger fiddle often conflicted, except during the climactic A classes. If a player or fan of a given fiddle type attended every competition bracket featuring that instrument, he or she would have little opportunity to hear the other fiddle type, save during dance evenings. These contests are rich and indeed crowded, and audience members are expected to pick and choose what to attend. This was recognized in the nature of the "comprehensive ticket," no longer a pass to everything, but rather to all competition and to just a few small concerts; the big concerts are ticketed separately. There are enough concerts that these begin to fall into types. One major evening concert is devoted to celebrating traditions of the host area (one or several small concerts usually do this too), and the other main concert offers one or another progressive approach to programming. In Trysil, the "new" large concert was a straightforward but attractive "Folkemusikk i gamal og ny drakt" (Folk music in old and new garb), offering tunes in both traditional and innovative arrangements and instrumentation. In Lillehammer, the committee arranging concerts for the Olympics sponsored as previews three major evening concerts, one exploring Grieg's relationship to folk music; one fancifully linking tunes to the four "grunnelementa" of air, earth, fire, and water; and one joining Norwegian performers with those from countries connected to Norway by much-traveled seaways (actually, mostly from various British traditions). These concerts seemed in the end to have been too many and their conceptions overly abstract; the next year's annual meeting of the National Fiddlers' Association restricted the number of large evening concerts at the National Fiddle Contest to two. The competition category of *gruppespel* (chamber-sized fiddle groups, smaller than a fiddle club) was presented as an evening concert in Trysil.

Local traditions (of the host clubs) are also underlined visually at the National Fiddle Contest. The logging heritage of Trysil was portrayed in a photomontage at the back of the community hall stage (see Plate 15). The specific history of Lillehammer was not depicted in the usual manner, that is, in a backdrop, but was certainly evident. Maihaugen, the site of many events, offers Norwegian rural history to tourists year-round, and our walk between that venue and the Olympic Kristens Hall passed in front of the Olympic ski jump, still green in late summer (see Plate 14).

Certain aspects of programming at each National Fiddle Contest reflect the event's conservativism. A fiddle club that includes accordions (generally with an upright bass and a guitar) must compete with fiddles only, leaving groups like my home club, Spelemannslaget i BUL Nidaros, at a disadvantage. The tune genre *gammalvals* is allowed in solo fiddle competition, but not in the dance brackets. Club competition *(lagspel)* is a very popular category, though most clubs are less than fifty years old, while many instruments with a long tenure in oral tradition—among them the clarinet—may not compete. That such rules are inconsistent is known to many; the National Fiddle Contest has its own traditions to obey, logical or not. Nevertheless, such inconsistencies did become part of an acrimonious and divisive debate that shook the institutional folk milieu to its core recently. This was the *gammaldans* controversy, discussed in the next chapter.

CHAPTER FIVE

Reconfiguring the Norwegian Folk Music World: The *Gammaldans* Controversy

The restiveness of the fiddle constituents in the National Fiddlers' Association described at the end of the second chapter eventually found a focus in what came to be known as the *gammaldans* controversy, a wrenching debate that would change the shape of the institutional folk milieu drastically. The term *gammaldans,* which translates literally—if somewhat paradoxically—as "old dance," came into use during the first third of the century to describe Norway's adaptations of nineteenth-century pan-European social dances and their music (principally waltzes, mazurkas, *reinlenders,* and polka types). Some of these adaptations flourish today in the ballroom and salon, and more are jolly songs that make up much of Norway's domestically produced popular music. Yet another significant repertoire of *gammaldans* is in oral tradition among the same amateur fiddlers, accordionists, and other instrumentalists who are the main custodians of other oral tradition music in Norway. Such *gammaldans* tunes exist in regional variants (though the variations may be less pronounced than in the older *folkemusikk* repertoires). But although *folkemusikk* now shares behavior and some elements of style with art music in the context of Norway's folk revival, *gammaldans* in traditional style retained just its older function accompanying dances—until quite recently.

Given those facts, should the music of *gammaldans* be reclassified as folk music? Does it deserve—or need—a home in Norway's folk music revival? This very public debate was in its last stages when I lived in Norway in 1988–89. I talked with fiddlers and dancers on both sides of the issue then and during the summers of 1991 and 1993.[1] And I was able both to follow the debate and to track its antecedents in the *Spelemannsblad.*

The reasons behind many Norwegian folk musicians' hostility to *gammaldans* reach back into the prehistory of Norway's folk revival. As mentioned in Chapter 1, toward the end of the nineteenth century, when the Norwegian folk music revival very slowly began to gather momentum, traditional music had been much weakened in the Hardanger fiddle strongholds of the western mountains. The two customary enemies of instrumental folk music and associated dance—religion and changing fashions—had been especially effective there, though influencing all of Norway.

Of the late nineteenth-century fiddlers who stubbornly remained dance oriented, many were seduced away from older genres by new dances arriving from Europe, and by a different dance instrument, the accordion, now made more widely available through advances in mass production. *Gammaldans* came to be viewed by many fiddlers in the central Hardanger fiddle counties as a scourge, antithetical to *folkemusikk,* even as the less-threatened fiddle area welcomed the genres that would eventually be known collectively as *gammaldans,* and often allowed accordions to play alongside fiddles. Although *gammaldans* has continued to flourish throughout Norway, it has been especially vigorous where the fiddle is played.[2] Any contest featuring *folkemusikk* during the day sees contestants and audiences relaxing in the evening by dancing . . . to the genres known collectively as *gammaldans.*

Beginning to Argue the Worth of *Gammaldans* Music

The *gammaldans* controversy proper started in 1980, nearly a century after folk music contests had started in Norway. In the 1880s, *gammaldans* clearly had been a threat to *folkemusikk* in some areas, but by 1980 oral tradition tunes and performances of *gammaldans* were well out of the popular mainstream, now a rural survival with much in common with *folkemusikk.* And this timing of the beginning of the controversy also makes sense in terms of the expansion of the National Fiddle Contest (illustrated in Fig. 5). By 1980, possibilities for new competition categories based on the older *folkemusikk* were about used up: no additional logical brackets by age, already accepted instrument, or within the dance sphere offered themselves. The next logical step was to go outside the *folkemusikk* genres.

The opening salvo of the debate came during an interview with a brash young ensemble originally formed to play for *gammaldans* from the province of Møre og Romsdal (within the northern part of the West in the fiddle area, though the Hardanger fiddle is present there, too). Members of the group—I suspect principally their fiddler, Arild Hoksnes—criticized the revival's elitism by referring to *høgstatusområde,* or high-status areas (Telemark, Setesdal, and, within the fiddle area, the Gudbrandsdal), all of which produce excellent players but, even more, benefit from being viewed through a romantic haze. Hoksnes thought folk music ought not be defined by instruments or, at the least, that more instruments ought to be considered legitimate: for example, Møre og Romsdal was home to extensive use within oral tradition of the clarinet. Rather, the identification of folk music ought to be based on social function. In sum, he wished to broaden the "grandparents' view" of folk music supported by the National Fiddlers' Association (*Spelemannsbladet* 1980 [5]: 8–9).

Hoksnes and his group, though small fry in the folk music world at that time, were already fine and knowledgeable performers. Their comments drew immediate fire from Johan Vaa, an influential dancer from Telemark, high in the councils of the National Fiddlers' Association, in an article entitled "Yes to the Old Days' Definition of Folk Music." ("Old days" meant "the good old days," offered as a positive alternative to "grandparents.") Vaa noted that the group from Møre og Romsdal had a right to their opinion, and certainly could play whatever they wanted. The question was what to call the results: he suggested "arranged folk music." Experimenting was good, and some combinations of instruments would sound good, but "ensemble playing in various forms must never push aside the pinnacle of Norwegian folk music, solo performance on the Hardanger fiddle and fiddle. In the "high-status districts" (not his term, he pointed out), music had remained vital without being "messed with" (*klussa med; Spelemannsbladet* 1981 [2]: 15).

Hoksnes's next foray, entitled "Nonsense, Johann Vaa," raised the temperature of the debate by posing several pointed questions: Did Vaa think that Møre og Romsdal's folk music was not worth as much as that from the high-status districts? (This question foregrounded the previously simmering conflict between the elitism of the folk-music revival and Norwegian egalitarianism.) Why should solo fiddle performance constitute the apex of Norwegian folk music? Do the high-status districts have the right to define folk music for the whole country? Is the age of the music critical? Just how old must it be? In Hoksnes's view, this was a debate about ideology, about national romanticism. Was it really water sprites, headless apparitions, and waterfalls that created Norwegian folk music? (*Spelemannsbladet* 1981 [1]: 3).

Vaa reacted immediately in an article entitled "What Is Folk Music?" He criticized definitions based on social function, as these could include music that wasn't "historically" folk music. He countered, not unexpectedly, with a definition emphasizing content: "Folk music is a type of music which flourishes within an environment defined both by geography and tradition. Each tradition area has its own characteristics in terms of instruments, rhythms, and tonality." This, he continued, squares with a section of the bylaws of the National Fiddlers' Association (a section presenting overlapping lists of genres of *folkemusikk* that each fiddle type could employ in contests). He excluded arranged tunes and those "inspired by" folk music, and argued that the rhythms of the older materials were better. For the comparison of pieces within a genre, he suggested the criterion of relative complexity. And, as for the worth of different districts' folk music, he argued for comparing how much they have aroused collectors' interests, and how well their proponents do in the National Fiddle Contest. Why was solo fiddling best? He found that hard to tackle head on, but noted that he could listen to it with pleasure much longer than to any kind of ensemble playing. After all, as Steinbeck pointed out in *East of Eden,* (here I retranslate Vaa's translation) "Collaboration has *never* borne living fruit in music or the other arts." In response to Hoksnes's sniping at national romanticism, Vaa quipped that defining folk music (i.e., excluding *gammaldans*) was "not a matter of pixies and waterfalls, but rather one of *å halde snørr for seg og bartar for seg*" (keeping facial hair and snot separate; *Spelemannsbladet* 1981 [2]: 15).

After further exchanges characterized by wit and heat rather than new substance, the debate ebbed. Then, when Ivar Schjølberg was elected leader of the National Fiddlers' Association in 1984 (he was the first—and to date only—active player of the fiddle to attain this office), he reopened the controversy by appointing a committee to look into how the National Fiddlers' Association ought to treat *gammaldans:* perhaps an annual contest as a companion to the National Fiddle Contest would serve. This bombshell provoked vigorous, at times savage colloquy along battle lines already drawn. This busiest phase of the debate brought into relief the growing pains that the National Fiddlers' Association was experiencing, and along the way revealed much about what Norwegians had come to believe folk music to be. I heard these arguments expressed verbally, and also read them in the *Spelemannsblad*. Opinions were sometimes so passionately and hyperbolically expressed in conversation that I was not always sure which statements were private and which I had license to repeat. For that reason, I will confine my reportage to the published record. The issues are the same, without exception, though the published versions are relatively temperate in expression.

Terms of the Debate

One critical issue already mentioned concerned defining folk music by internal properties and geographical context rather than also by its function and how it was cultivated. The anti-*gammaldans* position, that held in Telemark and in other high-status Hardanger fiddle areas, followed Vaa's earlier remarks. A policy statement of a new folk music organization (the NFD, discussed below) asserted that music and dance are high-quality art forms, created and cultivated with long, hard work. Their worth is not just that they link past and present: they have a musical and aesthetic uniqueness that is the fount of their vigor (*Spelemannsbladet* 1987 [2]: 23). *Gammaldans* was condemned as simple and frivolous, whether charming or not. Those on the pro-*gammaldans* side countered that the functions of old and new folk music were in general the same, that both types were linked with the dance, and that they learned and cultivated these musics precisely the same way. Interestingly, no one chose to argue that *gammaldans music* was as aurally rewarding as *folkemusikk*. This left unanswered a question with practical implications: Even if it would be justifiable to allow *gammaldans* music into the institutional revival system, would this music be suitable for the contests and concerts of the revival?

A second issue raised earlier by Vaa concerned fidelity to the official position of the National Fiddlers' Association and to that organization's history, including how it had traditionally balanced monistic and pluralistic nationalism. Anti-*gammaldans* advocates emphasized that the expressed purpose of the association was to cultivate the oldest layer of genuine, typical Norwegian music, and that a *gammaldans* festival was not in keeping with either the association bylaws or history. The counterargument was that the National Fiddlers' Association ought to adjust to serve the folk music and dance community of the whole country. The old guard, now sometimes referred to as "Telemark imperialists"—the fight was indeed partly a matter of turf—shouldn't be allowed to continue to define folk music for all of

Norway. The *gammaldans* advocates found that the definition of folk music in the association bylaws (a list of genres) was artificial, contradicting another section, which mandated fostering the oldest music in each area. This oldest layer in a number of locations in the normal fiddle areas was indeed some portion of *gammaldans*. The section of the current bylaws defining folk music was in fact narrower than in their original form, which had left the door open for *gammaldans* contest brackets they became necessary (rules from 1946, quoted in Mæland [1973]: 46, and discussed by Ingar Ranheim in *Spelemannsbladet* 1986 [1]: 3).

The anti-*gammaldans* forces were worried that folk music would be injured by *gammaldans,* as it had been in the past: "The accordion nearly killed off the old tunes. Isn't this the indirect reason the National Fiddlers' Association was formed?" (*Spelemannsbladet* 1987 [4]: 13). It was felt that threats posed by mass culture in general and *gammaldans* in particular were undiminished (NFD in *Spelemannsbladet* 1987 [2]: 23; Bernt Balchen, in *Spelemannsbladet* 1987 [2]: 13), threats posed by both *gammaldans* and its performers, who were asserted to be fundamentally different in character and aims. Conversely, those in favor of holding a *gammaldans*-based festival felt more confident in the ability of the National Fiddlers' Association to perform a greater variety of tasks without losing its integrity. Many of the organization's "most prominent members already play both *folkemusikk* and *gammaldans.* They [wouldn't] give up *folkemusikk* now." Further, in normal fiddle territory and in Hardanger fiddle areas outside the most prestigious ones, "fiddle and accordion ensembles have existed for a hundred years, and many accordion players imitate the fiddle" (Øla Grøsland in *Spelemannsbladet* 1986 [1]: 8).

Just how vulnerable was *folkemusikk?* Several proponents of the fiddle told me that while no one in their home areas disliked local fiddling, residents of the Hardanger fiddle area were somewhat polarized in their attitudes toward that instrument. The same esoteric qualities that were valued in the contest system inspired great affection for Hardanger fiddle tunes among some listeners in its district, but alienated others. The pro-*gammaldans* faction did not reply to another assertion by the anti-*gammaldans* group, that folk-style *gammaldans* music lacked clear boundaries. In Linton's analysis of nativistic movements, he noted that cultural materials selected for revival needed to be distinctive—*gammaldans* music is less so than *folkemusikk*—and their revival practical (1943:231). Pragmatism was easily served in one sense: *gammaldans* tunes were already in many a *folkemusikk* fiddler's repertoire. But the lack of boundaries remained ominous: Would opening the door to folk-style *gammaldans* music let popular pablum in?

More than a few members of the National Fiddlers' Association were sufficiently upset by the prospect of *gammaldan's* becoming part of the association's formal concerns that they threatened, in one way or another, to disrupt the society. In a first move, a few prominent Hardanger fiddle players from Telemark and other high-status areas skipped one National Fiddle Contest to demonstrate the gravity of the threat (*Spelemannsbladet* 1985 [5]: 7). Of the total number registered for the event, 15% failed to compete, compared with an average of 10%. When this straightforward attempt at a boycott failed, a longer-term solution was developed. A separate Telemark-dominated folk music organization was formed. While a few members of the new group were unrepentent purists, most who joined genuinely felt that, by sponsoring the National Festival for *Gammaldans* Music, the National Fiddlers' Association had irretrievably lost its way. In response, it was predicted that recruiting for the National Fiddlers' Association, which already went especially well in areas where *gammaldans* was popular, would improve were *gammaldans* sanctioned, and that areas of Norway which lacked older folk music genres might at last participate in the association (this argument referred especially to the four counties of the far north; Ivar Schjølberg in *Spelemannsbladet* 1984 [5]: 2, 1985 [3]: 7, and 1987 [1]: 6). In fact, between 1984 and today, association membership has doubled, somewhat more in the fiddle area. However, it is not easy to establish how much of the increase would have materialized had *gammaldans* remained in its old position; the North has not participated much more.

The controversy had become two related debates. The immediate question was whether or not to inaugurate a *gammaldans* festival under the auspices of the National Fiddlers' Association. The answer would be yes. The eventual decision was to hold an annual festival for *gammaldans* for a three-year trial period, then decide whether to keep it. The broader theoretical question, which bore on the first one, was whether *gammaldans* music was folk music. If not, it ought not to be allowed in folk music venues. A committee charged in 1986 by the governing board of the National Fiddlers' Association with defining folk music eventually adjourned without doing so. Too probing an inquiry would have made explicit a number of critical inconsistencies in the revival's history. For instance, the climax of larger contests is the *lagspel* category, in which whole fiddle clubs compete, each a visually and aurally splendid embodiment of local identity. These clubs, a twentieth-century development, with most formed in the 1950s or later, are much younger than *gammaldans* music! Since the *gammaldans* festival was to be given a chance in any case, the arduous—and perilous—attempt to define folk music was dropped. Nevertheless, the shape and character that the National Festival for *Gammaldans* Music assumed point to aspects of such a definition.

When, after the three-year trial period, the *gammaldans* festival was retained as a regular National Fiddlers' Association event, the most alienated members formed the splinter organization mentioned above, the NFD. The name initially suggested was Norsk Folkemusikk- og Bygdedanslag *(bygdedans,* rural dance, encompasses the dances done to *folkemusikk).* Today's *Spelemannsblad,* which has borne a half-dozen titles over the years, was then called *Bladet for Folkemusikk og Bygdedans;* the new organization was laying claim with its intended name to the center of the National Fiddlers' Association' mission. Because the name initially suggested was too similar to that of another group, the organization was called instead the Norsk Folkemusikk- og Danselag (NFD). It has never been large and never reached significantly beyond the most conservative parts of the Hardanger fiddle area; most members did not in the end quit the National Fiddlers' Association, but belong to both organizations. Although the NFD was formed in anger, most members did not really want to see institutional Norwegian folk music harmed, and the divisive potential of the NFD was minimized from the beginning. Its leadership seldom has drawn on the most rabid of the anti-*gammaldans* firebrands. And influential members Johan Vaa and Jan-Petter Blom insisted from the start on individual membership only; they did not wish to see any fiddle club leave the National Fiddlers' Association. The NFD now functions like many other large fiddle clubs, despite its unusual history and despite some vestigial inflammatory rhetoric. It sponsors meetings, concerts, and publications and, in part because one member, Hallgrim Berg, belongs to the Storting (Norway's Parliament), manages to corner at least its share of government and industry subsidies. This last factor nags, since such funding is important to the National Fiddlers' Association. Are grants to the NFD genuinely new money, or funding that would otherwise have gone to the national organization? In any case, the real price paid for the National Festival for *Gammaldans* Music has proved to be painfully high: the dissolution of many decades of unity—at least surface unity—in the Norwegian folk music world.

Birth of the National Festival for *Gammaldans* Music

Despite all this turmoil, the National Festival for *Gammaldans* Music has succeeded, and done so rather quietly. The first was held during July 1986 in Førde, and was sponsored by the Indre Sunnfjord fiddle club. Førde is in the northern part of the west coast of the main body of Norway (i.e., not its lengthy northern extension), and, although this fiddlers' club is based on the Hardanger fiddle, the area has nurtured both fiddle types for centuries, as well as both *gammaldans* and *folkemusikk*. It might seem that this location was chosen for diplomatic reasons, but in fact it was a matter of finding which reasonably sympathetic club could organize such a large affair on short notice.

The avowed purposes of the newly minted festival were (1) to have a contest for "traditional music" other than the music featured at the National Fiddle Contest, (2) to provide a meeting place for playing and nonplaying friends of Norwegian *gammaldans* music, (3) to strengthen local music traditions throughout the country, (4) to motivate performers of *gammaldans* music to improve, and (5) to have a contest of *gammaldans* music that would foster high respect for the music and its performers (thus to distinguish the National Festival for *Gammaldans* Music from a commercial alternative already in place, the cheerfully crass Titanofestival). Contest rules encouraged performers to display the richness of their repertoires by playing pieces from different genres and to draw on the oldest layers of *gammaldans* music flourishing in their locales (*Spelemannsbladet* 1985 [6]: 12–13; this last provision lopped off the potentially controversial "new" layers of this music used in, for example, the Trondheim area, where an evening of *gammaldans* usually includes, along with the staple waltzes, mazurkas, *reinlenders,* and polka types, one or several examples of foxtrot, tango, and western swing).

This first National Festival for *Gammaldans* Music included brackets for solo *torader* (a two-row button accordion; a solo bracket for modern piano accordion would have been too radical), fiddle clubs (which here could allow their accordions—generally two—with guitar and bass to accompany their masses of fiddles, something which is not allowed at the National Fiddle Contest), and the highlighted genre, *gammaldans* groups (which take various forms, but typically consist of one or two fiddles and accordions—any type—a guitar, and a bass). At Førde, ten *torader* players, eighteen fiddle clubs, and 26 *gammaldans* ensembles competed. The central Hardanger fiddle areas of Telemark and Setesdal were not represented, nor was northern

Norway. In all, the participants numbered around 500, with an audience totaling around 6,000 over the long weekend. The festival has grown since, and, although a few of the first ones lost money, most have been financially successful.

As it became clear that the majority in the National Fiddlers' Association were in favor of continuing to sponsor the festival, the *gammaldans* controversy became less heated. Debate at the 1989 annual meeting of representatives of the fiddle clubs, during which the vote to keep the festival took place, was more dutiful than antagonistic. One Einar Eimhjellen spoke for many when he remarked that, while the coming of the National Festival for *Gammaldans* Music was among the best things that had ever happened to the National Fiddlers' Association, the debate preceding it was the worst. During and even before this meeting, leaders of both camps tried to tone down the rhetoric. Ivar Schjølberg, head of the National Fiddlers' Association during the heat of the debate (he extended his tenure from an intended three years to four [1983–87] in order to see the first festivals launched), remarked that he would certainly "rather work for than discuss folk music" (*Spelemannsbladet* 1987 [1]: 6). Johan Vaa asked all to "play more and preach less" (*Spelemannsbladet* 1988 [2]: 2), and noted that "some have mumbled about resigning from the National Fiddlers' Association. On the other side are those who say 'have a nice trip. We're glad to be rid of you.' I despise [both] such positions" (*Spelemannsbladet* 1989 [4]: 4).

Interestingly, prominent voices on each side of the controversy turned away from the use of the red-flag term *folkemusikk*. Arild Hoksnes, who had sparked the *gammaldans* debate in 1980, went on after his university graduation to become the folk music consultant for the second program on Norwegian radio (the first program airs classical music, some pop music, and the "Folk Music Half Hour" mentioned above, while the then P2 concentrated on pop music). One product of his association with the radio was a series on *gammaldans* music that he later published (1988). Another was a radio quiz show on folk music, the "Radiokappleik." He chose to include *gammaldans* music in the quiz material, and declared that he would refer to "traditional" rather than *folkemusikk,* since "folk" customarily referred to just one slice of Norwegian traditions (*Spelemannsbladet* 1985 [4]: 19).[3] Vaa, who continued to be the most articulate voice on the conservative side, dropped both *folkemusikk* and *gammaldans* in a peace-making article of 1988, saying that "in many places *runddansmusikk* and *slåttemusikk* have the same participants and public, so that it would seem

reasonable for the same organization to take responsibility for both."
(*Runddansmusikk* is an uncommon term used, especially in Vaa's
home of Telemark, for *gammaldans* music: in each *gammaldans*
genre, couples circle the dance floor.) He went on to emphasize the
superiority of *slåttespel* (the short instrumental dance tunes that constitute most of *folkemusikk;* the vocal portion is *kveding*) and the pre-
eminence of the National Fiddle Contest, but his overall tone signaled
an adjustment to the new reality (*Spelemannsbladet* 1988 [10]: 22).

Portrait of the Festival in 1991

I attended the 1991 National Festival for *Gammaldans* Music. It was
held in the Gudbrandsdal, in the hamlet of Vågåmo, the home of Ivar
Schjølberg, who was in charge of the festival. The head of the National Fiddlers' Association at that time was that old adversary of
gammaldans, Johan Vaa, who, however, gave a conciliatory speech
during the festival's opening ceremonies. He stated that the threats
thought to have been posed by the festival had not materialized, that
runddansmusikk was, after all, genuinely Norwegian, and, though he
still didn't believe it measured up to *slåttemusikk,* it provided a valuable bridge to the real thing. He appeared with a bushy beard, which
he had sworn to retain until peace returned to Norwegian folk music
(parodying medieval King Harald Hårfagre, who shaved only after
unifying Norway). At the end of the festival, Knut Buen, a master
Hardanger fiddle player from Telemark who had led the *NFD,* and
Ivar Schjølberg, head of the National Fiddlers' Association during the
heat of the *gammaldans* controversy, buried the hatchet on behalf of
their constituencies by together ceremonially shaving Vaa.

The festival took place July 17–21. These were four long and very
full days followed by one (Sunday) kept short in order to give people
time to travel home. The participants included forty-seven *torader*
players, thirty fiddle clubs, and sixty-five *gammaldans* ensembles—a
great increase over the first festival. In addition, five groups competed
in an "open" class, which allowed instruments with a *gammaldans*
pedigree but little used in that connection today, such as clarinets and
assorted fipple flutes. Last, one category, chamber-sized fiddle ensembles, was shifted from the overfull National Fiddle Contest. Both
the number of contestants and audience sizes set new records. The
number of participants could continue to rise, as this festival has yet
to resort to scheduling two brackets of competition simultaneously in
nearby venues (routinely done at the National Fiddle Contest). But it

is hard to imagine fitting a larger audience into the community centers of the smallish towns which host the event. The Saturday night dancers packed the Vågå Hall so that entering and leaving was at a snail's pace, and the local fire marshal halted ticket sales.

The *gammaldans* festival has thus had to face the same problems of gigantism that dog the National Fiddle Contest, the event upon which it is in many ways modeled. But differences remain, and these reach beyond the statutory ones of allowed genres and instruments. Both the parallels and the differences illustrate how the new festival embodies aspects of what many members of the National Fiddlers' Association now believe folk music to be.

Both events have quiet audiences (as attentive as at a concert of art music) during the day's competitions, then lively dances until late at night. During the day, stage dress features folk costumes associated with the home region of each performer (or perhaps with their former home or that of their parents). Flowers adorn the stage (and often basketball hoops; these are multipurpose buildings), and local rural life and history are visually celebrated. Both the fiddle contest and the *gammaldans* festival supplement competition with concerts, some national or even pan-Scandinavian in character, others spotlighting local performers and traditions. Taken together, the costumes, stage decorations, and concerts point at aspects of national, regional, and local identity, and they do this in a romanticized manner, drawing on colorful and comfortable symbols of the past. The "folk" clothing, for example, is derived from the prettiest traditions of the eighteenth- and nineteenth-century land-owning peasant. Here, as in the music, a sort of antiquarian idealization is at work. However, at the *gammaldans* festival, a significant minority of performers opt for more casual garb, or combine, for example; a folk shirt with jeans, ever so slightly diluting the national-romantic atmosphere.

The music at the National Festival for *Gammaldans* Music, like that of the National Fiddle Contest, is defined by genre, though the statute is less precise ("the oldest *gammaldans* genres flourishing in a given tradition area"). These genres are younger than the *folkemusikk* genres performed during formal competition at the National Fiddle Contest, though none is less than a century old (however, individual pieces may be recently composed). In this sphere, the orientation toward content and the antiquarian flavor of the National Fiddlers' Association definition of folk music are preserved. Some modest loosening occurs in the domain of allowed instruments. It is true that instruments in the brackets of the festival as originally conceived (solo *torader,* fiddle club, and *gammaldans* ensemble) are treated the same way musical genres were: what is permissable is described in a list, thus offering more evidence of content orientation. But the new "open class" features clarinets, recorders, and other instruments, and concerts parade other unusual ensembles. In these "experiments," what seems to be a dramatic relaxing of attitude is carefully based on historical research, on a more accurate, rather than a receding, antiquarianism. But the rigor of the research in the end leaves less of an impression than does the sight of "new" old ensembles on stage.

Perhaps the most interesting development in the festival affecting the unexpressed redefinition of folk music is a clever, technologically aided nod to the dance origins of *gammaldans* music within this concert-like competition. The top five contestants or groups in each competition bracket have their final confrontation in the evening, playing for a full hall of dancers. The judges are across the hall from the performers and wear headphones to hear the contestants. They watch the dancers, and in awarding scores, consider how well the musicians seem to inspire movement. Eyes assess function while ears evaluate musical content.

But what of the imagined threats of *gammaldans* to *folkemusikk,* both by reducing the time fiddlers devote to practicing it, and by fragmenting the organization that encourages these fiddlers' devotion to *slåttemusikk?* The demography of the National Festival for *Gammaldans* Music I attended did surprise me. Although a fair number of Hardanger fiddle *gammaldans* groups exist, few competed here—or would in 1992–94—and no ensemble from an established Hardanger fiddle area got into the *gammaldans* ensemble finals, the festival's climax.[4] The entire event was strongly skewed toward the fiddle areas of Norway, much more than had been expected.

Some of the contestants at the festival were new to National Fiddlers' Association–sponsored competition, including some *torader* players and a *gammaldans* ensemble from northern Norway (which received a vigorous egalitarian welcome . . . and a low aesthetically based score). However, I had seen many of these faces before at the National Fiddle Contest or at smaller contests, but in the audience and during dancing in the evening rather than on stage. Many accordionists, guitarists, and bass players belonging to fiddle clubs had played in the evenings (only) at the National Fiddle Contest, when dancing mixes some *folkemusikk* with more *gammaldans;* contest rules kept these performers off the stage during the day. They and the fiddlers they accompanied did not have to change their practice habits very much to get ready for the *gammaldans* festival: they would now receive recognition for the already sizeable parts of their repertoires devoted to *gammaldans* music.

I have noted that few Hardanger fiddle players attended this festival. What of the fiddle players: Would they reciprocate by abandoning the National Fiddle Contest? Spelemannslaget i BUL Nidaros has a history at the National Fiddle Contest of being loved by the evening dancers, but of not faring well during the day's competition, when only fiddles may play. In 1991, this group chose to skip the National Fiddle Contest in order to concentrate on the festival, where they indeed scored higher than they ever had at the fiddle contest. Also, two *gammaldans* ensembles drawing on this fiddle club made their division finals. I would not be surprised to see this organization attending the festival at the expense of the fiddle contest. But I cannot imagine many groups following suit. There will be no mass defection from the National Fiddle Contest. In fact, the signature performers at the *gammaldans* festival, the ones that score well every year, are the same fiddlers and fiddle clubs that dominate the fiddle competition at the fiddle contest. Of the sixty-five *gammaldans* ensembles that competed at the 1991 festival, the three scoring highest were from the fiddle's high-status district, the Gudbrandsdal. Eleven of the top-scoring sixteen groups were from there.

Of the sixty five ensembles, at least eight were not standing groups, but were created specifically for this event. Six of these eight pick-up groups were among the top thirteen scorers. And performance standards are rising overall. The egalitarian justification for *gammaldans's* deserving a contest parallel to the National Fiddle Contest seems not to have affected the process of competition. The contest/concert impulse is a central mechanism in this revival's motor. *Gammaldans* joined the revival sponsored by those that wished to resist the art impulse, but, to many *gammaldans* performers, a contest was a contest.

The previous chapter explored how fiddlers carefully select *folkemusikk* contest tunes from the complex and exotic end of the spectrum of tradition (see also Goertzen 1990), and therefore gradually create new canons of repertoire, as is done in many folk revivals (Feintuch 1993:191). The *gammaldans* ensembles that routinely score well at the National Festival for *Gammaldans* Music do their best to follow this model. For instance, Bjørn Ødde and his twin sons, Johannes and Kristen, joined with friends to become Odde og Koldens Orkester for the 1991 festival. They played a "Skotsk etter Sigurd Eggen" and another tune, and placed fifth. This *skotsk* had several striking aspects, including (1) the presence of three strains, which is only slightly unusual, (2) an extended strain (which is a more frequently encountered exoticism in *folkemusikk* than in *gammaldans* music), and (3) most odd, irregularity in the extended phrase (the second- and third-to-last measures function identically; either could be removed). Several of the high-scoring groups followed this general strategy in choosing pieces to play for competition at the festival—the same strategy these groups' fiddlers employ so successfully each year at the fiddle contest.[5] Plenty of *gammaldans* tunes sport interesting and locale- or region-specific musical characteristics: many of those transcribed from the playing of Knut Kjøk for this book are excellent examples. But the Oddes' "Skotsk etter Sigurd Eggen," though an unusual *gammaldans* tune, contains much less musical information than the tunes the Oddes play at *folkemusikk* contests and, to my ears, is much less rewarding. The rhythms and modes of *gammaldans* music really are not as interesting as those of *folkemusikk,* and this cannot help looming large in a listening-based forum. As an audience member, I enjoyed the fiddle contest much more than the *gammaldans* festival. I found that I endorsed parts of Johan Vaa's statement from 1981: I too could listen to solo fiddling (especially of pre-1810 genres) much longer than to ensemble performance of *gammaldans* music. This is, of course, not a judgment on the validity of the festival as folk expression. However, it has everything to do with the aptness of this traditional music for a revival based on concerts and contests.

I talked with Ivar Schjølberg about my reactions after the festival. He responded that "of course *folkemusikk* is more aesthetically pleasing. But that's just one value. *You* heard more of the festival than anyone—you should have taken it in smaller doses, and danced in the evening instead of sitting with your damned recorder." He was right, of course. The art motor is indeed operating in competition *gammaldans* music, but the more varied repertoires constituting *folkemusikk* have moved far more easily from dance-connected origins to an art-oriented present. The nature of *gammaldans* music is more stubborn: if it is to be fully enjoyed, its dance function cannot be neglected.[6]

The *gammaldans* controversy seems to be over for all practical purposes. In the end, the picture it presents is far richer than intellectually tidy. Feintuch has noted that "one prerequisite . . . for a folk revival is a shared sense of the tradition as well as a notion of how participants are related to that tradition" (1993:184). Did this debate displace what had long seemed to be a consensus view of folk music among members of the National Fiddlers' Association? The only un-equivocal result was to demonstrate that the consensus, if it had ever really existed, had definitely frayed around the edges. And a new con-sensus did not emerge beyond an eventual willingness to tolerate more differences of opinion than had previously been acknowledged. The National Festival for *Gammaldans* Music remains a discrete event: neither the National Fiddle Contest nor lesser contests have changed in response to its success. Members of the National Fiddlers' Associa-tion who do not care to attend the *gammaldans* festival have the op-tion of not changing the letter of their definitions of folk music, though the controversy must have forced some introspection. Since the National Festival for *Gammaldans* Music has sought legitimacy by modeling itself fairly closely on the much older and still preeminent National Fiddle Contest, the outcome has not been revolutionary. Nevertheless, the inflexible nature of *gammaldans* music, and the irre-sistible opportunity to rethink matters in a new event, have left some marks. The National Festival for *Gammaldans* Music as it now exists illustrates many small, careful steps away from an exclusively content-oriented definition of folk music toward one paying modest, but real heed, to function.

PART 2

Fiddle Tunes

CHAPTER SIX

Fiddle Tunes in *Folkemusikk* genres: Mode and Form

The second part of this book focuses on the music Norwegian fiddlers call their own. The preceding chapters presented a picture of Norwegian fiddling based on people, events, and culturally important ideas. In turning to the music itself, we can gain a more intimate and detailed picture of how these ideas have found fuel in sounding materials, in tunes and musical styles that have both mirrored and modeled the development of culture.

The last part of the book consists of transcriptions of tunes, an anthology to which I will refer throughout Chapters 6–8. These tunes were selected for two overlapping reasons. Each illustrates one or several points in the following discussions, and, as a group, they constitute a small but representative sample of the tunes played by these fiddlers today. The transcriptions are ordered in several groups, many defined by region and key within the main older genre (*springleik/pols* and other names), others simply by genre. Each numbered transcription may contain one or several melodies or versions of melodies. Tunes belonging to the more recent genres, grouped as *gammaldans* music, appear at the end of the anthology, followed by a pair of newly composed tunes in *folkemusikk* genres. The ordering of tunes within sections of the anthology tells a number of short tales, too. Some tunes are grouped within a transcription or follow one another in the anthology owing to perceived similarities of various kinds, others because of instructive contrasts—the reader who does not care to wade through the following analytical remarks but who is handy with a fiddle may find many of the points made in the prose suggested by the ordering of the music itself.

The groupings of tunes within the anthology are as follows.

Part One: Older Genres in the Gudbrandsdal and the West

I, 1.   Transcriptions #1–5: *Springleik*s in D major from the Gudbrandsdal

I, 2.   #6–12: *Springleik*s in D minor from the Gudbrandsdal

I, 3.   #13–17: *Springleik*s in A major from the Gudbrandsdal

I, 4.   #18–22: *Springleik*s in C, G, and F major from the Gudbrandsdal

I, 5.   #23–27: *Halling*s, with emphasis on the Gudbrandsdal

I, 6.   #28–34: *Gammalvals* (Old Waltz), with emphasis on the Gudbrandsdal

I, 7.   #35–41: *Springar*s from the West

I, 8.   #42–46: Bridal marches, most from the West

Part Two: *Pols* and *Polsdans,* from the East

II, 1.   #47–52: *Pols* in Røros and Brekken: from straightforward to complicated

II, 2.   #53–58: The most familiar *pols* family

II, 3.   #59–63: A variety of relationships among similar *pols*

II, 4.   #64–71: *Pols* in keys other than D major

II, 5.   #72–74: *Pols* types south of the Rørostraktom

II, 6.   #75–79: *Pols* types west and north of the Rørostraktom

II, 7.   #80–82: *Pols* types in the far North

Part Three: Special Effects

III, 1.   #83–93: Tunes in unusual tunings from various genres

III, 2.   #94–102: Programmatic and other listening pieces

Part Four: *Gammaldans* Music

IV, 1.   #103–106: An evening in the Gudbrandsdal with Bælg og Streing; waltz

IV, 2.   #107–109: Same Gudbrandsdal venue; mazurka

IV, 3.   #110–112: Same Gudbrandsdal venue; *skotsk* and other polka types

IV, 4.   #113–116: Same Gudbrandsdal venue; *reinlender*

IV, 5.   #117–119: Waltzes from the West, Northwest, and East

IV, 6.   #120–122: Polka types from the West and Northwest

IV, 7.   #123–125: Mazurka and *reinlender*

Part Five: New *Folkemusikk*

V, 1.   #126–127: Composing *folkemusikk* today

Conventions of Transcription

Sevåg and Sæta, in the notes to *Slåttar for Vanlig Fele* (Folk tunes for normal fiddle), state that they wish their transcriptions to offer "the most accurate description possible without sacrificing readability" (1992:I,47). That is my goal too, but as my point of departure is somewhat different, my choices do not always match theirs or the choices made for other publications of Norwegian fiddle tunes. Norwegian authors have written principally for an audience of Norwegians, many of them fiddlers, while I anticipate a largely American audience, including fewer performers. Nevertheless, I expect readers and fiddlers to move easily between this and other volumes containing transcriptions.

The first critical choice in notating these tunes stems from the fact that each is normally cast in a given tuning. Less than half of the pieces in general use on the Norwegian fiddle are played in the tuning typical of concert violin, that is, in fifths, low to high: G D A E. Instead, A D A E is the most employed tuning by my count (as it is for the Hardanger fiddle), G D A E is in second place, and A E A E is fairly common too, with a variety of other tunings brought in rarely for special effects. (Overall, the fiddle uses tunings outside these few less than does the Hardanger fiddle.) Most Norwegian fiddlers who customarily read music do so as if the tuning G D A E were in force. A transcriber must often decide whether to place notes on the staff as heard or as fingered. For instance, if the fiddle is tuned A D A E, a low *a*, that is, the lowest open string, would be notated as a *g* if the transcriber is telling fiddlers where to place their fingers. This is the traditional choice in Norwegian publications of Norwegian fiddling, and is what Sæta did. Since I expect fewer of my readers to be Norwegian fiddlers, and more to be American scholars and fiddlers, I am transcribing what is heard instead. This will not pose great difficulties for those who wish to fiddle pieces in correct tunings when the original tunings are those mentioned above. And this goes along with a current trend in Norway: more than a few fiddlers are adjusting melodies to minimize retuning. However, when tunes were played in rarer scordaturas, in which either or both of the highest-sounding strings are retuned, I include two transcriptions, one giving the tune as heard and one presenting it as fingered. (I will defer description of the more exotic scordaturas to a section specifically about tunes employing these.)

In notating multiple stops, Sæta and his predecessors used smaller noteheads for pitches not bearing the melody. I have used slashes instead, in the interest of graphic clarity. Another change concerns ornaments. He writes these out in small notes, while I have employed the following abbreviations, many of which are common in the notation of art music:

♪ = grace note

Most grace notes in these repertoires are appoggiaturas and, like most ornaments employed in Norwegian fiddling, steal the time they occupy from the preceding note. All such ornaments are slurred to the note that they precede.

〰 = simple mordent; for instance, grace notes on *g* and *a* preceding a note on *g*.

tr = short trill.

〰 = inverted mordent. Other, less common turns are written out.

n = neutral pitch; a note so marked is raised (or lowered) a quarter tone or less.

/ = glissando; slide between notes.

+ = note played using left hand pizzicato.

o = harmonic; note produced by touching but not pressing the string.

A notehead consisting of a slash is the less-important member of a double stop, as mentioned above. A note bearing two stems, one pointing up and the other down, represents a unison double stop (e.g., when the note *a* is played simultaneously on the open *a* string and by placing the fourth finger on the *d* string). To avoid clutter, I have chosen not to write out the open string member of a double stop consisting of grace notes immediately preceding a unison double stop.[1]

Rhythms are particularly interesting in the oldest surviving genre in triple time. In a typical *springleik, pols,* or other regional cognate of the principal older triple-time dance, a few more beats are divided into 3 than into 2. I therefore used a time signature of 9/8, although duplets are so common that a meter freely mixing 9/8 and 3/4 is heard. In the interests of avoiding clutter, I have not marked duplets as such: whether a beat is divided into 2 or into 3 smaller notes should be clear in context.

Throughout the fiddle area, the second beat in a three-beat measure is lengthened. The precise amount of this temporal emphasis varies by region—the Gudbrandsdal is especially strongly affected—and also by player and performance forum. In general, the slower the overall tempo, the longer the second beat is held relative to the others. Our first player, Mari Eggen, plays in contests (and for interviews) at relatively slow tempos, and thus places much emphasis on the second beat of each measure: the relative lengths of the three beats in each measure are about 5/6/5. Thus, an eighth note occupying one-third of beat 2 is longer than such a note within beat 1. These transcriptions will not reflect this, but instead will only clarify the internal relationships within a given beat.

I first recorded nearly all of the tunes given here in 1989 or 1991, but then tried to videotape these again, in 1993, during my last visit before finishing this book. While the purpose of videotaping was to be certain of bowings, I also found that the 1993 versions often differed in small ways from the earlier recorded performances. Unless otherwise specified, the following transcriptions are of the most recent, videotaped versions. Copies of all of the transcriptions went out to their performers for perusal and perhaps correction.

Introducing the Issues: A Sample Performance

Rather than immediately launching into a discussion of musical features of broad repertoires, I will first introduce these analytical topics briefly through a close look at a single, relatively simple melody, a "Springleik etter Amund Slåstugun," performed by Mari Eggen, given as #1 in the Tune Anthology. This piece is from the Gudbrandsdal: giving pride of place to this area follows normal practice in scholarship on music for this instrument. Although I do wish to be as even-handed, as fair to the different districts of Norway as many Norwegians in the folk music world wish to be, it is impossible to overlook the primacy of the Gudbrandsdal in contest and concert, and in strength—second to no other area—in playing for dances. D major is far and away the commonest key in Norwegian fiddling. In music for the Hardanger fiddle, a majority of pieces are fingered in D, but, because of the ways the instrument is tuned, usually sound a minor third higher, in F; on the fiddle, well over half of the composite repertoire is both fingered and sounds in D. The fiddle's second-highest string generally is tuned somewhere between A 440 and A 444. Although customary violin tuning is fairly common, a tuning in which the key of D is favored is even more usual. In this most popular tuning, the lowest string is a step higher, thus A D A E. Like the vast majority of these melodies, this first *springleik* is a straightforward bipartite dance tune, each strain of which may be seen as falling into symmetrical halves, the first cadencing incompletely—often on the dominant, as is the case here—then the second half repeating the first, but landing firmly on the tonic. As is usual (but not invariable), the strains emphasize contrasting tessituras.

In well over half of the tunes in this genre, both strains (or all of them, in longer pieces) are regular, eight bars each. But, in a substantial minority of tunes, including this one, one or both strains are extended. (Shortened strains are rarer. Odd-length strains add or subtract complete measures from the norm—only older players long separated from the dance add or drop beats.) The commonest in a wide variety of extended forms is that found here, 5 + 5 measures. A typical contest performance would consist of a strain, its repetition, the other strain, its repetition, then all of that again, thus AABBAABB, or, less frequently, AABBAABBAABB. Dance versions are generally AABBAABBAABB or even longer.

Rhythmic density tends to follow a pattern in each phrase, especially within the first strain played. Typically, the first measure has a distinctive rhythmic profile. Whereas nearly all measures include quarter (and perhaps dotted quarter) notes and eighth notes, the longer values predominate as phrases begin. On the average, the following measure is busier, and the next even more active, with some—or much—thinning out at cadences. Each strain cadences on its last measure's second beat. The half-cadence ending the first phrase may reflect the rhythmic profile of the full cadence, as in this tune's second strain, or may be busier, as in this first strain.

Movement between notes is both by step and by leap, with conjunct motion favored, though thirds are common in eighth-note triplets. In most of the fiddle area, pitches are almost never repeated immediately except within cadential measures (the district not following this rule is that surrounding Røros, and allied styles in the East). Some contours are broad shapes (as in this tune's first strain), while others feature sequences falling into single measures, this being more common in second strains, including the one in this tune. As in fiddling throughout northern Europe, longer notes in strong rhythmic positions tend to be stable from version to version of a tune, while passing and short notes vary more. This variation is in general more restricted than in vocal melodies, perhaps owing to the reinforcement of aural memory with a tactile component.

The first note of this and of many of the tunes starts an eighth note before the first full measure begins; forms of introduction other than this simple anticipation are very rare. Flourishes that in younger genres might precede the first measure are here contained within it, often placed so that the emphasis on the second beat is immediately made clear. That is the case in the first strain of this tune, which lands on the tonic in that second beat. In addition, first strains are more emphatic harmonically than are second strains. That is, the key is made apparent, often by outlining the tonic chord in the first measure or two, as is done in this piece. Succeeding measures in the phrase may flow naturally from the first, or may consist of formulas that occur in many melodies.

Norwegians are not given to colorful verbalizing, and vivid tune titles are few. Instead, a majority of melodies are referred to by genre together with the name of the source of the version. Thus, this is a *springleik "etter"* (in the manner of) Amund Slåstugun, a fiddler from Eggen's area. Whether *"etter Amund Slåstugun"* is part of the formal title is questionable. (In Sevåg and Sæta [1992] this information is placed off to the side.) The player named in a title may be living, more often a past great, or, perhaps most commonly, a player from one or several generations past who was associated with a specific locale. Citing his name, therefore, asserts a personal and a local pedigree for that version of a tune. As a natural result of this approach to naming tunes, many pieces have the same name. When fiddlers perform in a group, the leader lets the others know which tune is next by quietly and quickly playing its first few notes. The most telling identifiers of many tunes are thus their musical incipits.

Mode

Norwegian fiddlers (of both fiddle types) sort their large repertoires in several overlapping ways. Perhaps the most straightforward way is by genre, which refers both to past (and often present) function of a tune and to the general musical characteristics of a given genre. A second, less clear-cut method is by *current* customary uses of tunes— for dances, in contests and concerts, or for private or in-group pleasure. These three uses overlap with one another and with groupings according to genre, of course. For instance, a given *springleik* that was formerly used in dances may continue in that function today and, if complex in certain ways, may also appear in contests and in concerts.

A third way that Norwegian fiddlers sort their repertoires is by musical characteristics, generally starting with mode. The primary inspiration for this is practical. Since changes of mode often require retuning one or more strings, fiddlers and fiddle ensembles, when playing a series of tunes, will stick to tunes with a given final for a while, perhaps thirty to forty minutes. For instance, tunes in D major and ones in D minor may be performed in the same set, since they are played in the tuning A D A E, while most tunes in G major must wait until the fiddle is retuned to G D A E. Staying in a tuning does more than minimize delays between pieces. A certain coherence settles over an evening of short tunes gathered into sets by mode, because characteristics associated with each mode tend to make pieces in it somewhat similar. This modest, but very real, trend toward unity within a mode receives impetus on a intimate level, from past genetic flowering of one tune into several similar ones and, on a broad level, from assorted restrictions on tune shapes that are imposed by the physical nature of the violin and from traditional associations of certain moods with given modes.

Scholars of European folk music have often centered their analyses on mode, too, partly because this can mark given repertoires as distinctive—perhaps old—and as separate from the tonal harmonic system of European art music. Modern Norwegian fiddlers do value tunes that are in unusual modes, partly for similar reasons. Tunes in odd modes help show that folk music is older than and different from the popular and art repertoires that surround and are considered to threaten folk music in modern Norway. Every fiddler knows and savors a few such distinctive, unusual tunes. Nevertheless, most surviving Norwegian folk music is squarely in the major mode, in fact a simplified and straightforward major mode leaning especially heavily on the first and fifth degrees of the scale, that is, tonic and dominant. (A very few *folkemusikk* tunes have passages emphasizing the fourth degree, the subdominant—see tunes #20, #28 and #42—though this becomes more common in the music of *gammaldans*.) A species of the minor mode is firmly in second place (this is less true for the Hardanger fiddle). Details of these modes, however, and of the interplay between mode and physical aspects of the violin are fascinating. I will discuss correlations of mode with range first, then explore correspondences between aspects of form and the common modes within given genres. Some general attributes of the tunes are tabulated in Figure 10. Although this figure refers specifically only to the tunes transcribed for this book, this sample was chosen to be as typical a cross-section of the repertoire as possible. Rare instances in which tendencies emerg-

Figure 10. Mode, form and range in this sample of fiddle tunes in older genres. *Note:* These tunes were not entered: 69a (rare version of tune), 92 (*gammaldans*), 101 (Swedish), and 102 (Hardanger fiddle tune).

Genre of Tune (in some cases divided by key)	Aspects of Form						Range		
	Strain Length			Strain Order					
	Normal	1st Long	2nd Long	Low, High	High, Low	+ Strains	Full	Omit Low String	Shift Up
Springleik, D	#3,4a,5,19c	83	1,2,4b	1,4,5,19,83	2,3	4	1,2,4,5,83	3,19c	3,19c
d	7a,8,10,12	6,11,95a/d	9,11	8,9,10,11,12	6,7a,95a/d	10b,11	7a,10,11	most	12
A,a	13,14,16,91	15	15,17	most are	high/high	17	91	13-17	15,16
G,C,F	18,19,21,85	20/2,93/5c		19,20,85,21a	18,22,93/5c	21a	18,20	most	21a
Springar, D	35,36,37		38	35,36	37,38		35,38	36,37	
other keys	40,87	41,95b	21b,39,41	21b,41,95b	39,40,87		40	most	21b
Pols/Polsdans, D	47,48,49,50 51,53,55,58 59,69,75,78	62,63,79 81	52,54,57,60 61,63,68,77 81	47,48,49,50 51,53,55,58 68,75,79,82	52,54,57,59 60,61,62,63 69,77,78,81	55 (prelude), 75,77	49,50,52,53 54,55,57,58 61,75	47,48,51,59 60,62-3,68-9 77- 79,81,82	
A	70,89	88,90	71,76,90	70	71,76,88-90	70(p),71	71,90	70,76,88,89	
G	64,65,66,67		56,80	56,64,67	65,66,80		67,80	56,64,65,66	
Random etc. d/D	most		72a,73c,74a	74a,74b	72a-c,73a-c	medleys		all	
Halling	23 only	all others		less relevant		usually	24,27,7b	23,25,26	
Waltz	28,29,30,31 34,84,86	33	32	28,29,30,33 34,84,86	31,32	29,31c 32,84,86	28,34	29,30,31,32 33,84,86	32
March	42,46	43	43,44,45	42,44,45	43,46		44	42,43,46	45
Listening piece	97,98,100	94,96,99	94,96,99	97,98,100	94,96,99	94-97,99	94,96	97,98,99	

ing in this figure do not fairly represent those in the general repertoire will be noted.

Just as major is overwhelmingly the most common mode, D major is the commonest key. A solid majority of folk fiddle tunes in the Gudbrandsdal are in D, and that majority is much augmented in the West and in the Røros area (this emphasis weakens for *gammalvals* tunes, and is least telling in the music of *gammaldans*). When a dance evening is organized by key, D often comes first, G next, and A major later yet, with its brilliant tunes calculated to maintain spirits into the small hours. No one mood is associated with the key of D major. Tunes in this key explore the full traditional range of the fiddle more often than not, and do so more consistently than do tunes in any other key. By "full traditional range," I mean the range available in first position in the tuning typical for the mode. In the case of D major, that range extends from the *a* of the lowest open string to the *b* reached by the left hand's fourth finger on the *e* string. Thus, the tonic, *d*, is padded above and below at least to the dominant, *a*, yielding, in the terminology developed to describe the chant repertoires of the Catholic church, an expanded plagal impression. Tunes in D major rarely leave the lowest string unexplored, and almost never go into positions. Just as it seems quite natural for this to be most common key, since sharp keys in general and D major in particular are easy to finger, this plagal feel issues from matching this key with the range of the fiddle in first position. In my sample, the two performances of *springleiks* in D that exceed first position are clearly exceptional—#3 a seldom-encountered tune that goes high through an odd method of construction, that is, building a second strain by transposing the first, whereas #19c is a very rare version of a tune that usually is in first position in a different key.

Tunes in both G major and A major tend to be plagal in the lower range, taking as their lowest gesture some movement from dominant to tonic. The dominant in each case is the pitch of the second-lowest string in the tuning most typical for each key, G D A E for tunes in G major and A E A E in A major. While most tunes in these two fairly common keys do not explore the lowest string with their melodies, the pitch of that string remains important. It may be touched very briefly in the course of the melodies of one or two tunes in a set. More critically, it will be drawn upon for double stops. In the upper range, tunes in G major usually extend up to the *b* on the *e* string, that is, to the mediant in the key, thus taking part in producing the sweet, unstrained effect of many tunes in this key (see #18). The range is just a scale step beyond what can be reached in A in first position; nevertheless, the general flavor of the two keys is very different. Tunes in A frequently explore positions above first, but that is very rare in G. In general, G gives much less of an impression of power than is characteristic of D, and less of a tendency toward virtuosity than infuses A.

Tunes in A major fall into two groups. Some reach up to the *a* or *b* on the *e* string, thus, in Gregorian chant terms, being authentic (the high *b* acting as an ornament to the tonic *a*; see #13 and #14). But tunes in this key from the Gudbrandsdal and in the West often have contours that flow naturally higher, requiring shifting into positions. Of the tunes in this sample, those that require changing the location of the fiddler's left hand are listed in the column on the far right of Figure 10. Tunes #15 (a "Springleik etter Fel-Jakup") and #16 ("Melovitte") are in the horizontal column devoted to *springleiks* in A major from the Gudbrandsdal. Tune #12 ("Vigstadmogleda," just above #15 and #16 on the chart) has one strain in D minor, which stays in first position, and another in A major, which requires shifting. The waltz in this group that exceeds first position, tune #32 ("Holnurkjen") is an irregular and uncommon one in A major. The remaining tunes in this sample that require shifting are rare, and are exceptional in ways other than in range.

Why do so many tunes in A major require shifting up? Perhaps the fact that the primary key, D major, is plagal, pushes the general repertoire in that direction. In order for tunes in A major to reach more than one pitch past the tonic *a* on the *e* string, the fiddler's left hand must move up the neck of the instrument. Doing this makes the range explored more familiar, but at the same time requires abnormal technique. Employing one virtuosic maneuver encourages other explorations, with the general result that A major, although the home of many tunes typical in most ways—including level of difficulty for the performer—also features many of the hardest tunes to play. Certain of these showpieces in A major are designed to be played in the most common true scordatura, A E A C♯; quite a few of tunes in this subset feature pizzicato and flashy drone passages (see tunes #88–#92, to be discussed below).

D minor is far and away the most frequently encountered of the minor keys in Norwegian fiddling. In general, minor is not common, and tends to be unstable to some degree (it is least rare in the Gudbrandsdal and, within the broad domain of the *pols*, in the *rundoms* of the Southeast; see #72 and #73). D minor is a species of melodic minor: the notes *b* and *c*, that is, the sixth and seventh degrees of the scale, tend to incline in the direction the melody is going. The seventh degree is invariably raised when resolving to the tonic, and generally natural in descending contours. The sixth degree tends to be raised, especially on the *a* and the lowest strings. The note *g* may also be inflected upward on occasion in order to ornament the dominant, *a*, as in the first full measure of tune #6. The resultant mode complex could be called melodic minor with a sharp wash, with a push toward major (see #9, #10, and esp. #11). That D minor is not merely a modal shading of some tunes in major is underscored by the range explored by tunes in minor. While melodies in D major are often plagal in the low range, extending down to the open low *a* string, those in D minor are usually authentic in that range, either not using the low *a* string at all or dipping down just to an ornamental *c♯* rising to a unison double stop on the tonic *d* (i.e., *d* played both on the open *d* string and stopped with the third finger on the low *a* string).

Other keys are rare. Tunes in C major (#20, #21, #40, #69), F major (#22), B♭ major (#30), and even G minor (#31b–c, #95c, #97, #100), A minor (#17), and C minor (#98) do pop up in many regional repertoires, perhaps as legacies of art influence. Each key has its own characteristics. For instance, many tunes in C are especially irregular in form (Norwegian fiddlers consider this a sign of a tune's age), and many lean heavily on the third degree. A handful of old waltzes in the Gudbrandsdal are in B♭ (see #30). Local wisdom says this key was deeded by military bands—that is, local youths became acquainted with the key and pieces in it during military service. Another factor may be the influence of keyboards (on which flat keys are often perceived as easy to play) on this early nineteenth-century genre. The older the genre, the more those sharp keys easiest to finger on the fiddle are emphasized. Tunes in F major may require one of several drastic scordaturas (see tunes #85, #86, and #87), each different from the tunings already considered in this section in that one or several low strings are tuned *down* from standard violin tuning. When this is done, timbre and volume both suffer; it is even worse when, in a rare tuning associated with D major, the lowest string is retuned all the way down to a low *d*.

The keys of C, F, and B♭ major all require the use of half position for the first finger of the left hand on one or more strings. Half position is not comfortable for many fiddlers, and neutral intervals often result as the first finger starts to edge towards its accustomed home. Other neutral intervals also probably result from fingers' drifting out of unusual locations. The second finger can move a bit out of each of its normal posts toward a spot between these; the fourth-finger *b* on the *e* string often is somewhat flat. But although the pattern of intervals that are on occasion neutral argues convincingly that these arose as simple inaccuracies, over time these errors were institutionalized, modified to shape their own logic. In the hands of sensitive fiddlers, the resulting temperament becomes quite lovely. Few performers employ neutral intervals today, but a few younger fiddlers would like to learn how to play these.

Certain modifications of mode may also have come into being for physical reasons. The fourth degree of the scale is often inclined upward to emphasize the dominant (see tunes #6 and #37). In a fair number of tunes, especially *pols* in D major, the fourth degree in the upper register, *g♯* on the *e* string, occurs even when this note is not leading to the dominant, and thus starts to yield an impression of Lydian mode (see tunes #53, #57, #58, #59, #60, #62, #63c, #72b, and #73). Why do hints of and stronger impressions of Lydian mode turn up so frequently in Norwegian fiddling? Groven (1964) speculated that Lydian mode issued naturally from the harmonic series, that is, the series of upper partials produced by instruments such as the *seljefløyte* (willow flute). Mary Barthelemy's version of "Sofie Råen"—I quote the first four measures as the lowest line in #59— illustrates this: the note *g″* is automatically sharped throughout her performance. It is possible that the playing of such instruments, once much more common than today, influenced fiddlers. But a more plausible (and more prosaic) explanation may be offered. When the fiddle is in its commonest tuning, A D A E, pitches in the scale of the commonest key, D major, issue from the lowest three strings when each is fingered precisely the same. The left-hand index finger is a whole step from the nut, the middle finger a whole step up from that, then the ring finger up a half-step. It would be natural to replicate that same fingering pattern casually on the top string. There, the middle finger a whole step up from the index finger is on the note *g♯*. Indeed it is only in this octave—only on the *e* string—that *g* is frequently sharped in the key of D major in Norwegian fiddling. The fourth degree is raised regularly, though much less frequently, in the keys of G major (see tune #93) and A major (see tune #41 for an example in the tuning A E A E and #88 and #89 for examples, yielded again by fingering patterns, in the scordatura A E A C♯). As in the case of neutral intervals, a habit that may have begun as a pattern of errors was transformed over time into a distinctive and attractive feature.

Extra Resonance: Unusual Tunings and Multiple Stops Reinforcing Mode

For much of the history of fiddling in Norway, the typical performance situation was a single fiddler playing for dancers who, because of their physical activity, could not be completely quiet even if that was intended. Various strategies were employed by solo fiddlers to obtain extra volume, and each had interesting musical by-products. This may be among the reasons behind the Hardanger fiddle's addition of sympathetic strings, which resonate when certain pitches are bowed, that is, pitches the same as those of the sympathetic string or bearing a close relationship to those pitches (an octave, a fifth, or some combination of related frequencies away). Related to this idea is the tuning of the four bowed strings (of either fiddle type) so that open strings not being played directly resonate sympathetically with important melody notes. The strings in question are generally—but not always—the lowest or two lower strings. The effect begins to work even in the common fiddle tunings. In these tunings, A D A E, G D A E, and A E A E, the lowest strings are tuned to pitches critical to the most-used keys, which are respectively D, G, and A major. Those strings are then available for unfingered double stops, yielding a drone effect, and they also increase volume and enrich timbre through sympathetic resonance on dominant or tonic.

Other, rarer tunings, which therefore may be called scordaturas, go further in the direction of not merely facilitating fingering but also adding volume and highlighting important pitches in specific keys. The extremely rare tuning D D A E, for example, takes the low string an octave below the third string to offer a tonic drone in D major. Since that D is a fourth below the G for which the string was intended by the manufacturer, the string becomes quite slack, hard to keep in tune, and with a timbre that blends poorly with those of the upper strings. Its value as a tonic drone is exploited in a few seldom-heard pieces such as those given here as #83 and #84. The latter selection, a "Vals i form etter Einar Turtum," illustrates what would seem to be quite an old scordatura used in conjunction with a modern genre—though not too modern a genre, since this waltz is clearly a gammalvals. This is a contest piece in which the lesser rhythmic interest of its genre (in comparison with the *springleik*) is compensated for by exploring range and sonority. The first two strains underline their contrasting ranges through the use of *d* as an occasional double stop / drone in two ranges. The second and third strains begin with the same idea in different octaves; the third strain summarizes by exploring the ranges of both strains and by using both *d* strings as drone. The exploiting of the *d* drone is further highlighted in the second strain by sometimes placing *d* off the beat, nicely coupled with *springleik*-derived off-the-beat bowings (see measures 12–14). I first heard this piece in a contest, which has indeed become the typical venue for pieces in such inconvenient, but attractively exotic, scordaturas.

Another rare scordatura, F D A E, is called Tjorhælstille in the upper Gudbrandsdal. Although this positioning of the low string lacks the disadvantages of the previously considered tuning, since *f* is just a step away from *g*, this tuning is rare simply because the key of F is uncommon (see #85 and #86). This key is also served by a more drastic retuning, F C A E, named Kolagut tuning where it is most used, in the West. Although this scordatura is at first hearing remarkably striking, it actually follows a common pattern; the tonic and dominant are given on the two lowest strings, just as in the more common tunings of G D A E and A E A E. This allows for the near-constant drone through double stopping that is characteristic of much fiddling in this part of Norway. Arne M. Sølvberg, who knows of four traditional pieces in this tuning, describes tune #87 as a Tatarslått, meaning that it is associated with Norway's traveling people, a group analogous to Gypsies elsewhere. He played this tune and a *halling* he had composed in the same scordatura at the 1989 National Fiddle Contest, which he won. That he employed this very special tuning was a modest but significant factor in the judging. No one else from this part of Norway has ever won the fiddle division of the National Fiddle Contest.

The tuning A E A C♯ is probably the most common and most widespread of the true scordaturas today. It takes the common tuning of A E A E a step further in exploring double stops and the general resonance of the key of A major. This is the only scordatura I encountered that uses the third degree of the scale as a frequent drone. It also is the "tightest-sounding" scordatura, both in the general sense that the interval between lowest- and highest-pitched string is at its narrowest and, more specifically, in the close interweaving of melody and double stop in the fiddle's upper register. *Solungstille* (sun-tuning) is the term used in the upper Gudbrandsdal for both A E A E and A E A C♯. It is said that toward the end of a long dance, when the sun was rising, shifting to *solungstille* brightened up the music and restored the spirits of tired dancers (see #91, "Solung Springleik"). Indeed, over half of the pieces in A E A C♯ that I have heard supplemented thorough use of characteristic double stops with flashy sections full of pizzicato chords (see #90 and #92); plucking is quite rare outside the key of A major.

The mode employed with this tuning is always A major. However, considerations of easy fingering often point this major mode toward Lydian (as was seen in another way in D major, especially in the Røros area). In "Hjulmaker" (#88) and other pieces from that area in this tuning, placing the first finger in normal position on what is now the *c*♯ string produces a *d*♯, which in A major is the sharped fourth degree. Also, a common double stop, produced when the first finger stops both the *a* and the *c*♯ strings, to include *b* natural must sharp *d*. Certain characteristic progressions result from the use of this double stop, among them parallel major thirds (see the ends of measures 8, 12, and 16), and the resolving of the major third between *b*♮ and *d*♯ to the unison double stop on *c*♯, further emphasizing the importance of that scale degree in this scordatura (see measures 6, 9, 11, and 15). The handful of pieces in this tuning within a given style area seem rather similar, constituting what might be thought of as clusters somewhere between tune and style families (compare #88 and #89). I do not imagine these pieces converging further: once a fiddler has taken the trouble to tune his instrument in this way, he or she is likely to run through the small repertoire of appropriate tunes found in his or her part of Norway. These tend to be aurally intricate or physically taxing pieces, thus amplifying the tendency toward demanding virtuosity characteristic of A major.

Last, I will mention the tuning G D A D—called *spakrostille* in the Gudbrandsdal, named for a specific location—which allows an upper-register drone on the dominant in the key of G major (see #93; terms for tunings are best discussed in Jenstad [1994]). Such exotic tunings are more common on the Hardanger fiddle, which remains more closely wedded to solo performance and to playing for listening.

A consideration of mode in music for the Norwegian fiddle would be incomplete without at least a few words about different approaches to double stops. I have pointed out that modes are tied to tunings, tunings which in turn make certain double stops merely a matter of tilting the bow, and others nearly as easy. Most double stops include a melody note, whether a stopped or an open string, and a neighboring open string. In the next-largest group of double stops, the note that does not belong to the melody either is stopped, but not new (i.e., it was the melody note during the previous beat), or both notes in the double stop are stopped at once with the same finger. In both cases, two notes may be fingered, but only one needs to be found (these generalizations hold for both fiddle types). These varied types of double stops can most easily be sampled in the *pols* beginning with tune #49.

However they are created physically, double stops perform several functions. They increase volume, important when a dance is accompanied by a single fiddler, as was common in the past. They can be ornamental when rationed sparingly (see, e.g., tune #84, second strain). This function includes timbral ornaments too, specifically those unison double stops on tonic or dominant created by playing an open string at the same time as the same note stopped on the adjacent lower string. And, most important, double stops provide a pitch reference that functions in a manner somewhere between that of a drone and a harmonic reference. In any tune containing many double stops, most pit a repeated note against a melody which is passing through several pitches. Such a note is reiterated as long as is convenient, perhaps a measure or two—thus acting as a temporary drone—then it is replaced by a different note with a related function in the key. The commonest added note in D major is the open *a* string, the dominant in the key, with the open *d* string in second place, and the open *e* string in third place (the supertonic and a member of the dominant chord, played when the implied harmony is the dominant). Less common, but found in many pieces, are what might be called resolving double stops, which have a harmonic function. These generally include the note stopped with the first finger on one string and the note stopped with the third finger on the next-lowest string, for instance *b* on the *a* string and *g* or *g♯* on the *d* string, resolving to a unison double stop on *a*, which will be either the tonic or dominant of the key. Nearly all double stops in the common keys are accounted for in the group of categories described in this paragraph. Ornamental multiple stops are especially important in the Gudbrandsdal, whereas the drone/harmonic technique is in fullest flower in the *pols* of the Røros area.

Fiddlers from the Røros area who have an opinion about double stops assert that the constituent pitches of a given double stop are equally important. I found that true in a broad sense—double stops as a general part of texture are absolutely essential. However, it was seldom a problem to figure out which member of a multiple stop was carrying the melody forward. The other pitch was (1) most usually an open string, (2) next most common, a note stopped with the index finger, either held over from the previous beat or stopped with the index finger over two adjacent strings, and (3) much less common, some other note held over from the previous beat. In very few situations did a player begin to stop notes simultaneously with different fingers.[2] The double stops in Røros are much like those in complex Hardanger fiddle tunes (see tune #102). In both bodies of musical literature, the luxuriant variety of notes that do not belong to the melody almost—but not quite—manage to constitute true polyphony. The textures present not two independent voices, but rather one voice that is almost constantly commented upon by a constellation of notes outside it, yet intimately related.

Form and Gesture

Some aspects of form seem tied to mode, and some not. It must be kept in mind that these are large and dense repertoires which nevertheless contain great variety. All patterns are challenged by exceptions, but patterns do remain. I base the following generalizations on a general appraisal of a large array of repertoires for fiddle, and have tested them statistically against the complete body of the more than 2,000 performances I have collected (Fig. 10 will again be useful for referring to specific examples of general principles).

The principle that tunes have two strains is held to most strictly in the key of D major, in the Røros area, and in the *springleik/pols* composite genre and the march. A *gammalvals* often has three or more strains; this is one of many factors illustrating the lack of a clear dividing line between old and newer waltz. The genre of the listening piece *(lydarslått)* also is unpredictable in this regard. This is a relatively young genre, composed to a great extent of adaptations of tunes originating in other genres; it is explicitly for listening, and thus tends toward length and complexity.

Patterns of how strains are ordered do seem loosely tied both to locale and to mode, as well as to genre. Tunes in D major and D minor generally start with the lower strain (this is truer for tunes in the Gudbrandsdal than for ones from elsewhere). Waltzes also tend to start with the low strain. In the Røros area, most *pols* in A major and most *rundom*s, which are generally in D minor or D major, begin with the high strain. This aspect of form is otherwise unpatterned.

Strains irregular in length may be found throughout the reach of the fiddle—tune #33 features a compression, but most irregularities are expansions. The overall tendency, in all genres and in all geographic areas, is for the second strain to be more likely to acquire "extra" measures than the first (this is not borne out consistently in

Fig. 10, but emerges clearly from the larger sample). The first strain has the more straightforward and assertive profile in terms of rhythm, of harmony—outlining the tonic chord generally more clearly and quickly than does the second strain—and also of form. The second strain will rely a bit more on repeated figures and on melodic sequences, which tend to spill into an "extra" measure or two.[3] How this works in specific tunes varies greatly (see the pieces listed in the appropriate columns of Fig. 10).

While many tunes bear lengthened strains owing to what might be termed melodic exuberance, others work on a very different principle. This is the "organic" construction that is at its most complex in the highest-status Hardanger fiddle areas of and neighboring Telemark. In that repertoire, growth of a piece is frequently achieved through presenting a short idea (usually two measures), then repeating that idea, then repeating again with slight variation, repeating that form, then treating the gesture with additional freedom, and so on (see #102 for an extended Hardanger fiddle piece with its roots in Telemark). This form of construction infiltrates the normal fiddle repertoires principally in the genre of the *halling,* a genre much more important in the Hardanger fiddle areas. Within the sample presented in this book, the *halling* given as #24 used much of the principle, while that given as #23 uses none, and #25 an intermediate amount. Tune #24, a "Storhallingen hass Fel-Jakup," as performed by Leif-Inge Schjølberg, follows the Hardanger fiddle model by consisting of a series of measure pairs which are often varied slightly when repeated (see Kvifte 1981 and Hopkins 1986). For instance, the first beat of the first full measure is broken up when repeated in measure 3. Then, the next pass through this measure pair breaks up its cadence. In general, a given idea picks up steam, rhythmic density, with repetition. For an even better example of this, compare the ends of the second through fourth measures of the penultimate line of music. Most ideas are presented thrice. The resulting performance, even if not as engagingly fluid in form as many a Hardanger fiddle *halling,* is quite exciting. This sort of construction does occasionally find its way into the *springar/springleik/pols* genre for fiddle, doing so most frequently in the West, where many players perform on both fiddle types. For instance, a *springar* in the repertoire of Arne M. Sølvberg, our #41, has an unusual form. It is basically the usual rounded binary form, repeated; the first strain is longer in the 1993 performance. The forms of the two performances, with numbers of measures per phrase given in subscript, are as follows:

1989: $A_6 A_6 B_{4+4} A_5 A_6 A_6 B_{4+4} A_5$
1993: $A_7 A_7 B_{4+4} A_5 A_7 A_7 B_{4+4} A_5$

Measures 2–3 in the 1989 version, and measures 2–4 in the 1993 performance represent the sort of intensified repetition—an accelerating device—typical of Hardanger fiddle music.

A third way of loosening up structure may or may not result in odd lengths of pieces in terms of number of measures, but certainly shows how tunes can begin to escape the punctuation of the measure line, that is, making sense on the level of the beat and of the phrase but being relatively fluid between those levels. This is best viewed in the Røros area, within the genre of *pols,* many of which show remarkable horizontal flexibility. For instance, some versions of tunes start on the second, rather than the first, beat of the measure—compare Johnson Nyplass's and Schjølberg's versions of "Storhurven," tune #50—as do quite a few tunes. In "Storhurven," the versions are synchronized immediately after their different starts, but other tunes exhibit more variety. For instance, anthologized versions of "Leken hass Gammel-Møller," #66, begin three very different ways, and one of these remains a beat out of step with the others for almost four measures. And some distinct tunes are differentiated in the first instance by where, within the measure, similar opening gestures start (compare #59 and #60).

Another dramatic type of flexibility appears in the anthologized versions of #63, "Leken hass Nils Toresa." Although the modest contrast between the versions by Brekken's Magne Haugom and Røros's Harald Gullikstad seems typical for community-based variation of reasonably common tunes, Brekken-raised Tron Westberg's second strain, six measures long in all versions, is especially odd. The rhythms are smoothed out in a way that suspends meter, placing four beats in the space of three for an extended period (a period that starts on the second beat of the measure!). He has played this version for dancers, who must rely on his foot taps, which maintain the 9/8 measure, to get their bearings. Westberg pits four against three now and again, following the model of one of his main sources, Jørgen Tamnes, who was the source for this tune. Tamnes fits an uncommon profile for a senior fiddler: his memory is excellent and repertoire large, but technique limited. He changes bows uncharacteristically seldom; Westberg has copied and made attractive this "sawing" bowing style, and derived fascinating, unusual rhythms from models that may not have been deliberately idiosyncratic. Indeed, many Røros pieces seem incomplete without the dancers, whose physical motions (and consequent sounds) grouped in threes provide the sense of measure lacking in some fiddle tunes.

The variety and commonness of strains irregular in length help demonstrate that form in these "simple" dance tunes is not something to be taken for granted, not just a rigid mold into which gestures are poured. Instead, we witness gestures that reinvent these short forms each time, perhaps with regular results, perhaps not. This tussle between the propulsive gesture and the habits of symmetry is engaging and powerful. And it is an important part of a larger picture in which patterns of various kinds and on various levels are heard as strong and original because they are involved in a struggle. We hear triple meter in the *springar/springleik/pols* complex of genres as vigorous partly because of the lengthening of measures' second beats that continually threatens to subvert the meter. Bowing pushes us forward by changes within beats at least as often as between them. And, most important, surprises in the dance and suspense in the tune may coincide, or may instead play off of each other. In form and subsidiary elements, just as in mode and related features, these repertoires of short tunes demonstrate over and over the complexities that both make them immediately attractive and wear so well over the centuries.

CHAPTER SEVEN

Local and Regional Style, Genre, and the Individual Fiddle Tune

Possessing and meticulously maintaining distinctive local and regional folk fiddle styles are natural in a country where local identity is so important. Regional and local styles are differentiated in three main ways: general attributes of performance practice, exclusive attachment to or a marked preference for certain music and dance genres, and playing of tunes or versions of tunes specific to an area. While genre may vary more on the regional than the local level, performance practice and repertoire vary on the levels of region, general locale, and village. I will begin to illustrate the broad differentiation of style through multiple manifestations of what seem to me to be a single piece, the same one used to lead off the previous chapter, but now to be examined in three regional forms. This is the Gudbrandsdal tune "Springleik etter Amund Slåstugun," known as "Springar etter Gamle-Lars Tomasgård" in the West, and as "Litjhurven" (Little mess) in the Røros area.

The subtle and linear style of the Gudbrandsdal has been best suited to the contest system. This is partly a matter of an initial high degree of compatibility of the style with the needs of the contest and partly reflects adjustment over an extended period, dating back to when prominent fiddlers from Lom in the Gudbrandsdal, Olav Mølloken and Hans Brimi, began competing in the National Fiddle Contest early in this century (see Fig. 3), men who influenced much of the valley's playing. The qualities which together produce this style's linear impression include the basic conjunct motion of nearly all melodies, the push of appoggiaturas—these most propulsive ornaments are at their most common in this style—bow changes that often start within beats or overlap beats, and reflection of forward motion in the frequency of irregular strains whose odd lengths seem to result from melodic exuberance (in "Springleik etter Amund Slåstugun," in the second strain). The style features ornaments that lean up or lean down, turns, and also double stops that are infrequent, that decorate or limn mode rather than becoming textural. The result is an aesthetically rich style that, while certainly proven in the arena of dance, is the most melodic and hence especially at home in a concert setting. This particular piece is on the simple side, a good demonstration of general attributes of overall fiddle style and, more specifically, that of the Gudbrandsdal. (A more balanced impression of the music being presented in contests by Gudbrandsdal fiddlers today may be obtained by scanning the first thirty four tunes in the accompanying anthology). In fact, Mari Eggen, a skilled performer—the only woman ever to win either solo fiddle bracket in the National Fiddle Contest—does not have this tune in the most active part of her repertoire. I recorded it from the playing of two younger fiddlers from her area at the 1988 District Contest. When Eggen was interviewed initially, through correspondence, she omitted this common tune; however, when I requested it during a meeting in 1993, she played it without hesitation. It comes from the meat-and-potatoes level of her local repertory, a level she would draw on at dances, but had left behind in the contest environment.

The "Springar etter Gamle-Lars Tomasgård," #35, is one of the most-played tunes in the West. This is an area with considerable variety in style source, because of the presence of both fiddle types and, more generally, of easy communication by sea and fjord. Here we see less-linear tunes and rather more of a dance orientation than in the Gudbrandsdal. More double stops appear, not for delicate variety, but rather for volume and rhythmic definition. This varies from tune to tune and within tunes: note that in this *springar* double stops are more common and more important to the general aural impression in the first strain than in the second, and certainly more critical overall than in the Gudbrandsdal *springleik*. Ornaments in the West include fewer propulsive appoggiaturas, but more and a greater variety of turns. Irregular forms are less sought out—compare the four-measure phrases in the second strain of this *springar* with the corresponding five-measure ones in the *springleik*.

Although the styles of the West and the Gudbrandsdal contrast quite a bit, the major Norwegian fiddle tradition most different from that of the Gudbrandsdal is that of South Trøndelag, a style complex centered in and around Røros. The *pols* "Litjhurven," several versions of which appear as #49 in the Tune Anthology, demonstrates this in a number of ways. A majority of pieces in the Røros area are in D major, like "Litjhurven," the other fairly common keys being G major and A major. The minor mode is almost unheard of. D major frequently has Lydian touches, that is, the same peppering of g#'s on the e string witnessed in the West. Although the same kinds of exceptions to the norm of bipartite tunes consisting of balanced phrases occur in this repertoire as in the Gudbrandsdal, they do so less frequently. In this tune, phrase structures are regular. Double stops are now pervasive, used in tunes like this one for volume and rhythmic definition throughout the piece. Ornaments, if present, are usually for decoration and articulation. The contours of Røros *pols* melodies are on average less involved than those of a typical *springleik*. This is not to say that the entire effect of a performance of a tune is any less rich. But much of the power and complexity of a *pols* come from factors other than the stringing together of pitches in a melody. These factors include rhythmic intricacies, metric ambiguity, dense ornamentation, and, above all, vigorous playing of a thick fabric of double stops. In short, a sense of line clearly takes second place to the web of sound.

Local Style: Subdivisions of *Pols* Territory

While the *pols* tradition now centers on Røros, related styles extend in several directions from there, thus offering a good illustration of how style areas in Norwegian fiddling subdivide. The copper mines near Røros, in operation over 300 years before shutting down in 1972, spawned a substantial settlement in an otherwise inhospitable area. This is a "cold spot" in Norway, fit only for marginal agriculture, principally raising cows and the hay to feed them. The mines brought about regular European influence, and patterns of communication based partly on proximity and partly on economics also allowed this community to export its culture. Places not too close by, but having mines, such as the Folldal, received the *pols*. So did points north and south from Røros, through trade connections. A series of waterways stretches south: lumber and other necessities flowed to Røros, and money and music flowed out. Much shipment of the mined copper was north, toward the ocean, with the same result.

The center of *pols* production and performance remained a small area including Røros and, a few dozen kilometers toward Sweden, the hamlet of Brekken.[1] Despite the proximity of Røros and Brekken, stylistic and repertorial choices are slightly different in the two towns. A broad picture of these differences may be obtained by playing through tunes #47–#71; fiddlers Haugom and Westberg are from Brekken, while Gullikstad, Nyplass, and Johnson learned principally from Peder Nyhus of Røros. In general, Brekken performances are slightly more extravagant, employing more ornaments. The versions of "Litjhurven" by Haugom and Westberg illustrate this and also explore a higher octave in the first strain of the tune. A common ensemble arrangement in the area, called *"grovt og grant"* (fine and coarse) consists of octave doubling, with the added octave being above or below the melody depending on where space is available—in Brekken, the solo version of "Litjhurven" is in the brighter upper octave, in keeping with a slighter flashier approach to performance typical of that town.

Whereas the style of nearby Brekken is close to, but distinct from, that of Røros, *pols* become quite different farther north, west, and south of the Røros area. For instance, the oldest layer of folk fiddling in much of southeastern Norway is dominated by *pols* types under various names. Tune #72 exemplifies the *random,* the commonest *pols* relative in that part of the country. *Random*s are played in sets, with a set of three being fairly standard in contests these days, whether the fiddler is competing as a soloist or accompanying dancers. At dances away from contests, sets of five are more typical. In past generations, sets may have been longer still. A *random* has two strains, like a *pols,* but these are repeated less often during a performance. In a typical sequence, the first *random* is played (probably without repeats), and closed with a slower tag. Fiddler(s) and dancers pause long enough for a deep breath, then launch into the middle *random,* pause, then play and dance the last. Most *random*s close with one of a handful of common tags. In the transcribed performance by Bente Kvile Buflod, if each of the two strains of each *random* is assigned a letter, the first *random* (A), will be just a (though this long single strain has two ingredients), the second cd, and the third ef. The form of the complete performance is: a a tag #1, c c d c tag #2, e f tag #2. When I recorded this set, it lasted one minute and fifty-one seconds, somewhat longer than the length of a typical performance of a *springleik* or *pols.*

Many of the common *random*s sound rather similar, particularly in their first strains which, like those of the three in this set, typically leap to the note *a* on the *e* string, and gradually descend. Thus, the effect of a performance of a set of *random*s is less disjointed than the description above might suggest. The impression created is less a mosaic than a series of variations or, since it is the first strains of the respective *rundom*s that are especially similar, a rondo. Another factor promoting unity in this subrepertoire is modal: D minor is common here, and both D major and minor are liberally peppered with the note g♯.[2]

Other Major *Folkemusikk* Genres: *Halling, Gammalvals,* and *Bruremarsj*

The *halling* is a solo male display dance of considerable age (couple forms exist too, but the solo form predominates). Most modern performances take place during the same contests in which fiddlers compete. In the course of a two-to-four-minute dance, the contestant gracefully proceeds counterclockwise around the stage, punctuating his passage with acrobatic feats, among these fancy push-ups and a variety of difficult leaps. The general pacing and overall effect are reminiscent of competition ice-skating. A woman, generally standing on a chair, holds parallel to the stage a long pole, at the end of which a hat hangs (perhaps six to eight feet above the stage). At the climax(es) of the event, the dancer flips entirely over, ideally kicking the hat off of the pole.

Competitors in this dance genre come from many places in both the fiddle and Hardanger fiddle districts. The Østerdal and the West provide most of the dancers from fiddle areas. However, the *halling* as a musical genre has been cultivated more thoroughly in the Gudbrandsdal, where the dance is seldom performed. When fiddlers choose their statutory two pieces for a contest, one is almost always a *springleik* or *pols* (by whatever name). The other may be a second one in 9/8, but more likely will be an old waltz, *halling*, bridal march, or listening piece *(lydarslått)*. Gudbrandsdal fiddlers favor the *halling* and listening piece for this slot. In fact, since the *halling* is generally not danced in the Gudbrandsdal, its music overlaps quite a bit with that of the listening piece.

Most *halling*s are in D major or D minor, a substantial minority in A major or minor, and very few in any other key. They are in duple time, almost always simple duple. The formal influence from music for Hardanger fiddle is at its strongest here. Some pieces are irregular, seeming to follow the Hardanger fiddle model of organic growth (discussed below, with #24). The two *halling*s in D major given here are at opposite ends of a spectrum, with #24 as much like a Hardanger fiddle *halling* as any, whereas #23 is a simple symmetrical two-strain tune.

This first *halling*'s rhythmic profile is typical: the first few measures open with the rhythm quarter/eighth/eighth, a rhythmic germ that propels many a *halling*. The phrase structure here matches that of many *springleik*s. The first strain, with its bold opening rhythm, has a broad shape yielding phrasing of 4 + 4, while the second strain is phrased 2 + 2+ 4. A *halling* generally goes the same speed in solo fiddle competition and in the dance competition, between 95 and 105 beats per minute (if understood in cut time). The lengths of performances contrast, however. A solo fiddler will generally pass through the material twice, thus, AABBAABB, whereas a dance version is often half again as long, and can end anywhere in the piece (within a few moments of the last—meaning second or third—try to dislodge the hat from the pole).

The plucked chords in this *halling*'s fourth measure are part of a general tendency in this genre to add forward motion through a modest variation in articulation. The second in pairs of passes through musical material often will include one or a few instances of changed bowings (yielding more direction changes per measure) or newly staccato phrase endings.

The waltz is the youngest of the "old" genres allowed to be played by the fiddle in most contests. The genre was vital and continually renewed throughout the nineteenth century and into the twentieth century in Norway, and its character gradually changed. It is the older waltz type, the *gammalvals,* that is permitted in contests. But the *gammalvals* is not a subgenre with clear musical boundaries, since (1) some variety in waltz type was present at all times, (2) there was no instant at which the old waltz abruptly was replaced by the Strauss waltz, (3) a strain from a waltz of one age might be joined with one from another time, and (4) a waltz of one period might borrow style characteristics from those of different-aged ones also in individual and regional repertoires. But an ideal profile of the *gammalvals* can be defined. It includes these characteristics: two, more often than three or more, strains; strains eight measures long (perhaps expanded or truncated—though irregularities of form are uncommon in this genre—but not as long as sixteen measures); and a rhythmic texture in which over half of the notes are eighth notes, most of the remainder quarter notes, and the very few half notes are almost all at cadences.

Although of all the older genres in the fiddle repertoire, the *gammalvals* is the least wedded to the key of D major, many fine waltzes belong to that key. Tune #28 is a fairly typical *gammalvals,* and shares traits beyond those already mentioned with many other members of the genre. Sequences are especially important in these waltzes—note how this *vals* begins. These sequences are not merely common, but also easier to hear in waltzes than in *springleik*s. This is because in these faster pieces (tempos average ca. 170–80, nearly half again as rapid as in the *springleik*), there are far fewer passing tones and other ornamental notes.

Also, although rhythms are more consistent than in the *springleik,* these can evade straightforward notation. A pair of eighth notes in a *gammalvals* from the Gudbrandsdal is imbued with a subtle energy: the first in the pair will be slightly louder, but the second slightly longer. A precise notation of length would be one-fourth to one-third of the way between two eighth notes and an eighth-quarter triplet. Small deviations from this most-basic surface rhythm add interest. For instance, a measure preceding a cadence either may smooth this rhythm out, to genuine pairs of eighth notes (this happens here in measure seven) or, in such a location, the usual rhythm may be sharpened (as here in measure 15, where what is heard is midway, rather than one-third, of the way from two eighth notes to an eighth-quarter triplet). Another minor but pervasive feature is that waltzes almost always begin with a pick-up beat or half-measure, which is very rare in the *springleik.*

The last major difference between these oldest waltzes and the genres that preceded them concerns their pitch structures. The oldest genres are clearly diatonic, but may offer a trace of pentatonicism through lack of emphasis on the fourth and seventh degrees of the scale. These degrees are heard in stronger positions in the waltz. In tune #28 each strain begins its first full measure with a note (not just an ornament) on the leading tone, and the second phrase of the second strain starts with a flowing phrase issuing from the subdominant.

The bridal march *(bruremarsj)* is now most common in the West. Throughout Norway, through the early part of this century, a wedding party's procession through its village was led by a fiddler or two playing a bridal march. Today, many members of the folk music community revive this practice for their own nuptials. Marianne Tomasgård, Gunn Gausemel, and other members of the Honndalstausene (an all-woman ensemble from the West) played at fellow member Bente Tomasgård's wedding during the summer of 1993. But, although the *bruremarsj* has not entirely lost its traditional function, for many fiddlers it has become more a concert and contest genre, as apt a vessel for creative musing as the listening piece.

The surviving bridal marches are in a musical language that points back at most to the eighteenth century; most are firmly in major. Tune #42, "Napoleanmarsjen," is in one of the common conventional forms, rounded binary, whereas #43, "Bruremarsj etter Magne Maurset" / "Bruremarsj etter Samuel Bergset," is full of formal surprises. Arne M. Sølvberg, who performed the latter version, believes this is the oldest bridal march in Nordfjord. This claim is supported by the many versions that coexist and the variety of irregularities that they contain. Both of the versions transcribed have straightforward second strains, in which a phrase appears once with a cadence on the second degree, then repeats, ending on the tonic. Tomasgård's version (the first one) does this in the first strain too, while Sølvberg's grows oddly, with a phrase structure of 2½ + 3 + 4 measures, then rests on the supertonic. His tempo is slower too—this seems like a good example of a march that has become a listening piece.

The Listening Piece: Program Music, Exoticism, and Modern Needs

Indeed, nearly all of the pieces given so far in this small anthology lead a double life today. They are historically functional music, most for the dance, with a few marches for wedding processions. But most of these melodies now are contest pieces too, intended to entertain critical audiences devoting their full attention to the music, and to convince discerning judges that given performances, while firmly grounded in tradition, are sufficiently distinctive and expertly presented to earn points and perhaps a prize. As vehicles for their virtuosity, clever performers choose pieces that stand out, generally owing to rarity or complexity. Some of these especially suitable pieces are programmatic (though many tunes with striking titles do not have these titles reflected in their music—see "Skejegge Loppe," i.e., Beard flea, #58). Tunes having a genuine program often fall into the category of the *lydarslått* (listening piece, #94–#102 in this collection). A few dance tunes whose music in some modest but undeniable way reflects an evocative title serve as a bridge between the dance genres and the *lydarslått*.

The most notable examples of *springleik*s in which a title is painted musically are those with names referring to the cuckoo, or *gauk*. The commonest and most widespread of these is simply called "Gauken"

(The cuckoo, #95a). It is a danceable *springleik* opening with a pair of harmonics outlining a descending fourth in imitation of the call of the cuckoo. Indeed, many Norwegian fiddlers call harmonics "cuckoo tones" (*gauktone, gauklåt, gaukemål;* Jenstad 1994:196 and 358). This special effect can be employed outside the "cuckoo" melodies: the "Bjønnhalling" (Bear *halling,* #25) starts with such a pair of harmonics. But when the title *"Gauken"* is mentioned or remembered, this gesture does evoke the memory of the bird call. Moreover, this opening idea is much more important in "Gauken" than in "Bjønnhallingen" for two related reasons. First, there is much less musical material in "Gauken." Its first strain is extended in a simple way, and the second strain is complementary in that it is shortened by a measure. That second strain presents only one measure of new material, the first one, which contains a routine sweep upward. After that seven-measure strain is played, its first four measures return, followed by the first four measures of the first strain, which reiterate the opening cuckoo call. If that patched strain is called B', a typical contest performance, whose form could be represented as A A B B' A A B B', would include no less than ten cuckoo calls.

Tune #95b represents "Gauken" as played in the West. It is there cast in A major, which allows plenty of the open-string double stops typical of this area's style. This "Gauken" is clearly the same tune as in the Gudbrandsdal, but it is less striking, less oriented in several ways toward listening independent of the dance. It is in major—minor is simply much less common in the West—and the form, although beginning with the same five-measure phrase employed in the Gudbrandsdal, then continues in a more symmetrical manner. The first strain is 5 + 5 measures rather than 5 + 4, and the second strain a simple 4 + 4, without the rounding off with the beginning of the first strain found in the Gudbrandsdal version. However, versions from the West that I have heard make a modest nod in the direction of this rounding off: they close with a harmonic.[3]

The epic battle with the Scots at Kringelen in 1612 is remembered in the titles of a number of melodies, all played today as listening pieces. Shepherdess Pillar-Guri (also spelled Prillar) warned of the approach of the Scots, under the command of General Sinclair, by blowing on her *lur* (straight wooden trumpet). A number of "Sinclair Marches," descriptive *hallings,* and "Guri Tunes" were written. Knut Kjøk's "Guri Tune" (#96), which he played as a powerful listening piece in the Fel-Jakup Konsert during the 1989 Gudbrandsdalsstemne, is in fact a compilation of three of these tunes.[4] Pillar-Guri is also remembered in tunes for the Hardanger fiddle, an instrument with a much larger repertoire of listening pieces. Knut's "Goroleikjen" is put together much like a Hardanger fiddle *halling* or *gangar* used as a listening piece (compare #102).

"Hestleiteren" (The stable boy, #97) is the commonest listening piece in the Gudbrandsdal, but "Budeiehull" (Dairy maid's call, #94) may be the most interesting. It is a true listening piece, one of just a handful commonly played in the Gudbrandsdal (even fewer flourish elsewhere in the domain of the fiddle). I hear this *lydarslått* as reworking and expanding the contents of the *springleik* "Gauken" (#95a). The "Budeiehull" begins with the same pair of harmonics, then meanders in a path that seems a compromise between those explored by #95a–b and #95d. Its second strain (measures 6 and following) recalls measures 12 and following of #95a. It also delays cadencing on the tonic similarly, and is rounded off with a section beginning with harmonics. The effect is not at all like that of "Gauken," however. The musing, exploratory course of this *lydarslått*, formal irregularity, generous rubato and ornamentation, and, in general, great amount of musical information presented identify this as a listening piece. Such pieces can draw on characteristics of many genres, both instrumental and vocal. The title "Budeiehull" allies it with the *lokk*, or cattle call, through which usually female tenders of herds once communicated with their charges over what were often long distances, mixing shouting, song, and speech. These pieces, now largely defunct outside the concert hall, are often rich in leaps and melismas. In the "Budeiehull," the opening harmonics, which evoked a bird's call in the "Gauken" group, now represent the penetrating yell with which a *lokk* often begins.

Other listening pieces draw on other vocal folk music genres. Religious "*folketoner*" in oral tradition are easily the richest genre of Norwegian folk song. "Folketone fra Hornindal" is widely known in the West. It existed in recent times as an instrumental tune, informally referred to as "classical," though its vocal origins are obvious. Now it has a text in some performances, "Om Kvelden" (In the evening). Lullabies *(bånsull)* are another apt vessel for the musing qualities of listening pieces. "Jenta ved Vogga, Bånsull etter Johan Hagen" (#99) has a program: A very young mother rocks a cradle sadly. After a while, she sees (or imagines) other teenagers dancing a *springleik* (painted in measures 39–50). They pass out of sight, and she returns to her rocking.

The listening pieces discussed above all appear in contests with remarkable frequency. The category of the listening piece as performed at home, for private enjoyment, can reach beyond Norway, and thus beyond what would be allowed in a contest. For instance, tune #101, "Ganlåt från Äppelbo," is a Swedish tune I heard several times during or just after interviews. Many Norwegian fiddlers enjoy listening to Swedish tunes, but seldom perform them. These would not constitute appropriate fare for dances or concerts, but now and again are picked up for fiddlers' private enjoyment. Foreign tunes like these, if learned at all, cross regional boundaries within Norway, and draw on genres without precise parallels in Norway.

Since the genre of the listening piece is far less important in fiddle territory than in the Hardanger fiddle area, it seems inappropriate to consider this genre without giving an example of the longer and formally more complex pieces played on Hardanger fiddle. Tune #102, "Førnesbrunnen" (Brown horse from Førnes) was "a horse that made its way alone across the mountains from Møsstrand to Rauland during the Black Death" (Gurvin 1960, 3:243; see also Hopkins 1986:89). Those locations are in Telemark, and older recorded versions of this common piece under this title are all from Telemark, the home of the most complex and highest-status Hardanger fiddle styles and tunes. More than a few players from there performed this tune at national contests during the early to mid-1950s, the only period for which it is easy to know which tunes were performed at the National Fiddle Contest, since the judges' comments then reproduced in the *Spelemannsblad* cite tune titles. The performer of this version of the tune, Annbjørg Lien, is from the West, and therefore plays both fiddle types, but performs her handful of listening pieces only on Hardanger fiddle. Her version of "Førnesbrunnen" is just a little longer (at just over four minutes) and slightly more intricate than those anthologized by Gurvin (1960, 3:196–223, 243–45). Although this piece clearly is shaped as a *halling*—titles of some versions in Gurvin cite that genre—Lien's performance, with its rhythmically flexible beginning and gradually slowing tempo (as the horse tires during his arduous journey) is a spectacular listening piece.

The Music of *Gammaldans*

On May 5, 1989, fiddler Knut Kjøk and his *gammaldans* group, Bælg og Streing (Bellows and strings) started off an evening of *gammaldans* during a local festival I described in Chapter 4, the Gudbrandsdalssteemne. Kjøk, whose accomplishments in contests I have already related, is also very highly regarded as a player for dancing, and his *gammaldans* ensemble is both respected and enjoyed. The fourteen tunes they performed that evening are serendipitously typical of *gammaldans* music in traditional style *(slåttestil)*. I transcribed these as well as I could from recordings made on the spot, although the ensemble playing and crowd noises obscured detail. Four years later I was able to videotape Knut playing these tunes alone; these performances are transcribed as tunes #103–#116. I also requested the same tunes from two other prominent *gammaldans* fiddlers—Arild Hoksnes, who learned most of his repertoire in Møre og Romsdal (in the Northwest), and Arild Plassen, of the county of Sør-Trøndelag (which contains Røros; Plassen is from the Folldal)—and asked Ivar Schjølberg what he knew of these tunes, too. Sometimes these fiddlers knew a given tune, and sometimes not; when a version by one or both differed instructively from Kjøk's form of the tune, I give multiple versions. Last, I asked these fiddlers and also accordionist (and folk music lexicographer) Tor-Erik Jenstad which titles each of them associated with these tunes (see Fig. 11).

Figure 12 lists the tunes Kjøk and his group played that evening by genre, and lists certain musical characteristics of each. The four basic genres of *gammaldans* were attended to roughly equally, in three sets of four tunes plus an abbreviated last set of just two tunes. The genres balance nicely in terms of meter and tempo. Of the triple-time genres, the waltz is much quicker than the mazurka, and of the duple time genres, the polka cognate *(skotsk,* i.e., schottische in the Gudbrandsdal) paced faster than the *reinlender.* I have reordered these fourteen tunes by genre in the Tune Anthology and in the following discussion: waltz, mazurka, *skotsk,* and *reinlender.*

Waltzes played by tradition-oriented *gammaldans* ensembles range in age and style from the *gammalvals*—whose style goes back to the late eighteenth century, regardless of the age of specific pieces—to the late nineteenth-century waltz. Unsullied examples of either type are the exception, making a purist attitude untenable. The first waltz of the evening, "Hardingvals" (#103), bears a number of modern characteristics. All sections are at least sixteen measures long, it is rhythmically sparse, and it has a harmonic rhythm no more rapid than a chord per measure. Many *gammaldans* tunes have been texted at some point or in some versions. This can result in varying titles corresponding to different texts (here, the commonest title, "Hardingvals," reflects a text beginning "*Jenta er mi*"),[5] and frequently also loosens any link a tune may have had to a specific key, since individual singers' ranges

Figure 11. Tunes played by Knut Kjøk and Bælg og Streing, May 5, 1989
(names by which these are known to Knut Kjøk, Arild Plassen, Arild Hoksnes, and Tor-
Erik Jenstad; also whether Arild Plassen and Arild Hoksnes play these tunes; tunes are
grouped by set)

Number	Knut Kjøk	Arild Plassen	Arild Hoksnes	Tor-Erik Jenstad
103	*Hardingvals*	no name	*Helgeland's Jenta*	*Harding Jenta*
110	no name	no name	no name (doesn't play)	no name
107	no name (says Swedish)	no name	didn't recall hearing	didn't know name
113	no name	no name	no name (doesn't play)	no name; has heard in several parts of Norway
104	*Jerusalem's Valsen*	no name (doesn't play)	*Kjenner Du, Kjenner Du . . .*	as AH
111	didn't recall name	no name (doesn't play)	similar: *Galopp fra Otrøy*	*Galopp etter* [?]
114	*Ringnesen #2*	*Ringnesen #2*	*Ringnesen #2*	*Ringnesen #2*
108	no name, then as AH	no name	*Kjære Tony Korporal*	as AH
112	*Skotsk etter Fel-Jakup*	no name (doesn't play)	no name (doesn't play)	no name
105	*Godvalsen*	*Godvalsen*	*Godvalsen hass Loms-Jakup*	as AH
115	no name	no name (doesn't play)	no name (doesn't play)	no name
109	*Kampar og Kari*	no name (doesn't play)	*Kjøkken masurka*	as AH
116	no name	no name (doesn't play)	no name (doesn't play)	no name
106	*B-dur vals etter Pål Skogum*	no name (doesn't play)	hasn't heard	no name

often inspire transposition. G major may be the commonest key for waltzes; this tune is cast in at least the three commonest keys for fiddle, as we see in these three fiddlers' versions.

Ornaments employed in the three versions match what these fiddlers are apt to use when playing *folkemusikk*. Kjøk favors appoggiaturas and turns, and some double stops, including unison doubles, in a fairly dense texture. Hoksnes's version includes his usual grace notes and turns, whereas Plassen adds to those ornaments the inverted mordent common in the Østerdal. But the most striking signal that this tune has been in oral tradition for some time, that it has become traditional in style, is a phrasing problem in the first strain. Should the

Figure 12. Characteristics of Tunes Played by Knut Kjøk and Bælg og Streing, May 5, 1989, during the *Gudbrandsdalsstemnet*
(tunes are listed in order of performance)

Number	Genre	Meter	Key	Striking Features			Other Special Aspects
				3+ Strains	Harmonizing	Odd Keys	
103	vals	3	A	3 strains			one strain lengthened
110	skotsk	2	G				modulates up, (to A
107	masurka	9	D		yes		KK harmonizes in middle
113	reinlender	2	D				last two B strain accompanists hold chords
104	vals	3	D	5 strains	a strain taken up an octave		one short strain
111	skotsk	2	G	3 strains		a strain in D	
114	reinlender	2	G		yes		KK harmonizes near middle
108	masurka	9	A minor				some obbligato measures, enc on major thir(
112	skotsk	2	A	4 strains	yes		KK harmonizes toward end
105	vals	3	A	3 strains	yes		KK again; accompanime drone near en postlude
115	reinlender	2	D				KK rhythmic play near end
109	masurka	9	D	3 strains	a strain taken up an octave		
116	reinlender	2	A	3 strains		a strain in D	KK prominent glissandos
106	vals	3	Bb		yes!	key "lifts" to C	KK harmonizes playfully for 2 3 of the performance

first full measure be considered a pick-up measure, as in a modern waltz, or as a flourish beginning the strain proper, as in a *springleik*? This confusion causes Kjøk's version to be extended irregularly, and may be at least part of the reason that his second full measure contains six eighth notes rather than the more striking pattern of a quarter-note and four eighth notes found in the other versions. A less-distinctive rhythmic profile allows this measure to be heard as a "real" second measure, as a continuation rather than the beginning of a phrase.

Two other waltzes played on this evening seem older. Tune #105, a ubiquitous and stable tune, is always known as either "Godvalsen" or "Godvalsen hass Loms-Jakup." Although not all fiddlers associate it specifically with Loms-Jakup (Fel-Jakup), it is generally considered a Gudbrandsdal tune that has traveled far. Hoksnes heard it first in Nordmøre: the tune had long flourished there because Fel-Jakup had often traveled there during the middle of the nineteenth century. The tune's high rhythmic density, eight-measure sections, and association with Loms-Jakup suggest that the tune would be as at home in the pre-*gammaldans gammalvals* category, but it is in fact much played during *gammaldans* evenings. The contours of the first two strains are graceful in a way typical for the genre; they are so attractive because they seem inevitable. The third strain's arpeggios invite comparison with, among other tunes in A major, "Melovitte" (tune #16). And this strain calls for ornamentation. Kjøk did this through bowing, at the dance performance playing the second pass through this strain using long slurs, each encompassing two measures. Hoksnes and Plassen both added graces during repeats. Both inserted grace notes on *a* and *c* before the *a* that is the second note in the first measure of that strain; Plassen added parallel gestures in several other measures as well.

I encountered this tune only in the key of A major. Its rhythmic density, which suggests that it might be an older waltz, probably stood in the way of its acquiring a text, which might have tended to destabilize key. And the figuration in the third strain would continue to hold the tune to its key.

Whereas the "Godvals" is widely traveled, #106, "B-dur Vals etter Pål Skogum," is not. It is common in the Gudbrandsdal, but much less so elsewhere: Hoksnes and Plassen didn't know it. Once again, density and eight-measure sections suggest that this tune would be at home in the subgenre of *gammalvals*. It is never texted, but always known either by the above title or simply as "B-dur Vals" ("B" in the Norwegian system follows German music terminology, i.e., it means B♭). The key of B♭, like C, is unusual enough to be frequently mentioned in the titles of tunes in that key. B♭ may be a legacy of the military band—insiders believe this—or perhaps simply comes out of art music.

Playing this tune to wrap up the contribution of Knut Kjøk and Bælg og Streing to this *gammaldans* evening worked well. It "lifts" harmonically, lying a half-step above the key of the previous tune, and abruptly modulating up to C under way. It is a waltz, as was the group's first tune of the evening, and a familiar one, the key of which would have jarred if the tune were placed anywhere else in the sequence. The tune's great familiarity allowed Kjøk to harmonize playfully for about two-thirds of the performance.

While "Masurka" (#107) is the least known of the three mazurkas Bælg og Streing played that evening, it is nevertheless representative of the genre in several ways. It has just two strains, as is usual (the third strain of tune #109 is slight). In a typical rhythmic profile, a Norwegian folk mazurka's first measure has more notes in the first beat than in the other two. This genre has a general affinity with the *springleik*, though the mazurka is a bit faster and somewhat less dense rhythmically (this one is a shade busier than average). Like the *springleik*, many mazurkas in oral tradition tend to break beats into triplets more often than into duplets or dotted figures, hence my decision to transcribe these in 9/8. Although some *springleiks* contain arpeggios, these are a real earmark of the mazurka.[6]

The dances I have classified as "polka types," the *skotsk, galop, hamborger,* and *hoppvals,* arrived or coalesced in Norway at scattered intervals during the nineteenth century. Their music, all of which is most easily notated in cut time or in 2/4, is also similar in pace, texture, and general feel, so much so that a melody can easily shift from one of these genres to another. Each part of the fiddle area has ended up favoring one of these dances over the others, so that we encounter the *skotsk* in the Gudbrandsdal, the *hamborger* in the West, the *gallop* in Møre og Romsdal (the Northwest), and the *hoppvals* in the Røros area.

Skotsk #110 and #111 have no title beyond that generic classification; #112 has a slightly longer name, "Skotsk etter Fel-Jakup." Duple-time *gammaldans* pieces are in general less likely than waltzes and mazurkas to have text or title. Many of the polka-type tunes migrate. When they cross geographical boundaries, that often means translation to a different dance genre. In the Gudbrandsdal, tune #111 is now a *skotsk.* Tor-Erik Jenstad knows it as a *galop* associated with the late Hilmar Alexandersen of Steinkjer, northeast of Trondheim. In fact, Kjøk learned the tune from a recording by Alexandersen. Jenstad and Hoksnes both mentioned how similar this tune is to one in oral tradition in Romsdal, from a small island and therefore known as "Galopp frå Otrøy"; Hoksnes's performance of this tune is given as #111b. Kjøk's *skotsk* and Hoksnes's *galop* both have three strains, one of them in the key of the dominant; in general, a *gammaldans* tune with three strains will have no more than one stray from the tonic key. The first strains of these tunes are clearly the same: Kjøk's second strain roughly parallels Hoksnes's third, and Kjøk's third one Hoksnes's second. These similarities of range and gesture may reflect genetic divergence. On the other hand, in strains containing little musical information, in a near-saturated repertoire with strong conventions, it would be rash to claim any specific type of relationship.

All of the dances during an evening will be about the same length in performance. Most of the tunes an ensemble will play will have precisely two strains, and will occupy typical length of time through following either the pattern AABBAABB or AABBAABBAABB. The shorter pattern is more common in contests, the longer one in dances. When a tune has three strains, the conventional long form becomes AABBCCAABBCC; Hoksnes and many others often abbreviate the return to play a more concise AABBCCABC.

*Reinlender*s can be found throughout Norway. Tune #113 has no specific name, but it is widespread. Tor-Erik Jenstad called it a Gudbrandsdal version of a tune from Westlandet; he had also heard it in Hardanger. Plassen, Schjølberg, and Hoksnes all associate the melody with the Kjøk family. Plassen, who also plays this tune, heard the group Bælg og Streing perform it at the first National Fiddle Contest he attended (he was not sure of the year). The rhythmic density and texture of this *reinlender* are typical, as is its mixture of linear motion and arpeggios.

Looking a last time at Figure 12, we can see that these fourteen tunes were very cleverly ordered during the dance evening in question. Tunes with unusual formal features, that is, having more than two strains, or strains of odd length, or strains in keys other than the tonic, are not in clusters, but rather doled out carefully. And all tunes end up with some distinctive feature in these arrangements. The "normal tunes" are granted special qualities: for example, #110 has a modulation added, #107 is granted an attractive harmonization, and so on. Whether or not the dancers notice these qualities I cannot say. The musicians' sense of play is always evident, and these dance tunes inspire movement, please the ear, and interest the mind.

The anthology includes an additional handful of *gammaldans* tunes selected for various reasons. Waltzes #117–#119 broaden the picture of the genre presented by #103–#106. Among the very commonest *gammaldans* tunes, perhaps second only to the *reinlender* "Ringnesen," Nordfjordvalsen" (#117) is played throughout Scandinavia.

"Vals i C Dur" (#118) is as rare as "Nordfjordvalsen" is common. Its most surprising aspect is, I suspect, the characteristic that has restricted its spread. It is driven by sequences, and these move it almost out of harmonic focus, certainly out of tonal comfort. Here we see the key of C once again the home of oddities, just as in *folkemusikk*. Last, "Bikkje Fredrik Vals" (#119), a waltz from the Røros area, illustrates a regional bowing pattern for waltzes (see measures 3, 8, and 11–13), a pattern that may be related to that in the *hoppvals,* the Røros area's polka type, or may simply be a legacy of the performance style of Peder Nyhus. In any case, this sort of local modification of *gammaldans* genres makes such repertoires more like *folkemusikk*.

The West's polka variant, the *hamborger,* is represented by "Hamborger etter Teiga-Ola" (#121), which illustrates a common seconding technique, and by "Randabygdaren" (#120). Bente Tomasgård, from the Horningdal in the West, taught this simple but ingratiating *hamborger* to Spelemannslaget i BUL Nidaros when she was studying in Trondheim. Although the *hamborger* is not a dance proper to the county of Sør-Trøndelag, the musical compatibility of polka types allowed this transfer; we played this tune many times during 1988–89. Last, "Red Wing" (#122), is often played in the Northwest. According to Arild Hoksnes, this ubiquitous American squaredance tune was brought to Norway by returned immigrants and by visitors from the United States and on early 78 rpm recordings.

The last *gammaldans* tunes in the anthology are a "Masurka etter Fel-Jakup" (#123), a difficult solo piece from the Gudbrandsdal, a "Masurka etter P. M. Bolstad" (#124) from the West, and "Jonsauk Draum" (#125), a long and virtuosic reinlender from the Northwest.

The Testimony of Tune Titles

The names Norwegian fiddle tunes bear range from the relatively unspecific to many rich in historical resonance, often classifying a tune simultaneously in terms of genre, region, and style. Even the shortest, least-detailed titles tell us quite a bit. For a tune to be called simply "Springleik," "Springar," or "Pols" is to place it in the complex of oldest triple-time dance genres and at the same time to associate it with a given broad tradition area, respectively the Gudbrandsdal, the West, and the Røros area. Modifications of these titles (in this genre complex) are then more specifically targeted geographically. For instance, the genre title "Springdans" takes us to a specific subregion of the Gudbrandsdal (just downstream from the championship area of

Lom and Vågåmo), and "Polsdans" to certain areas of the Northwest and far North (#76–#82). Outside that complex of genres, a fiddled "Halling" will often be from the Gudbrandsdal, though this designation can refer to the West or Southeast (#23; #7b), and a "Vals" could also be from anywhere, but a "Gammalvals" most likely from the Gudbrandsdal (#29). "Masurka" and "Reinlender" are not region specific, but polka cognates are, as detailed above. A few titles that refer only to genre are further limited to a few region-specific pieces, for example "Melovitte" (originally a minuet, #16a), which is played as a *springleik*—or less frequently a *masurka*—in the Gudbrandsdal, but as a *polsdans* in the Northwest, in Møre og Romsdal (#16b), and "Budeiehull," that is, Dairymaid's call, a vocally based listening piece from the Gudbrandsdal (#94).

Apart from rare exceptions such as those two tunes, referring to a piece simply by dance genre asserts that this is dance music, without need for further narrowing beyond naming the region where the dance would take place. However, many titles are more explicitly regional or local, through linkage with a specific fiddler. In discussion of tune #1 near the beginning of the previous chapter, I mentioned that this "Springleik etter Amund Slåstugun" associated that *springleik* with an individual's style, and thus with an intimate local tradition. Such individuals may be alive, recently deceased, or from the distant past, and may bear modest or great fame. Slåstugun, not so famous, was active during the mid-nineteenth century in Skåbu in the mid-Gudbrandsdal, thus quite near where the performer of this tune, Mari Eggen, was raised. Other tunes are attributed simultaneously to fiddlers of varying vintages and degrees of fame. For instance, tune #4, which Vågåmo fiddler Ivar Schjølberg called "Springleik etter Arnfinn Upheim"—Upheim, recently deceased, was in the Ringnesen line of tradition in Vågåmo—Knut Kjøk of neighboring Lom calls "Springleik etter Fel-Jakup," thus highlighting an earlier stage in tune transmission. Fel-Jakup's influence permeates the Gudbrandsdal. Referring to him in a tune title points to region rather than locale, but balances this dilution of specificity with his great prestige. (I should note that his name presents something of a problem in terms of geographic reference. He was formerly known more often as Loms-Jakup, i.e., Jacob from Lom, referring to the residence in the hamlet of Lom as it was constituted in the middle of the nineteenth century. The alternative appelation of Fel-Jakup means Jacob of the Fields, which has less value in terms of regional reference. The problem with the name Loms-Jakup is that the area called Lom during the fiddler's life has been subdivided into three hamlets, Garmo [where many of the best Lom fiddlers now live], Lom, and Skjåk, in which Loms-Jakup's home is located. But no one calls him Skjåk-Jakup today, although Loms-Jakup is, in modern terms, inaccurate. The increasingly common use of Fel-Jakup is in fact a diplomatic way out of the geographic conundrum.) Some current fiddlers get several generations and thus layers of regional or local associations into a single title—hence Arne M. Sølvberg's "Springar etter Samuel Bergset i form etter Alfred Maurstad" (#37) and "Bruremarsj etter Anders Reed i form etter Moses Paulen" (#45). In such cases, the first fiddler cited in the title is more prestigious, from an older generation, while the second, more recent tradition bearer adds local value.

A second group of titles refer to region by associating a tune either with an individual who was not necessarily a channel for that tune's transmission, or with a location. For instance, "Gamle Kringelen" names a dancer said to have liked tune #36 (alternatively known as "Springar etter Magne Maurset," using the title format described in the previous paragraph). "Drommen av Sulhusgubba" means "Sulhus's dream" (#60). Sulhus was a prominent fiddler in the Røros area, but is his "dream" something he composed or arranged, or a later fiddler's homage to him? Historical or legendary figures also appear in titles such as "Goroleikjen" (Guri tune, #96), discussed in the section on listening pieces in Chapter 6. Places cited in tune titles may be regions ("Rendalspolsk," #8 and #74, refers to a valley), towns ("Polsk fra Unset," within #74, honors a town within that valley), or, also quite common, specific intimate locations, often farms, such as "Vigstadmoin" (#6), "Flatmoin" (#20), and "Gamel-Husin" (i.e., old man living on the small farm "Husin" in today's hamlet of Skjåk in the Gudbrandsdal, #7a). The most detailed title of this sort comes from the Røros area, and seems to be poking gentle fun at the practice. Tune #52 is "Millom Abrahamsvolla og Køråsvollom, Bortover all Veil," meaning "All along the way between [those two farms]" (which border a slender lake situated between Røros and Brekken).

A third set of titles is more generally evocative, usually calling up outdoor life and the old days, perhaps without geographic reference, though the performers employing these titles may recall or supply such a reference in their own minds. These include "Bestamor" (#9, Grandmother) and "Kvennhusbekken" (#17, Mill creek). While Vagåmo fiddlers recall that this tune was composed by local fiddler Petter Eide, others may associate the tune with the mill creek nearest them. "Litjhurven" (#49) and "Storhurven" (#50) mean "Little mess" and

"Big mess," and "Skegge Loppe" (#58) means "Beard flea," presumably more numerous in the past than present. Times more important formerly may be cited: "Sup-Leken" (#54) makes reference to the ritual serving of soup during an old-fashioned wedding, and the *reinlender* "Jonsauk Draum" names St. John's Day, June 23, celebrated more in the past than now. "Gauken" (#95) means "Cuckoo," and Hestleitaren" (#97) "The boy who leads the horse." Many of these generally evocative titles also refer to a fiddler or location, hence "Bjønnhallingen etter Teodor Bakken" (#25), "Bear *halling* in the manner of Teodor Bakken"; "Finnvalsa etter Torger Iverstugen" (#31), "Lovely waltz in the manner of Torger Iverstugen"; "Jenta ved Vogga, Bånsull etter Johan Hagen" (#99), "Girl by the cradle, lullaby in the manner of Johan Hagen"; and "Hund-dengar'n: Polsdans fra Nordmøre" (#79), "Dog-beater: *polsdans* from Nordmøre."

A smaller group of titles note special, unusual musical characteristics of tunes, aspects that are noteworthy because they mark the musical outer limits of repertoires. "The "Forspellpols" (#55) is called that because it features a prelude, and almost no other piece does. And the "Vals i C Dur" (#118) is cited as being in the key of C major because few waltzes are. But, once again, such pieces are generally known alternatively or also as "after" someone. The "Andre-Posisjon Springleik" (#21a), "*Springleik* in second position," is also called "Springleik etter Pål Skogum," and "B-Dur Vals" (#30), "Waltz in Bb," is as commonly called "Vals etter Ivar Bråtå" (Skogum and Bråtå were fiddlers from Vågåmo). Among many titles joining reference to technique and to a fiddler are three pieces from the West, "Springar i C-dur etter Anders Reed" (#40), "Springar på Oppstilt Ters etter Magne Maurset" ("*oppstilt ters*" means "raised third string," i.e., retuning the D string to E to play in the key of A, something much less common in the West than in the Gudbrandsdal or the Røros area), and "Kolagutt Springar etter Petter Paulen" (#87; the Kolagutt tuning is F C A E, for certain tunes in F). Last, a very few tunes, generally from *gammaldans* repertoires, cite words that have been sung to the tune (see tunes #104 and #109).

The vast majority of tunes, therefore, name a locally affiliated fiddler through whose hands the tune has passed, regardless of what other ingredients a title might have. Tune titles as a group invoke local or regional style and genre. Indeed, this is done more efficiently than is the literal job of a title, distinguishing individual tunes. That is, even within a small community, there will be several tunes called, for instance, "Pols etter Marta-Johannes" or "Springleik etter Pål Skogum," tunes which then must be distinguished by musical incipit in group performance. To summarize, in this commonest form of title, style and locale are described by naming a fiddler, but the specific identity of a tune is not quite established: it may be one of a handful or one of a large group (there are many dozens of tunes "etter Fel-Jakup").

Musical Resemblances and Relationships

Assessing similarity and difference between tunes in repertoires such as those of the fiddle of Norway is an imprecise and generally unrewarding task. Some affinities are easy to hear, and some differences indisputable. But similarities signaling genetic relationships generally cannot be distinguished from ones resulting from stylistic convergence in these repertoires. This is because there are so many very short tunes within rather narrow boundaries of style—that is, because these are what could be called "saturated" repertoires. My approach to identifying similar tunes proceeded on two tracks. One was the intuitive approach, listening unsystematically to as many performances as possible and trying to recall whether I had heard similar tunes. Of course, this would presume that what I heard as similarities would also be considered that by tradition insiders. And this, I found, was in fact the case. Insiders judged tunes to be alike according to essentially the same criteria that American fiddlers tacitly use. These are, in order of importance, general contour, diagnostic tones (pitches in rhythmically strong positions), and melodic/rhythmic formulas with distinctive profiles occurring at tunes' beginnings.

In addition to watching for affinities among tunes intuitively, I attempted to index my own transcriptions systematically. After experiments with small samples, I chose an approach joining mode with an encoding of general contour, giving weight to diagnostic tones. Each strain received a seven-digit number. The first step was to choose the most important pitch heard during a given beat, which was usually the first nonornamental pitch (i.e., the first pitch occupying an eighth note or longer note). Although this may sound like a potentially controversial process, it was in fact quite straightforward. This was done for the first two measures and the first beat of the third measure, thus for seven beats in tunes in triple time (the last beat of each measure of tunes in duple time was ignored). Each pitch was then given the number of its scale degree, so that, for instance, any *a* in D major would become the number five. Tune #1 thus became two indexed items, the first strain encoded as 513/513/4 and the second as 571/243/1. The second step was to rearrange each series of digits, working on the assumption that the first beat of each measure was a diagnostic tone, more stable and important than were the second and third beats. The new order of digits would be: first beat of the first measure, first beat of the second measure, first beat of the third measure, second and third beats of the first measure, second and third beats of the second measure. Using this reordering, the initial encoding of the first strain of tune #1 became 554/1313. In the third step, I made as many photocopies of each tune as it had strains, so that each strain, rather than each piece, could have a place in the comprehensive index. Last, the rather forbidding stack of copies of transcriptions—totaling a little short of two feet in total thickness—was divided into groups by mode, then, within those groups, ordered numerically. Thus, tune #1 appeared twice in the D major grouping, once under the revised code number for the first strain, 554/1313, and a second time under the number for the second strain, which had become 521/7143. Then I played through each stack of transcriptions, sometimes comparing across stacks, looking for groups of strains and of complete tunes exhibiting various degrees and types of affinity.

I would have been delighted had this admittedly cumbersome process revealed any system of relationships between tunes, however intricate. This simply did not happen. The main relationship this process brought to light was that of near-precise correspondence; that is, it gathered multiple performances of the same piece. Even this minimal result was welcome, of course, in repertoires where so many tunes are entitled just "Springleik" or "Pols." I also found that this body of music contains remarkably few floating strains. If two first strains matched well, so would their second strains.

Might I find tune families in this repertoire? The principal articulator of this most-discussed organizing principle of European folk music, Samuel Bayard, described the tune family as "a group of melodies showing basic interrelation by means of constant melodic correspondence, and presumably owing their mutual likeness to descent from a single air that has assumed multiple forms through processes of variation, imitation, and assimilation" (1950:33). He noted that contour and diagnostic tones (notes in rhythmically prominent positions) tend to be relatively stable, and thus good signposts for identifying related tunes, while rhythms and modes are much more likely to fluctuate without reference to genetic connection (1939:125). Bayard and earlier devotees of tune family theory derived it from their study of the

British-American traditional ballad, particularly the seemingly oldest layer, called the Child ballads. It is of considerable interest that when Bayard published a massive collection of fiddle tunes from Pennsylvania, a body of music much more like that considered in this book than are the Child ballads, he rarely found the concept of the tune family applicable, and did not propose any parallel model as a substitute (1982). Instead, he referred to resemblances in an unsystematic, yet rather detailed, manner, classifying these as "slight, elusive, 'bearing some,' possible, general, considerable, 'quite a bit,' double-edged, especial, striking, substantial, strong, close, or unmistakable" (Goertzen 1986:181). Cowdery reexamined the tune family concept in his more recent work with Irish traditional music. He proposed three general types of relationship: "outlining," essentially with closely corresponding contours throughout; "conjoining," in which relationships were seen between sections of tunes but not for complete pieces; and "recombining," in which local and total similarities are considered, even if sections compared do not occur in the same order in the tunes in question (1990:90–92). Although I found a few groups of tunes I considered related in the repertoires of the Norwegian fiddle, the repertoires were simply too dense to distinguish regularly and reliably between resemblances that were genetic and those that were coincidental. I was left in essentially the same position as Bayard (i.e., after he shifted his attention to instrumental music), and with some relationships that match up well with Cowdery's categories.

When I assembled the sample of tunes to be presented in this volume, I chose individual items partly in order to be able to illustrate the different sorts of resemblances between tunes I had noticed; this sample is therefore significantly above average in the number and variety of similarities exemplified. These are the sorts of relationships I found.

1. Versions of the same piece which are so similar that both insiders and outsiders would consider it absolutely indisputable that they were the same; see multiple versions of tunes #4, #5, #9, #10, #19, #25, #49, #50, #59, #63, #66, #69, #98, and within the *gammaldans* music sample, versions of #103 and #104. In such instances, it is common for titles to be more different—through assertion of contrasting local affiliations—than are the performances themselves.

The modest differences between what are clearly versions of the same tune follow several distinct patterns. Tune #2 illustrates the simplest case of what might be called personal-local versions of a melody; that is, some minor differences characterizing these versions were learned from the performers' different teachers (each comes from a different community in the Gudbrandsdal), whereas other differences are the products of the fiddlers' creativity. Ornaments vary from version to version, though these tend to fall in characteristic spots, and incidental double stops, as well as a few passing notes, vary too. Such modest discrepancies also separate #19a and #19b, and #59a and #59b; many more examples appeared in the sample from which the Tune Anthology came. Some other tune versions are distinguished by varying modal impression or key, and concern particularly the instability of minor. Most commonly, one version of a tune in D minor will have nearly all *f*'s natural, whereas another version will have many sharped (see #5, #10, and #25). And for versions to be in different keys can mean more than contrasting ranges. In "Kvardagspols," #69, Tron Westberg's version in C (rather than the usual home for this tune in D) also features a remarkable number of double stops in which the secondary note is the third of the implied chord, thus changing the modal flavor along with the key. And #19c, in which "Riksbanken" shifts from its usual home of G to D, requires position work, which in turn inspires further virtuosity—a change in key here causes a change in character. Versions of #49 have a strain in different octaves, and #59c illustrates how instrumental idiom can affect melodic lines: the willow flute is less able to produce rapid conjunct figures than the fiddle. Other types of differences concern alternative beginnings (#50 and #66), widely varying employment of ornaments (#98), contrasting lengths of sections (#4, #103), and surprising bold differences in rhythm (#63c). Many such differences are quite bold, but in all of these cases the readings presented are clearly different versions rather than different pieces.

2. Tunes so similar that an insider would consider them possibly or probably, but not certainly, the same piece; see #8a ("Springleik etter Hans Teigplassen") versus #8b ("Gamel Ringnes'n") and #43a ("Bruremarsj etter Magne Maurset") versus #43b ("Bruremarsj etter Samuel Bergset"). Here again the titles tell much of the story, linking tunes with performers (from different generations, such as in the case of Vågåmo fiddlers Ringneset and Teigplassen, or from different communities within a given region, as for Western fiddlers Maurset and Bergset) who may have imposed enough of a personal stamp on versions of formerly more similar pieces to begin the process of building new tunes. This relationship squares fairly well with Cowdery's term "outlining." In tunes #43a and #43b, forms are quite different, taking these versions a long step toward being distinct tunes. The case of tune

#8 carries personal/local variation over generations to the brink of creating separate tunes. At the risk of offering too much detail, I will look at this case intimately. Sevåg and Sæta printed two versions of "Springleik etter Hans Teigplasen" (1992; 1:199) and eight of "Gamel-Ringnes'n" (1992:I, 195–98). Just one of those versions of "Gamel-Ringnes'n" mentions that central Vågåmo fiddler in its title (Ola J. Ringneset, 1811–1902), whereas the others are *springleiks "etter"* Ivar Bråtå (1827–1916), Ola Nystugen (1875–1946), Sigurd Eggen (1883–1964), or no one in particular. Bråtå, Nystugen, and Eggen all were musical heirs of Ringneset at some remove, as was Teigplassen (1866–1951). The eight versions of "Gamel-Ringnes'n" (none called precisely that) in Sevåg and Sæta were collected in Vågåmo, Lom, Skjåk, and Heidal—the last community is nearest to Vågåmo, the others up to a few dozen kilometers northwest, that is, upstream from Vågåmo.

The two versions of "Springleik etter Hans Teigplassen" both mention his name. One, played by Jakob Skogum of Vågåmo, has exactly that name, and the other, called simply "Teigplassen," is from Redvald Fjellhammer, of Sør-Fron, which is southeast, that is, downstream from Vågåmo. Of the ten different springleiks attributed to Teigplassen anthologized by Sevåg and Sæta, all—apart from the performance by Fjellhammer just mentioned—are from performances by residents of Vågåmo. Since Teigplassen's influence is focused almost solely on Vågåmo, it would seem that this "Springleik etter Hans Teigplassen" began life recently as his distinctively personal version of the certainly more widely distributed and probably much older tune here called "Gamel-Ringnes'n." It is a tune version that has split off to become a separate tune. When two melodies that coexist in a fiddler's repertoire are so similar that they might be confused, and that similarity is noticed, one tune might melt into the other, or, conversely, one might be changed so as to remain distinct from the other. This may have happened in Redvald Fjellhammer's repertoire. His version of "Gamel-Ringnes'n" is the only one that I have encountered that is in G rather than in D major or D minor (Sevåg and Sæta 1992:I, 197).[7]

3. Very similar pieces that an insider would nevertheless consider distinct; see #6 ("Vigstadmoin") versus #7a ("Gammel-Husin"). Relationship types 1–3 represent progressive differentiation that could take place within an area. Here, differences that individually might mark versions of a single tune add up, cumulatively creating an impression of two distinct tunes. These differences include plenty of passing notes, rhythmic profiles that remain contrasting through these

pieces, and also form. "Vigstadmoin," #6, with the striking 6 + 6 phrase lengths in its first strain, is the more common piece.

4. Pieces that an outsider would likely consider the same—an insider might or might not concur—but which are separated by boundaries of geography and thus style; see tunes #95a versus #95b ("Gauken"); #38a versus #38b; #71a versus #71b (form is critical here); #8a–b versus #8c (note very different densities); #16a and b, #21a and b; #31a–c, perhaps #35 ("Springar etter Gamle-Lars Tomasgård") versus #49 ("Litjhurven") and, in the *gammaldans* music sample, #111a and b (illustrating the looser affiliation of strains characteristic of *gammaldans* music).

5. Very similar pieces separated by geography and style; see #6 versus #59 and #60.

6. Similar pieces separated by boundaries of style that are linked to their being in different genres; see #7a (a *springleik*) versus #7b (a *halling*), and #95a (a programmatic *springleik*, "Gauken") versus #95 (a full-blown listening piece, "Budeiehull").

7. Possible tune families, with what I call a dissolving affinity (i.e., the members of which become less similar the further the tunes proceed); see #53–#58 and, in a looser group, #59–#63. Tunes #95a–d, the group centered on "Gauken," have a shared program depicted in the opening gesture of each, and so also exhibit a kind of dissolving affinity. This sort of relationship might be termed "conjoining" by Cowdery.

8. Tunes containing many parallel gestures, which however do not appear in the same order. Tune #2, a "Fel-Jakup Springar," to use Reidar Skjelkvåle's title, has a regular first strain and an extended second strain (5 + 5), just as did tune #1. The second strain of #2 begins with a clearer assertion of the key than does the first strain; perhaps the current first strain gained that position because its first measure is more distinctive (Skjelkvåle mentioned that his father began with the other strain). This second strain has a close relationship with the first strain of #1, reshuffling conventional formulas at the level of the measure. That is, measures 1–3 of the second strain of #2 are almost exactly the same as measures 1, 3, and 2 of the first strain of #1. Similar reorderings of melodic gestures are fairly common in this repertoire, yielding an effect compatible with Cowdery's category of "recombining."

9. Tunes with a shared stylistic feature so distinctive that a genetic connection is easy to imagine, whether or not it exists; see #88 ("Hjulmaker") and #89 ("Kjolstad Lek Nr. 2"), both of which are *pols* thoroughly exploiting the unusual tuning of A E A C♯.[8]

CHAPTER EIGHT

Musical Change and Cultural Forces Late in the Twentieth Century

I heard over half of the melodies in the Tune Anthology in contests, some after I had recorded them in interviews. This "over half" includes about three-fifths of my recorded tunes from the Gudbrandsdal, which is the area most oriented toward competition and most successful in it, half of those from the West, and three-sevenths of those from the *pols/polsdans* district of Røros and elsewhere in the East, the area least invested in contests. In an attempt to balance many fiddlers' contest orientation, I made a point of seeking out pieces that were either too common or not sufficiently complex or flashy to suit the listening format. But this century, and particularly the last few decades, has pushed the entire fiddle repertoire in the direction of suitability for contest just as has been true for the Hardanger fiddle (Ånon Egeland, personal communication).

Tunes in contests tend to be presented in a compact form with limited repetition, generally the first strain twice, the second twice, then all of that repeated (in rare cases twice). Overall tempos are slower than is typical for the dance, especially in the Gudbrandsdal, yielding more room for melodic ornaments and rhythmic nuance. The tempos of several recent performances of a very common *springleik* from the Gudbrandsdal, "Vigstadmoin" (#6), illustrate this point:

Helga Norman Møller	103	July 14, 1993
Mari Eggen	114	Spring 1989
Knut Kjøk	123 (in an interview)	July 6, 1993
Knut Kjøk	133 (accompanying dancers)	July 15, 1993
Rikard Skjelkvåle	134	July 15, 1993
Ivar Schjølberg	135	July 5, 1993
Torodd Hosarøygård	136	Sept. 3, 1988

The tempos fall into two groups, one ending with Kjøk's first version, played for listening, the other beginning with his second version, accompanying a pair of dancers as they competed during the 1993 National Fiddle Contest. The second group of tempos is relatively tight: 133, 134, 135, and 136 dotted quarter-notes per minute is quite a narrow span. This is the range of tempos at which *springleiks* typically are danced in the Gudbrandsdal today (although only the second Kjøk version was actually recorded during a dance). Skjelkvåle (grandson of the famous Rikard, nephew of Reidar), Schjølberg, and Hosarøygård, although recorded by me either during competition or in interviews, may be described as dance-oriented fiddlers; that is, they differentiate less—or not at all—between their solo playing and dance accompaniment. But this is not to say simply that customary dance tempos have governed their playing speed: dancing was revived after fiddling was, and revived from a much more profound level of neglect, so that dance tempos followed those of instrumentalists as much as the converse a few decades ago.

At a contest held in the Gudbrandsdal in 1958, one Peder Skavrusten (of Heidal) played "Vigstadmoin" at a tempo of at least 138.[1] This was in keeping with most *springleik* tempos at that event. The most obvious general conclusion is that tempos have gradually slowed down during this half-century, in both dances and contests.[2] This would correspond with an increasing emphasis on careful listening. Today's contest tempos are in a broad range, from the dance-oriented playing—relatively fast and relatively consistent—to the slower and more varied tempos of contest-oriented players. The very slowest tempo noted here for "Vigstadmoin" is by the youngest player, Helga Norman Møller (aged nineteen then). She is not originally from the Gudbrandsdal (though she lived there briefly), but rather from Trysil (in the East, south of the Røros area), and learned "Vigstadmoin" from master teacher Sven Nyhus, who is originally from Røros. The very unusual result was certainly not Gudbrandsdal playing, though her version was to my ear beautiful. It was untraditional both in tempo and in ornamentation, and earned her a low score in the B class at the 1993 National Fiddle Contest. She employed twice as many turns as did Mari Eggen, whereas Ivar Schjølberg played half as many ornaments as Eggen in the version he learned playing for dances with the Vågå Spel- og Dansarlag. Schjølberg's level of ornamentation fits well with that heard in Skavrusten's version, and in other playing at that local contest in 1958. Most modern contest playing, in addition to favoring especially distinctive tunes and variants, also tends to feature tempos slowed to accomodate plenty of melodic and rhythmic ornamentation.

While trends in contest fiddling seem reasonably clear-cut (these are explored further below), how dance playing will develop in the future remains in doubt. An anecdote illustrates how this issue evades simple characterization. Six-time National Fiddle Contest winner Bjørn Odde played both a contest and a dance version of "Riksbanken" (#19) during a 1989 interview. The tempos of the dance and contest versions were respectively 128 and 121; in the contest version, the second beat was lengthened more, and rhythms more varied overall, essentially the same differences distinguishing Knut Kjøk's dance and contest versions of "Vigstadmoin." Odde traveled the fifteen miles or so from his home in Garmo (Lom) to the Schjølberg home in Vågåmo for this interview. As he played both versions of "Riksbanken," Frøydis Schjølberg and her contest dance partner danced. They stated that they enjoyed dancing more to the version that Odde had said was for solo contest performance because its subtleties offered more challenges.

The more experienced and successful contest fiddlers make sure that the two tunes they play in a contest complement each other and present as much aesthetic and technical material as is reasonable, forming a temporary but convincing two-movement suite of, for instance, a *springleik* and a *halling,* or a *springar* and a bridal march. Most important, the tunes presented in listening venues are usually chosen with great care from the rare and unusual, and perhaps technically challenging, end of the spectrum of tradition. Favored tunes may be striking in the tuning used (#87), through requiring position work (generally third position, for the key of A, but even second position, as in tunes #21 and #45), may be odd in form, as are so many of the pieces in the Tune Anthology, or they may be unusual in various ways owing to their following a program suggested in the title (see the discussion of listening pieces in the previous chapter). Still other contest tunes stand out for reasons having to do with rhythm or meter. For instance, the most remarkable feature of the *springleik* transcribed here as #5, a rare tune now becoming less rare, is the complexity of rhythm at the start of both phrases of the first strain. This tune is genuinely difficult to play, and perhaps a little distracting to dancers, but a pleasure to listen to—in other words, an ideal contest piece. Its second strain is more conventional in contour but, since versions taken from the playing of Pål Skogum have this strain in minor, adds modal variety. This unusual feature makes the tune yet trickier for the player, since underlying fingering patterns alternate by strain. In a further example, the *gammalvals* "Lomsvogga" (#34), though simple in many ways, has one strain that sounds in 6/8, the other in 3/4 (the eighth note and thus the measure is the same length in the two strains).[3] Moreover, the complexities of the pieces best suited to the contest/ concert environment are intensified through the manner in which these tunes are performed. This can best be understood through examining the impact of judging at contests on the linked issues of tune choice and performance practice.

Judging at Contests: Tradition, Art, and Winning

Contest judges help shape tradition by encouraging certain styles and trends and by doing so in ways that reinforce the values of the revival and of Norwegian culture in general. Panels of judges are composed of experts, many past winners in the performance medium being judged, but occasionally including academics or other people widely recognized as authorities. Relying heavily on past winners ensures considerable continuity in taste. It is also significant that judges work as cooperative teams, and that a balance of expertise is sought through generally including one judge each from the Gudbrandsdal, the West, and the Røros area.

Judging today at the National Fiddle Contest—or, for that matter, at any contest—is not overtly different from how it has been for decades either in assessment of style or manner of awarding points. A new scoring sheet, with slightly revised categories, came into use in 1993. With this, the process was supposedly inverted: rather than removing points for flaws, judges are now to award scores for virtues. But since most judges choose a total score as their first act, then divide that score to fill whatever boxes there may be on a scoring sheet, the new scheme simply employs a modified technique of legitimizing a judge's first intuitive ranking. The problem of some players' polishing just a few contest tunes remains, as does the tension between art-style performance of tunes in dance genres and playing that is genuinely dance oriented. Most top fiddlers are, on balance, more art oriented, and nearly all successful contestants have learned to choose pieces that will catch the judges' attention through their distinctiveness, usually as a result of complexity. This general principle is far from rare in European folk revivals: "unusual" often translates as "genuine and old." When Norwegian fiddlers at the National Fiddle Contest act out this common practice, that is, when they exaggerate style through continual selection of especially striking tunes, their doing so serves two additional purposes. The local specificity of each tradition drawn on is underscored, since odd pieces by definition reveal distinctive earmarks of authenticity. And the listening-oriented forum is well served with plenty of material for a satisfying aesthetic experience.

Figures 13 and 14 classify the ways in which tunes played by fiddlers in the A and B classes at the 1993 National Fiddle Contest were distinctive, that is, how these renditions differed from a purely hypothetical unadorned performance of a simple bipartite tune in major. Identifying such ear-catching traits is a crude mechanical exercise, but nevertheless one that the performers themselves also seem to do, whether consciously or not. Fiddlers are listed in the order in which they placed in the contest: Amund Bjørgen won the A class, Øystein Rudi Ovrum came in second, and so on. A capital letter in the "key" column indicates major or Lydian mode, while a lower-case letter indicates melodic minor or some other pattern including a low third degree. "Meter" correlates with genre: the meter "9" (i.e., 9/8) identifies the genre locally named *springleik, springar, springdans, pols, polsdans, rundom,* and so on. It is a contest rule that a player's two tunes must be in different genres; the unwritten corollary of this rule is that one tune will be in some 9/8 genre. Pieces in 2 (most conveniently notated in cut time) are either *hallings* or listening pieces (*lydarslått,* in the column labeled "comments"). Tunes in 3 (3/4) are *gammalvals;* those in 4 (common time) are marches. "Irregular" means that one or more strains are not in four- or eight-measure sections. "Extra" indicates tunes with more than two strains. An "x" in the "key" column indicates either that a tune was not in major or that strains are in contrasting keys. "Beats" indicates a notable lengthening of the second beat of each measure. An "x" was also awarded if a rendition was rich in double stops (or a drone), ornaments, or variation of volume; if it was paired with great success with a complementary tune; if it was in an unusual scordatura (these are spelled out under "comments"); or if some other striking aspect merited listing in the column labeled "special."

Each "distinctive" aspect of a tune earned it a point in this tally (two marks in a box indicate, for example, that two strains were irregular). Total scores appear in the penultimate column. Over half of the fiddlers in the A class played in the already intricate styles of the Gudbrandsdal: fiddlers from elsewhere included Rue (from the West), Nyplass (Røros), Westberg (Brekken, near Røros), Ivar Schjølberg (Ålen, near Røros, though he resides in the Gudbrandsdal), Sølvberg

Figure 13. National Fiddle Contest 1993, Solo Fiddle A Class (attractive aspects of tunes)

name	(key/meter)		irreg.	extra	key	beats	doubles	orn.	vol.	special	paired	points/pair	comments
A. Bjørgen	d	2	xxx	xxx	x		x	x	xx	L	x	13	listening piece
	d	9		x	x	x	x	x	x	S		7	s=GDAD
												20	
Ø. R. Ovrum	g	2	x	x	x		x	x	x	L	x	8	listening piece
	D/d	9			xx	x	x	x	x	R		7	R=unusual rhythms
												15	
K. Odde	D	2	x	x			x	x	x	B	x	7	bouncing bow
	G	9				x	x	x	x	R		5	unusual rhythms
												12	
L. I. Schjølberg	A/a	9	x		xx	x	x	x	x	S	x	9	s=AEAE
	A	2	xxx	x	x		x	x	x	S P		10	s=AEAC#, Lydian; pizzicato
												19	
T. R. Rue	F	9	x		x		x	x	x	S	x	7	s=FCAE
	F	2	xxx	xx	x		x	x	x	S		10	s=FCAE
												17	
M. Eggen	D	9	x			x	x	x	x		x	6	listening piece
	d	2	xx	xx	x		x	x	x	L		9	
												15	
E. Bjørke	A	9				x	x	x	x	S	x	6	s=AEAE
	A	2	xx				x	x	x	S		6	s=AEAE
												12	
J. Nyplass	D	3	x				xx	x	x		x	6	
	D	9	xx			x	xx	x				6	
												12	
K. Kjøk	A	9	xx			x	x	x	x	S; up	x	9	s=AEAE; third position
	D	2	xx				x	x	x	B		6	bouncing bow
												15	

	Key	No.											
T. Westberg	G	2	x		x		xx	xx	L	x	14	8	listening piece; neutral intervals
	D	9	x			x	xx	xx				6	rhythmic displacement
T. J. Rødølen	d	9	xx		x	x	x	x		x	15	7	
	g/G	2	x	x	xx		x	x	L			8	listening piece
I. Schjølberg	D	2	xxx	x	x		x	x		x	11	8	a few neutral intervals
	D	9				x	x	x				3	
A. Sølvberg	F	9	xx		x		x	x	S	x	14	7	s=FCAE; odd rhythms
	d/D	4	x		xx			x	L; up			7	listening piece; second position
M. Larsen	d/D	2		x	xx		x	x	P	x	16	8	pizzicato
	d/D	9	x	x	xx	x	x	x				8	
T. Hosarøygard	g	9	x		x	x	x	x		x	11	6	
	G	3	xx	xx			x					5	
A. Fedt	d/D	9	x	x	xx		x			x	11	6	
	d	4	xx		x			x	L			5	listening piece
S. Bjørnsmoen	d	9	x	xx	x		x	x	*	x	14	8	medley with postlude
	d	2	xx	x	x	x	x	x				6	

Note: Categories more fully described include irregular strains, extra strains, key (if not major, or if there is more than one), uneven beats (i.e., when, in a triple-time piece, the second beat is very long), double stops or drone, generous use of ornaments, varied volume, special aspects (described on right), and when paired pieces are complementary.

Figure 14. National Fiddle Contest 1993, Solo Fiddle B Class
(attractive aspects of tunes)

name	(key/meter)		irreg.	extra	key	beats	doubles	om.	vol.	special	paired	points/pair	comments
K. Bjørgen	d	2	x	x	x		x	x	x	B	x	8	bouncing bow
	d/D	9	x			x	x	x	x			7	
												15	
Ø. Eriksen	D	3					x	x	xx		x	5	
	C	9			x	x	x	x	x	R; up		7	odd rhythms; second position
												12	
Å. Svenkerud	D	9	x			x	xx	x	x			6	
	D	9	x			x	xx	x	x	B		6	bouncing bow
												12	
G. Sindre	G	9	x				x	x	x	R	x	6	odd rhythms
	G	4	x				x	x	x	R		5	odd rhythms
												11	
R. Skjelkvåle	D	3	x	x	x	x	x	x	x		x	6	complex rhythms
	d/D	9	x				x	x	x	R		6	
												12	
T. Aasegg	g	4			x	x	x	x	x	G	x	6	genre: *bånsull* (lullaby)
	G	9				x	x	x	x			3	
												9	
A.L.Jensen	F	?	xx				x	x		S	x	6	s=FCAE; free rhythm
	F	3				x	x	x		S		4	s=FCAE; neutral intervals
												10	
I. Lotsberg	D	9					x	x			x	3	
	D	2	xx				x	x				5	
												8	
M. Vestrum	D	9				x	x	x	x		x	5	
	D	3					x	x	x			3	
												8	

P. I. Myrbekk	d	2	x			x	x	x			x	5	9	
	A/a	9	xx				x	x				4		
T. Hoff	G	9			x	x	x	x			x	4	8	
	G	3		x		x	x					4		
H. N. Møller	d	9	x		x	x	x	x			x	7	11	not her home tradition!
	D	3			x	x	x		R			4		odd rhythm
I. L. Valdal	d	4	x	x		x	x					4	7	
	d	2	x			x			P			3		pizzicato
R. Henden	G	9	x			x	x					3	7	
	g	4	x		x	x	x		G			4		genre: psalm
S. Simenson	A	9	x		x	x	x	x				5	9	weak tradition?
	D	9			x	x	x	x				3		
O. K. Graav	G	9				x	x	x				3	5	
	G	9				x	x	x				2		
K. Taklo	G	9	x				x	x				2	3	
	D	4					x	x				1		
K. A. Nakken	G	3		x	x		x				x	2	3	
	G	9			x							1		

(the West), Larsen (the Østerdal, residing in nearby Oslo), Fedt (the West) and Bjørnsmoen (the Østerdal, but in a profession keeping him away often). Their homes are plotted in Figure 15: note how many cluster in the county of Oppland, which contains the Gudbrandsdal. Even the most cursory examination of the charts in Figures 13–14 demonstrates that high scores in terms of complexity correlate convincingly with high ratings from the judges. And a few glitches in the numerical progression, that is, where high scores in terms of complexity appear low in the chart, can be easily explained. Knut Kjøk (halfway down Fig. 13), who scored a "15" on the complexity scale, has won the competition several times, but made audible errors during this outing. Marit Larsen (fourth from bottom of Fig. 13) has some difficulty concealing her classical training. And Helga Norman Møller (Fig. 14, about two-thirds of the way down) played a tune that clearly was not in her home tradition. Outside of these three exceptions, the numerical progression is smooth.

The evidence in these charts is not enough to prove a direct correlation between complexity and victory, of course. What is demonstrated is that the performers who are especially musical and technically proficient couple those qualities with a clear-cut strategy, one favoring complexity, and that the judges and contestants are generally in accord on how this works. The tunes chosen through this strategy form a new contest canon, but a revolving one. A few years ago, a complaint was voiced repeatedly: the same tunes were being played over and over again at contests. As a result, relative rarity became desirable, and suitable tunes began to rotate in and out of fashion. For instance, "Vigstadmoin" (#6 in the Tune Anthology) was common in contests in the late 1980s, then was used less, then returned as one of the tunes Amund Bjørgen used to win the 1994 District Contest. In the end, the Norwegian fiddle's contest canon is partly one of specific tunes, but more one of types of tunes drawn from the complex portion of each regional repertoire, an approach in which the letter of authenticity may be overcoming the spirit.

Nineteen ninety-three was a year in which many players on normal fiddle at the National Fiddle Contest chose to draw on a numerically very small genre, the listening piece; seven of these were played by A-class fiddlers in 1993, although just one (and a rather lyrical bridal march) was aired in 1989. The *lydarslått* (listening piece) is unmistakeably a concert selection, and the inclusion of so many at a given contest evinced a conscious attempt to cater to a panel of judges known to favor artistic over danceable playing. Indeed, Rolv Brimi (of

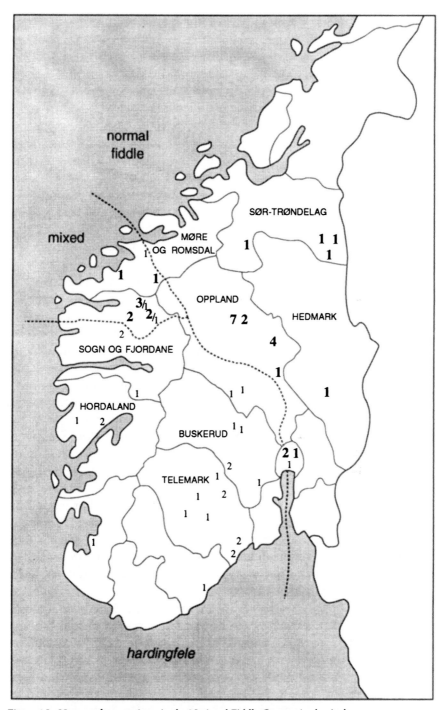

Figure 15. Homes of competitors in the National Fiddle Contest in the A classes, 1990–93 (both fiddle [bold-face numbers] and Hardanger fiddle)

Lom), one of the judges, remarked in a speech at the end of the 1993 contest that he was happy to hear so many listening pieces, since these and bridal marches allowed the widest scope for personal expression. And one dance-oriented player later confided that he and another top fiddler expected that this art-oriented panel of judges would not favor their playing. Amund Bjørgen, the most exquisitely lyrical of active fiddlers in the A class, was the winner. Back in 1989, with a panel of judges less keen on artistic nuance, most contestants refrained from performing listening pieces. Indeed, the winner was a dance-oriented fiddler from the West, Arne M. Sølvberg.[4]

Ivar Schjølberg once told me that he believed lyrical playing to be on the whole easier to judge than dance playing, and that ranking performances in the two approaches was difficult indeed. I agree that this becomes a matter of comparing apples and oranges. (At the first contest I attended in Norway, the 1988 District Contest, I drew on my experience as a judge at American fiddle contests, and ranked all of the top lyrical players just as did the judges . . . but failed to predict that dance-oriented Schjølberg would win.) Moreover, the problem of fairly comparing fiddlers in different styles grows as performers from style areas new to the National Fiddlers' Association choose to compete at the National Fiddle Contest. Judging courses do abound, and panels of judges are assembled with a view to gathering complementary expertise. For example, the 1993 National Fiddle Contest judging panel for solo fiddle included one knowledgeable fiddler from the Gudbrandsdal (Rolv Brimi), one from the Røros area (Inge Godtland, who recently moved there), and one from the West (Gunn Sølvi Gausemel). But each of these areas is large and its styles rather varied. And other styles, for examples, styles from the North, fall outside most panels' competence. Most fiddlers nurtured in a fiddle club have learned what in general to expect at contests, and most fiddlers today are indeed members of clubs. Fiddlers from areas where there is little folk music activity will not have a fiddle club to join, and these fiddlers may in other ways be out of step with contest norms. However, fewer and fewer active fiddlers do not have a club to join, and, of these rare unaffiliated musicians, fewer are choosing to participate in contests. Of the fifty-nine players of the fiddle that competed in solo brackets at the 1989 National Fiddle Contest, just four were listed without club affiliation, two each in the A class and B class. In 1993, just two registrants for solo fiddle competition were unaffiliated with a local club. Both were in the B class, and neither actually competed. Two of the unaffiliated contestants from 1989, Ståle Andre Paulsen and

Susanne Marete Lundeng (both from the North), made no secret of the fact that they found the judging process wanting, and both stopped competing. (Paulsen returned in 1996, but expressed reservations about doing so.) They both remain very active otherwise, and regularly release CDs; they are interested in folk fiddling, but less so in the modern institutional folk milieu.

The contest system, in rewarding certain kinds of playing, discourages other kinds, and cumulatively streamlines tradition. For instance, perhaps half of the oldest, D class competitors at contests I attended employed vibrato (some finger vibrato, but others in classical style, involving the wrist). I asked two judges how they coped with this. Both replied that the older players didn't really know that classical-style vibrato was "wrong," and they weren't penalized for it, but that younger players would not meet with this flexibility. Thus, purist attitudes in the contest system filter some kinds of variety out of modern playing. Nevertheless, the overall dynamic remains complicated: every art-oriented player accompanies dances sometimes, and the most dance-oriented have some lyricism to draw on. Two champion players, Knut Kjøk and Leif-Inge Schjølberg, manage to strike a fine balance between approaches, and they do have followers. Judging panels with different collective attitudes will continue to alternate unsystematically, training judges will become ever-more pluralistic (i.e., meant to cope with many different styles) . . . and most judges will continue to favor their intuition over their training when they award scores. The tensions between dance and concert orientation and between central and peripheral styles will continue, and will continue to enliven the Norwegian folk music revival.

Tunes and Repertoires Today

Even as modern communication, ease of travel, and exposure to tunes from far away during contests and concerts have helped many fiddlers greatly to increase their knowledge of their own and other Norwegian folk music repertoires, many have narrowed the repertoire they publicly play. Although some of the very best fiddlers make a point of continuing to put their own creativity on the line when they perform, more and more fiddlers believe their function is to preserve faithfully their share of a precious heritage. The more good tunes that they hear in highly skilled performances, the more humble they must become, and the less they are apt to think of their own compositional efforts. The contest category of *nyskaping,* of writing new tunes in *folkemu-*

sikk genres, has shrunk in recent decades as a result. It had long been more the province of players of the fiddle than of the Hardanger fiddle. Seven players entered the *nyskaping* bracket in the 1989 National Fiddle Contest, and received remarkably low scores for their trouble; low scores had become the rule for the category. Soon the bracket became "unjudged," and by 1993 the category had evaporated at the National Fiddle Contest, though a few fiddlers still present new tunes at the District Contest.

The new tunes that have entered *folkemusikk* repertoires in recent years fit contemporary aesthetics. I transcribed two of these as tunes #126 and #127. I first heard #126, "Per Bergom," written by Erling Kjøk, when Bjørn Odde played it at the 1989 Gudbrandsdalsstemnet during the Fel-Jakup Konsert; I recorded it again years later from the playing of Kjøk's son Knut. Arild Plassen played his own composition "Pols på Rondeslåttet" (#127) for me in 1993, just a few weeks before I heard a younger fiddler employ it in competition at the National Fiddle Contest in Lillehammer. Both tunes serve current contest needs in that they are moderately unusual, the first primarily in its length and the second in its elastic phrasing in the first strain. Simpler tunes either are not being written or are not deemed suitable for contests and concerts. I have heard more elaborate new compositions than these two, but audiences awarded those tunes applause that was merely polite. It cannot be easy to write melodies that are in line with the highly focused aesthetic desiderata now current. Most fiddlers today choose instead to preserve, to look back, to take care of, rather than to add new melodies to, the repertoires they hear at folk festivals.

Is the total number of tunes and versions of tunes in active use shrinking, staying the same, or growing? At the same time that progressively fewer new tunes are being composed, the fiddle club system may be threatening the existence of some versions of tunes. Nearly all clubs spend much of their practice time preparing for contests, just as do the fiddlers who choose to compete also as soloists, and with a parallel implication for repertoire: fewer pieces are practiced, quite intensively. In addition, a fiddle club must choose a single version of a given tune to work on, thus, in the more star-studded clubs, perhaps causing alternative versions known by some members to lose their place in those players' personal repertoires, and consequently reducing overall variety within local repertoires. Further, the only way for groups to achieve a solid unison is to play through the chosen version of each tune precisely the same way every time. This must cumulatively undermine many players' inclinations and abilities to ornament freely, to vary bowings, rhythms, and passing notes at home, too. Fiddlers may on occasion self-consciously compose, but will spend most of their time carefully replicating. Unplanned, incremental change of tunes, transformations through spontaneity and serendipity, must become increasingly rare.

Although habits fiddle clubs adopt in order to be effective at contests tend to cut down on the number of tunes in general use and on the number of versions of a tune current in a community, and tend to fix the identities of given tunes, this matrix of trends militating against variety is balanced in the creative activities of a few fiddlers. These individuals, who include most of the performers mentioned by name in this book, seek out rare versions of tunes from older tradition bearers in their communities, often then record these versions for CDs or play them in contests—thus bringing such rarities into public view—and often work toward assembling local traditional materials in local archives. Thus, while few literally new tunes are being regularly played, it is similarly difficult for a tune or a version of a tune to be completely forgotten. And some master fiddlers still compose, and many create new personal versions of tunes in order, in the words of Leif-Inge Schjølberg, to "give something back to the tradition" (personal communication, July 1993). Whether or not the dichotomy between how clubs and how star soloists affect the aggregate of fiddle repertoires is as clear as presented in these paragraphs, it is certain that strong forces are at work both shrinking and expanding the total number of tunes and versions of tunes in active use. The most prestigious repertoires, tunes, and versions of any age naturally remain those that fit the aesthetic needs of contests, but the preservation of tunes reaches beyond institutional desiderata to be as comprehensive as the time and energy of fiddlers allow. The old, recent, and new coexist in a living museum, in a dynamic equilibrium of diverse trends within a lively, thoughtful, and varied environment.

Folk Music and Dance Events: Proliferation, Gigantism, and Change

New events built around folk music and dance stretch and crowd the calendar. In 1992, Vågåmo's Trond-Ole Haug, then editor of the *Spelemannsblad,* warily described *"stemneinflasjon,"* the proliferation of such events. He, like many in the leadership of the National Fiddlers' Association, was glad that recruiting was going well, that the folk music milieu was growing in regions in which it was already established, and that new areas of the country were being assimilated into association activities. But he expressed mixed feelings about the sheer number of folk music events packed into each "hectic" summer (*Spelemannsbladet* 1992[10]:2). No one can go to all events. If, over time, fiddlers choose to attend just those events nearest their homes or most suited to their specific abilities, the folk music world will increasingly fragment. This would not be all bad: it might help solve very real problems of festival gigantism.

Folk music events are most at home in hamlets with 2,000–3,000 citizens like Trysil and Vågåmo, the populations of which increase significantly—even double—when the National Fiddle Contest or the National Festival for *Gammaldans* Music comes to town. In such locations, many residents are involved in planning a festival, the town government gets behind it, and, when an event takes place, the whole city center is inundated and, ideally, profits from the influx of performers and aficionados. A somewhat larger city like Røros still provides a fairly good site, but even Lillehammer (pop. ca. 22,000) began to feel too large. The very small towns that provide the best settings for folk music events cannot host these comfortably if they continue to expand. The combinations of rooms that house events—the community halls, school auditoriums and gyms, and occasionally movie theaters—generally seat at most a few thousand visitors. Healthy growth imperceptibly yields to claustrophobia. One can imagine this situation leading to a bifurcated clientele, composed of contestants and other performers who would monopolize most lodging weeks ahead of an event, and day visitors from the local community, leaving little room for an important transitional group, that of casual enthusiasts from elsewhere in Norway.

One plausible response to gigantism would be for fiddlers and other event participants to stop attending some national events, instead concentrating on nearby and instrument-specific activities. Figure 16 tabulates numbers of solo competitors on each fiddle type at the National Fiddle Contest during the six years 1989–94. There are more soloists overall on the Hardanger fiddle, notably in the A class (though more total performers on fiddle, if the rank-and-file majority of each fiddle club is counted). There has long been a tendency for fewer Hardanger fiddle players to compete when the National Fiddle Contest is in fiddle territory, and vice versa. This was at first a matter of ease of transportation, and that factor, while less significant now, continues to play a modest role. Also, any event is flavored by its site; fiddle players feel somewhat more welcome in fiddle territory. Whatever the combination of factors, the numbers of solo fiddle contestants in 1993 and

Figure 16. Solo Competitors on Fiddle and on Hardanger Fiddle in the National Fiddle Contest, 1989–96 (divided into groups by class of competition)

Location:	1989	1990	1991	1992	1993	1994	1995	1996
	Trysil	Nordfjordeid	Voss	Fagernes	Lillehammer	Rauland	Førde	Vågåmo
Hardanger fiddle A	21	13	19	21	12	26	13	14
B	21	23	36	26	24	32	28	34
C	19	21	20	19	20	23	23	26
"recruit"		5	4	2	2	2		
D	2	8	10	8	6	7	6	7
Totals	**63**	**70**	**89**	**76**	**64**	**90**	**80**	**81**
Normal fiddle A	25	23	13	14	17	8	8	19
B	7	21	19	16	18	18	8	27
C	24	25	19	31	29	14	16	22
"recruit"		5	7	9	8	3	18	
D	3	5	2	5	2	0	2	4
Totals	**59**	**79**	**60**	**75**	**74**	**43**	**44**	**72**

1994 suggest that attendance may be increasingly polarizing, with players of one fiddle type going to the "national" contest only when it is in the area proper to their instrument. These statistics would be insufficient to prove anything on their own, but they do support a number of generally held opinions. The broader points are these: There are overall more solo competitors playing Hardanger fiddle, despite the larger overall number of fiddlers in the National Fiddlers' Association, illustrating that the Hardanger fiddle remains more oriented toward solo performance. This disparity is exaggerated in the D classes, of older fiddlers, since the tradition of solo playing is older for Hardanger fiddle. Recent polarization in attendance is best shown by comparing total number of fiddlers of each fiddle type in contests in Hardanger fiddle territory with totals in contests in the normal fiddle area. In Hardanger fiddle territory, an average of eighty-four soloists on Hardanger fiddle took part in contests during this period, including twenty in the A class; on fiddle turf these numbers dropped to seventy-three and thirteen. This reflects relative ease of transportation and perceived level of welcome, factors present for decades. More dramatically, the average total number of soloists on fiddle in contests in fiddle territory was seventy-three, with eighteen in the A class, versus, in Hardanger fiddle territory, an average total of fifty-six with eleven in the A class. This larger drop reflects not just the factors of travel and mental comfort, as for the Hardanger fiddle, but also the existence of an alternative to the National Fiddle Contest in the National Festival for *Gammaldans* Music.[5] Indeed, a fair number of players of the fiddle seem to be choosing to attend the *gammaldans* festival and the District Contest rather than the Fiddle contest. The District Contest is specifically for fiddle and always held in the fiddle area, and the *gammaldans* festival, although conceived nationally, tends to draw mainly players on the fiddle and their ensemble mates, and has also almost always been held either in the fiddle district or in mixed-fiddle territory. Once a fiddle club puts on a large event, its members expect to rest for a few years. That the *gammaldans* festival generally lands in fiddle territory may cause the fiddle contest to be held less frequently there over time, and therefore slowly to return it to a Hardanger fiddle–dominated event.

Cumulative changes in the shape of the National Fiddle Contest and other events reflect the expansion of the National Fiddler's Association and progressive diversification of the folk milieu. There are increasingly more contestants in the old instrument brackets and in folk song because more folk music enthusiasts are seeking distinctive niches (e.g., cultivating antiquarian exotica) rather than places in the fiddle mainstream. The trend toward more "theme" concerts during contests is in response to the desires of audiences. Of course, change also meets with resistance now and again. For instance, it was argued in the 1994 annual meeting of the leadership of the National Fiddlers' Association that the National Fiddle Contest must return to being primarily a contest, that concerts should be fewer than in the 1993 contest in Lillehammer.[6] But can the clock really be turned back?

The younger generation, fiddlers in their thirties, now take most of the top prizes at contests (especially in the fiddle A class), and it will not be long until these performers assume leadership of the National Fiddlers' Association (in recent decades, most members of the steering committee have been in their forties or fifties). Aksdal recently summarized the effect of the *"generasjonsskifte"* on musical performance. He observed less variation in style both between performers in a given area and between neighboring areas, and wondered whether this might eventually result in a single national fiddle style. Fewer pieces were being played, fewer forms of each piece survived, and players varied tunes less during performance. He also bemoaned the rarity today of microintervals and the retreat of drone orientation in favor of lyrical lines and technically challenging double stops, and noted in general that dance-oriented performance was progressively rarer (1993:8–9). These modifications are natural results of changes in the training of fiddlers and in the culture in which they are raised, factors I explored in Chapter 3. They affect most young fiddlers, though several of today's young leaders manage to combine old and new aesthetics, techniques, and repertoires.

Although no European folk revival has been more consistent internally or more faithful to tradition than the revival of Norwegian folk music and dance, revivals always evolve, and even this remarkably compact revival has gradually but profoundly changed. It began as a series of small contests for Hardanger fiddle meant to salvage a threatened, but still extant, tradition. As decades passed, areas and instruments that had been less threatened at first came under the spreading umbrella of an institutionalized folk revival. Gradually adding the fiddle to this revival was invigorating, but brought into relief tensions between local and national approaches to defining identity, and set the stage for an exceedingly complicated contest dynamic featuring interplay between concert-style and dance-oriented fiddling.

Today's *generasjonsskifte* represents more than the elevation of fiddle technique, the contest orientation of learning tunes, and the creation of something of a canon of complex contest pieces. It is above all a generational shift in attitudes. Folk music as a natural and pervasive part of daily life is no longer a more or less distant—and no doubt idealized—memory, but something many young stars have never experienced. As the revival as a resuscitation has given way to revival as re-creation, fiddlers' attitudes toward repertoire have changed from matter-of-fact respect and an affection tinged with romantic nationalism to an even more nostalgic, ritualized veneration.

The Folk Milieu, the Media, and the Norwegian Public

No Norwegian can avoid knowing something about Norwegian folk music, about Norway's two fiddle types, and about the contest-centered institutional folk world. Events are well publicized, and receive some attention on the national media. Hours of TV and radio airtime devoted to folk music will seem few to Americans, but the Norwegian media have fewer total channels—though these media are now diversifying to better match American-influenced European norms. In the 1980s, it was customary for Norwegian TV annually to air an hour-long show on the National Fiddle Contest. That was just an hour, but, since most viewers then received just one channel, it was an hour that everyone watching television that evening saw. I watched this report in 1989, and saw a fiddle once and a Hardanger fiddle nineteen times. In this forum, within Norway but outside the folk milieu proper, the appeal of the Hardanger fiddle as national symbol and antiquarian visual object is irresistible. Much the same balance held in the televising of folk music in the cultural program of the 1994 winter Olympics. Both fiddle types were shown, but the Hardanger fiddle was featured, partly because that is the instrument of Telemark, the birthplace of a style of skiing. The lesson to be drawn from these instances is that the most general programs on folk music take a top-down approach that is centrist and focuses on the most specifically national instrument rather than a populist, but more involved, task of balancing the heritage of parts of the nation.

In 1992, shortly before an expansion of Norwegian radio, the best-known regular folk music show remained the "Folkemusikkhalvtime" (Folk music half-hour), airing at 6 P.M. Sundays on Program 1, then the art-music station. A temporary change in the show's schedule provoked a furor; for quite a few people, listening to this program is a part of their weekend ritual. Other half-hour shows on P1 included one following the venerable "Folkemusikkhalvtime" concerning international folk music, one presenting new Norwegian folk music hybrids (essentially representing the Oslo-centered urban folk revival), and a dance half-hour Saturday nights. P2, the pop music station, presented another half-hour dance, and, on alternate Fridays, "Trend og Tradisjon," under the leadership of the Trondheim-based team of journalist Arild Hoksnes and academic Bjørn Aksdal. This and the same team's occasional folk music quiz show—the "Radiokappleik"—were essentially educational, but presented a relatively liberal picture of folk music, a picture including *gammaldans* and giving more time to younger performers on the fiddle than did shows on P1 (see Goertzen 1996).

The Norwegian media are growing and becoming more specialized. Beginning in 1993, there were two pop music channels, but these together devoted less time to traditional music than there had been on P2. This retreat was part of a new general trend to separate light entertainment from education. The "Radiokappleik" had last been heard in 1991, and "Trend og Tradisjon" then left the air. The more education-oriented P1, renamed Kulturkanalen (Culture channel) P2, now has a weekly "Folkemusikktime," an hour rather than a half-hour, and the international half-hour has shifted to a different night, and retains its other two folk music shows. The fiddle does get a fair amount of airtime on the "Folkemusikktime." Much of this time is devoted to older fiddlers and music, and periodic coverage of festivals and contests allows some time for this particular instrument's music. The overall effect of the changes in the broadcast media, changes that are more a part of the history of these media than of folk music, has been conservative, to present folk music more as "good" than as fun and relevant to daily life. At the same time, leaders of the National Fiddlers' Association know more about the media than they did formerly and are better equipped to take advantage of its reach and power. The new (autumn of 1994) editor of the *Spelemannsblad,* Arild Hoksnes, although a folk music insider, has degrees in both music and journalism, and immediately revamped the journal. He expects to work with the Nynorsk Pressekontor (Press Office for New Norwegian) to relay folk music news to the print media efficiently, which will certainly result in better publicity for the major contests and festivals, and may also increase general public awareness of many aspects of Norwegian folk music.

The Norwegian general public encounters folk music outside the media in several growing forums. Anyone who lives in a smaller community, or visits such communities regularly—these two categories encompass much of the Norwegian citizenry—can dance regularly, if he or she wishes, to traditional music played by either a local fiddle club or a *gammaldans* ensemble emphasizing traditional style. Local music schools are becoming more interested in folk music. In 1990, some thirty out of 280 community music schools offered folk music formally (*Spelemannsbladet* 1990[1]: 13), often by turning prominent local folk musicians into adjunct faculty. When such schools hire full-time violin instructors with folk music interests—Mari Eggen is one such teacher, and Hannah Normann Møller intends to become another—the folk-music component in general musical training grows larger. Both Eggen and Møller play the fiddle—fewer Hardanger fiddle adherents have formal musical training. And, not least in importance, folk music events such as those described in the previous chapter simply take over one or another small community now and again.

"Springar etter Gamle-Lars Tomasgård": Decentralizing the Revival

In 1993, Leif-Inge Schjølberg became the third young musician whose services to Norwegian folk music were recognized with an annually awarded prize named for a legendary player of the fiddle, the Hilmar Alexandersens Musikpris. In a newspaper interview about this achievement, he said, "In our days we nearly drown in Coca-Cola, pop music, and pizza. I believe that it is important to be conscious of our own roots; that yields good character. . . . Different meters and rhythms can tell us much about the music's origins. That is what is unique about Norwegian folk music, and that is what I wish to take care of." He added that "it is easier to play folk music in 1993 than it was in 1983" (*Rønning* 1993:25).

In early July 1993, I was present at a memorial concert for Hilmar Alexandersen (1903–93) that the three prize winners gave. Knut Hamre, a reserved young player of the Hardanger fiddle, Leif-Inge Schjølberg, and northern extrovert Susanne Lundeng were on the same stage. All three have spent many, many hours at the feet of older fiddlers in their districts, all three have helped with local archives, and each has done well in contests (though Lundeng entered only a few) and has performed widely. Nevertheless, they represent markedly different constituencies and trends. On this evening, Hamre quietly played winding Hardanger fiddle tunes in the art-oriented style that took over much of his instrument's performance over a century ago. Schjølberg, equally reserved, showed how the vitality of dance rhythms can coexist with artistic nuance in his rare tunes from Vå-gåmo in the Gudbrandsdal. And Lundeng enthralled some in the audience and alienated others with spritely traditional tunes, played with charisma and showmanship, as well as her own Lisztian rhapsodies on *pols* motives. Where on that stage was the future of Norwegian folk music? It still seems to lie in the hands of fiddlers, each serving as an ambassador for his or her local tradition to the increasingly appreciative general populace of Norway. But which fiddle type will Norway best nourish? Will concert style or revitalized dance style dominate fiddling, or will these approaches mix in new ways? Will fiddling remain carefully channeled in the contest-dominated institutional folk milieu, or increasingly bypass the National Fiddlers' Association? These questions were posed—and perhaps an answer offered too—by the presence of these three very different fiddlers on one stage.

Schjølberg's remarks in his interview home in on several of the themes of the Norwegian folk revival. Norwegian fiddlers play to maintain Norwegian identity, to offset the debilitating effects of Norway's being inundated in international consumer culture, through a nurturing of traditional cultural materials that are clear markers of enduring national worth. Schjølberg invoked musical elements that not only distinguish Norwegian fiddling from musics outside Norway but also are distinctive from area to area within the country, symbolizing that the skein of local identities is critical for Norwegian culture in general and for folk fiddling in particular. Fostering musical distinctiveness, though originally done in the service of local identity, becomes a goal in itself, leading to some degree of exaggeration of style, to choices in repertoire and in performance practice that suit the modern needs of the contest/concert environment.

The last remark of Schjølberg's that I plucked from the interview is also significant: it has become "easier" to play folk music in recent times. The same cultural factors that made membership in the National Fiddlers' Association more than double in recent decades have also inclined the general populace of Norway to be more interested in folk music—certainly, folk music and dance events, although increasing in number, continue to draw capacity audiences. As it has grown in size, the folk music and dance institutional milieu has also grown in self-confidence, becoming better able to tolerate new initiatives (such as the initially controversial National Festival for *Gammaldans* Music), and also more welcoming to people that share some, but not all, of members' collective habits and goals. It is in this connection that both the prize honoring Hilmar Alexandersen and Susanne Lundeng's winning of that prize matter greatly.

Hilmar Alexandersen lived in Steinkjer, north of Trondheim—well away from any of the areas central in the folk revival. Although he entered a few contests early in life, he did not attend regularly later and, though an honored member of the National Fiddlers' Association, was much less a participant in the revival than a source for participants, a nineteenth-century fiddler in activities and attitudes. Rather than cultivating a faithfully delimited local repertoire, he supplemented his rich knowledge of tunes from around his home with many drawn from elsewhere in Norway, and he thoroughly mastered both types of fiddle. He played more than 300 weddings, concertized and recorded widely, and, in time, earned accolades both in the form of numerous prizes and through pilgrimages made to him in out-of-the-way Steinkjer by younger fiddlers. When the Norwegian Music Festival—not a part of the institutional folk world—decided to sponsor a prize for activity in folk music, it was natural for them to name it for a distinguished folk musician who was also not part of the institutional milieu.

The first two winners of the prize to play normal fiddle, Susanne Lundeng and Leif-Inge Schjølberg, contrast greatly in background and in how they now fit into Norway's folk music world. Schjølberg is a revival insider, a second-generation winner of the National Fiddle Contest, heir to the rich fiddle tradition of Vågåmo, in the center of the fiddle's highest-status district, the Gudbrandsdal. His own balance of measured creativity and informed faithfulness to tradition represents how the folk music world as a whole can maintain stability without stagnating, how the milieu can remain strong and vital by supporting and incrementally reevaluating insider values of long standing. Lundeng is in some ways his opposite. She is classically trained—she could easily fill a chair in a symphony orchestra—and had to learn her tunes outside the milieu, but through doing that filled in a previously "blank space" on the folk music map of Norway. She is the kind of extrovert, rare in Norway but more common in the North, who can entertain international audiences more easily than obey the subtle etiquette of the Norwegian institutional folk world.

One or a few unusual individuals like Lundeng, regardless of how prominent they may be, will not change the tenor of the institutional folk milieu: they are *visitors* to it, exceptional by definition. But a growing number of fiddlers have attitudes, practices, and repertoires that place them squarely between insiders such as Schjølberg and outsiders like Lundeng, and offer a real challenge to the stability of the revival. One such individual, Marianne Tomasgård, mentioned previously in this book both in the section on fiddlers in Chapter 3 and as the performer of the anthologized version of the "Springar etter Gamle-Lars Tomasgård," is in fact among the fiddlers who spent a great deal of time at the feet of maverick Hilmar Alexandersen. She moves comfortably within the contest system—she is among the handful of women in the fiddle A class—but is not very strongly invested in the system and, without fanfare, does as she thinks is best.

Although nearly all older fiddlers are male, at least half of the youngest ones are female (for both fiddle types). A few of the skilled female fiddlers grew up in families containing (male) fiddlers; Marianne's father, though primarily a dancer, fiddles too, and Gamle-Lars Tomasgård was her great-grandfather. But many young women belong to less tradition-rich families than do their male counterparts, and have less access to the mostly or all-male inebriated evenings during which some important transmission of tunes takes place. Comparatively more women begin as classical violinists—or at least study violin seriously at some point—and then pick up much of their fiddling from contemporaries, often in the fiddle clubs. Indeed, Tomasgård, though raised in a tradition-rich family, earned a master's degree in violin performance from the University of Houston. She, like Mari Eggen (whose father fiddles, but who also earned a degree in music), managed to become convincingly bilingual musically, but many young women—and an increasing number of young men—still show their violin background, to their disadvantage, in the folk milieu.

The often uneasy relationship between classical and folk performance techniques is not a simple issue. Education is highly respected throughout Norwegian society. Quite a few of the top Gudbrandsdal fiddlers (male champions) have received some coaching for their bow hands from classically trained Sven Nyhus, who plays orchestral music on viola, *pols* from his birthplace near Røros on normal fiddle, and music for Hardanger fiddle (his current performance focus) with equal facility. And the Oslo conservatory where Nyhus teaches has recently initiated a concentration in folk music. Nyhus has long given fiddle workshops throughout the country, and used to be criticized often for teaching kids to play just like him, kids who ought instead to be learning their local traditions. His style is indeed compelling, and has inspired much imitation, though I have also heard of several instances in which students asked him specifically to help them learn their home traditions exclusively and he readily complied. In a way, the tension here is between different historical periods. Today, adhering to one's local repertoire, performed in a distinctive manner, is mandatory, but Nyhus is an eclectic living legend much more on the nineteenth-century model. Teaching has also become the main way that fiddlers earn money through music apart from working in *gammaldans* ensembles. In past eras, fiddlers who were part-time music professionals played for weddings and the like, but today fiddlers are more likely to earn a music-based paycheck playing for school classes; Tomasgård has done much of this.

Tomasgård also exemplifies the increasingly precarious correspondence between physical home and "local" folk music tradition. Her father, from the Hornindal in the West, relocated to Nannestad, north of Oslo. He found that his new local tradition was not a vibrant one, and continued to cultivate that of his original home. Marianne chose to nurture that music, too, even though, while she spent much time as a child in the Hornindal during her father's vacations, she has never lived there herself. More and more young people are finding themselves in similar situations. Rather than growing up in the hearth of a tradition, and naturally cultivating that tradition all of their lives, they *choose* one of the several traditions to which they have some kind of connection, then choose to continue to cultivate it despite changes of residence for schooling, marriage, army duty, or profession. What local traditions will their children consider their own? Will more players follow the example of Brekken-raised *pols* virtuoso Tron Westberg, who, following a move to Hardanger fiddle territory, has become musically bilingual? Will the current norm, the cultivation by individuals of single, discrete local traditions seem increasingly artificial as this becomes more of a conscious decision and less the natural product of being raised in a tradition area, that is, when this becomes a choice resisting, rather than reflecting, the actual patterns of their lives? Answers to such questions will become increasingly complex, adding pressure on the coherence of the institutional folk milieu.

Last, Tomasgård's musical choices do not fit contest norms. In the 1988 District Contest, she played a *hamborger* for one of her two tunes. *Gammaldans* tunes are by statute excluded from this competition, but she felt, she later told me, that the judges knew *her* tradition. This was a good venue for her mildly heretical tune choice—the panel of judges was on the liberal side, including *gammaldans* scholar and proponent Arild Hoksnes. The other tune Tomasgård played on that occasion was the "Springar etter Gamle-Lars Tomasgård" (#35 in the

Tune Anthology). What is most remarkable about this choice is how prosaic it is within the context of contest fiddling. It is a fine meat-and-potatoes dance tune, with strains nicely balanced, but lacks typical contest characteristics; that is, it is by no stretch of the imagination complex, unusual, or rare. The West is home to many tunes that meet contest desiderata; selecting this *springar* instead for that venue—which I witnessed many fiddlers from the West do—is a statement that the performer feels no need to bend his or her taste for the sake of a good score, an attitude which undermines the inherited contest system.

Marianne Tomasgård's playing of tunes like the "Springar etter Gamle-Lars Tomasgård" in contests is, in a way, old-fashioned; it is an assertion that the appropriate fiddle tune for any setting is one that works well as a functional dance tune. This attitude is true to her adopted local tradition in the West, where many fiddlers continue to emphasize dancing over competition, and true to the broad sweep of the history of Norwegian folk music, but quietly ignores a century of tradition specific to the mainstream of the Norwegian institutional folk music milieu. This may be true of several other of Tomasgård's attitudes. She doesn't separate her local *folkemusikk* as thoroughly from other repertoires as do modern contest-oriented fiddlers—neither did eclectic giants of the fiddle through the centuries, from Fel-Jakup to Hilmar Alexandersen to Sven Nyhus. She has acquired the maximum formal musical education that is readily available, unlike many contest fiddlers, who are sensitive to potential contamination of their local styles by classical technique—but it is only recently that fiddlers have become leery of classical technique, as is demonstrated by the frequent use of one or another kind of vibrato by older players.

When the Norwegian folk revival expanded from the center of the territory of the Hardanger fiddle—Telemark and neighboring counties—to take in peripheral Hardanger fiddle areas and places where the normal fiddle is played, not just new repertoires but new attitudes were encountered. Adjustments had to be made in both the center and periphery, though, for the most part, fiddlers from the annexed areas were required to adopt the attitudes long held in the revival. Progressive chafing against this domination climaxed in the *gammaldans* controversy. Today, the old and continuing tension between center (Telemark) and outlying areas is echoed by differences between the highest-prestige fiddle area, the contest-dominating Gudbrandsdal and places that have become important in the revival more recently, like Tomasgård's West, and also locations just entering the milieu, like Lundeng's

North. Norway's critical value of egalitarianism continues to be sorely tested in the folk world when theoretically equal repertoires (and attitudes) prove to be uncomfortably dissimilar. Expanding the territorial scope of a nativistic music revival can be fraught with pitfalls if the "natives" disagree.

I argued earlier in this chapter that extant repertoires—that is, the sum of what can be found in archives, in the playing of older fiddlers, in the repertoires of fiddle clubs, and in the esoterica known to champions—now constitute an enormous diachronic living museum of Norwegian fiddle tunes. Something similar holds for performance practices and for attitudes toward fiddling. Contrasting approaches that can be associated not just with locales but with historical eras coexist, largely peacefully, but tend to decentralize and could disrupt the institutional folk music milieu. Yet no cataclysms on the order of the *gammaldans* controversy loom. The modest threats to the unity of the milieu are at the same time promises of enduring vitality. What Norwegian culture needs from its folk music world may change slowly or suddenly, but the richness of the repertoires and diversity of the attitudes now encompassed by the Norwegian institutional folk world augur that this revival will continue in good health, nurtured by musicians who, through their fiddling, help define and sustain local and national identity.

Tune Anthology

#1. Springleik etter Amund Slåstugun

Note: How these tunes are gouped is shown on p. 126.

#2. Fel-Jakup Springleik

#3. Springleik

#4. Springleik etter Arnfinn Upheim

#5. Springleik

#6. Vigstadmoin

#7a. Gammel-Husin
   b. Halling

#8a. Springleik etter Hans Teigplassen
   b. Gamel-Ringnes'n
   c. Rendalspolsk

#9. Bestamor

#10a. Gammel-Køyllin i form etter Torger Iverstugen
   b. Gråkøyllin

#11. N'Eina Kveen

Leif-Inge Schjølberg

D.C. al Fine

#12. Vigstadmogleda

#13. Springleik etter Ivar Storodden

#14. Fel-Jakupspringleik

#15. Fel-Jakupspringleik

#16a. Melovitte

Kristen Odde

AEAE

Fine

D.C. al Fine

#16b. Polsdans fra Tomrefjord

Arild Hoksnes

GDAE

Fine

D.S. al Fine

#17. Kvennhusbekken

#18. Springleik

Reidar
Skjelkvåle
GDAE

D.C. al Fine

#19. Riksbanken

#20. Flatmoen

#21a. Andre-Posisjon Springleik

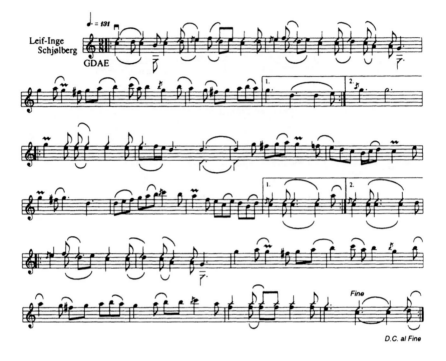

Leif-Inge
Schjølberg

D.C. al Fine

#21b. Springar etter P. M. Bolstad

#22. Springleik etter Pål Kluften

Mari Eggen

FDAE

#23. Halling

Leif-Inge Schjølberg

GDAE

#24. Storhallingen hass Fel-Jakup

#25. Bjønnhallingen etter Teodor Bakken

#26. Halling etter Martinus Helgesen

Helga
Norman
Møller

AEAE

#27. Skomakarhallingen etter Paul Berstad

Arne M. Sølvberg

ADAE

#28. Vals

Bjørn Odde

GDAE

#29. Gammalvals

#30. B-Dur Vals

#31a. Finnvalsen etter Torger Iverstugen
    b-c. Finnjenta

#32. Holnurkjen

Reidar
Skjelkvåle

GDAE

D.S. al Fine
(without repeats)

#33. Vals etter Hjalmar Fjellhammer

Øystein
Rudi Ovrum

GDAE

#34. Lomsvogga

Knut Kjøk

GDAE

D.S. al Fine

#35. Springar etter Gamle-Lars Tomasgård

Marianne
Tomasgård

ADAE

D.C. al Fine

#36. Gamle Kringlen

#37. Springar etter Samuel Bergset
i form etter Alfred Maurstad

#38a. Springar etter P. M. Bolstad
  b. Springleik

#39. Springar av Anders Reed

#40. Springar i C-dur etter Anders Reed

#41. Springar på oppstilt ters
     etter Magne Maurset

#42. Napoleanmarsjen

#43a. Bruremarsj etter Magne Maurset
    b. Bruremarsj etter Samuel Bergset

#44. Bruremarsj etter Bø-Mari

Gunn Solvi
Gausemel

ADAE

#45. Bruremarsj etter Anders Reed
     i form etter Moses Paulen

Arne M.
Sølvberg

ADAE

#46. Bruremarsj frå Fron

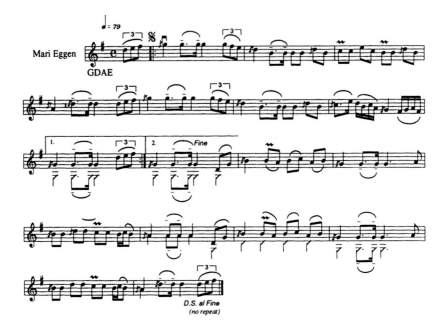

Mari Eggen
GDAE

D.S. al Fine
(no repeat)

#47. Pols etter Steffa Henningsgård

Use last measure again
to start repeat of
each half of
second strain.

#48. Brurleken åt Sulhusgubba

Harald
Gullikstad

ADAE

D.S. al Fine

#49. Litjhurven

#50. Storhurven

#51. Pols

#52. Millom Abrahamsvolla og Køråsvollom (Bortover all veil)

#53. Tore Spranga

Harald
Gullikstad
ADAE

D.C. al Fine

#54. Sup-Leken

Jens Nyplass
ADAE

D.S. al Fine

#55. Forspellpols

#56. Når 'n Olav Braut av Båggån
(informal title)

#57. Pols etter Marta-Johannes

#58. Skejegge Loppe

#59. Sofie Råen

#60. Drommen av Sulhusgubben

Siw-Marit
Johnson

ADAE

#61. Pols etter Henrik Møllman

Jens
Nyplass

#62. Kvernings-Anders

Harald
Gullikstad

ADAE

#63a-b. Leken hass Nils Toresa

#63c. Leken hass Nils Toresa

#64. Per Persa-Leken

#65. Pols etter Jorgen Wehn

Jens
Nyplass

GDAE

#66. Leken hass Gammel-Møller

#67. Leken hass Christian Dahl

Jens Nyplass

GDAE

D.S. al Fine

#68. Pols

Jens Nyplass

ADAE

D.C. al Fine

#69. Kvardagspols etter Henning Trøen

#70. Pols etter Henning Trøen

D. S. al 24, then
repeat prelude

#71a. Iver Kristesen Leken

b. Polsdans fra Lødingen

#72. Set of Rundoms:
   A. Kjerringa med Stoven
   B. Rundomen hinnes Tomine
   C. Rundomen etter Saming Sørjoten

Bente Kvile
Buflod

ADAE

tag (slower)

D.S. al 23 (no repeat), then skip to this tag

tag (slower)

#73. Set of Rundoms
    A. Rundom
    B. Rundomen hinnes Tomine
    C. Hussujo

Helga
Norman
Møller

B   (as B in previous set)

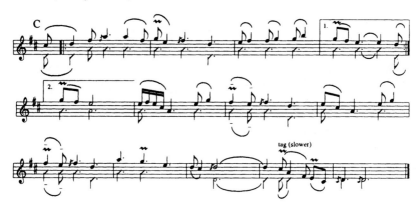

#74. Set of Rendalspolsks:
A and C. Polsk fra Unset
B. Polsk fra Rendalen

Stein Bjørnsmoen

#75. Åt Bønsa

Ivar
Schjølberg

ADAE

#76. Polsdans frå Åfjord

#77. Storpolsdansen fra Nordmøre

#78. Rytmisk Polsdans

#79. Hund-dengar'n: Polsdans fra Nordmøre

#80. Polsdans etter Ivar Rognryggmo

#81. Polsdans etter Morten Jønnso

play entire tune thrice

#82. Polsdans etter Konrad Hanssen Evensgård

#83. Kari Kluften

#84. Vals i form etter Einar Turtum

Kristen Odde
DDAE

Fine

D.S. al Fine

#85. Springleik etter Jakob Skogum

Leif-Inge
Schjølberg
FDAE

Fine

D.C. al Fine

#86. Vals etter Petter Eide

#87. Kolagutt Springar etter Petter Paulen

#88. Hjulmaker

#89. Kjolstad Lek Nr. 2

#90. Polsdans fra Drevja

#91. Solung Springleik

#92. Havdalsslåtten

#93. Den der Nest

#94. Budeiehull

Mari Eggen

ADAE

slurred second and
fourth pass only

slow; unmeasured

Fine

D.C. al Fine

#95a. Gauken

#95b. Gauken, Springar etter P. M. Bolstad

Repeat all twice, then
Da Capo al Segno

#95c. Gammal Gauken

#95d. Gaukmåtår'n

#96. Goroleikjen

#97. Hestleitaren

#98. Folketone fra Hornindal

#99. Jenta ved Vogga,
       Bånsull etter Johan Hagen

#100. Bånsull etter Ola Rønningen

Mari Eggen

GDAE

#101. Ganlåt från Äppelbo

Ivar
Schjølberg

GDAE

#102. Førnesbrunnen

#103a. Hardingvalsen
   b. Helgelands Jenta
   c. Vals (no specific name)

#104a. Jerusalemsvalsen

#104b. Kjenner du, Kjenner du, Jente på Lur?

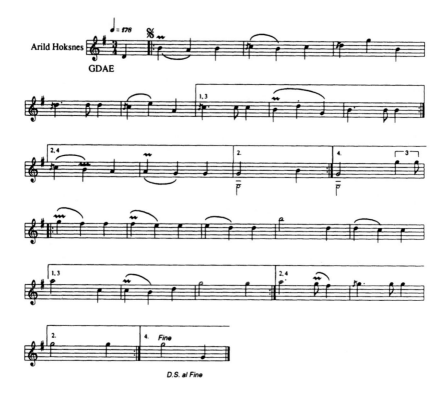

D.S. al Fine

#105. Godvalsen

Knut Kjøk

GDAE

last: serves as ending 4 and as coda

Fine

D.S. al Fine

#106. B-dur Vals etter Pål Skogum

#107. Masurka

#108. Masurka

#109. Kampen og ho Kari, Masurka

Knut Kjøk

GDAE

D.S. al Fine

#110. Skotsk

Knut Kjøk

GDAE

Fine

D.S. al Fine

#111a. Skotsk

#111b. Galopp frå Otrøy

Arild Hoksnes

GDAE

D.S. al Fine

#112. Skotsk etter Fel-Jakup

#113. Reinlender

Knut Kjøk

GDAE

#114. Ringnesin No. 2

Knut Kjøk

GDAE

#115. Reinlender

Knut Kjøk

GDAE

#116. Reinlender av Harald Haug

Knut Kjøk

GDAE

D.S. al Fine

#117. Nordfjordvalsen

Marianne
Tomasgård

GDAE

#118. Vals i C Dur

Arild Hoksnes

GDAE

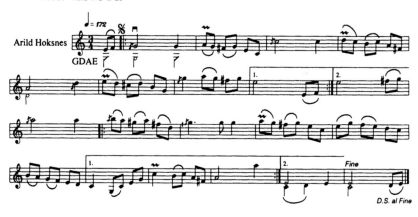

#119. Bikkje Fredrik Vals

Jens Nyplass

ADAE

#120. Randabygdaren

Bente
Storbakken

GDAE

#121. Hamborgar etter Teiga-Ola

#122. Red Wing

Arild Hoksnes

ADAE

#123. Masurka etter Fel-Jakup

Reidar
Skjelkvåle

GDAE

#124. Masurka etter P. M. Bolstad

D.S. al Fine

#125. Jonsauk Draum

#126. Per Bergom, av Erling Kjøk

#127. Pols på Rondeslåttet

PERFORMANCE INFORMATION

In nearly every case, the transcriptions in the Tune Anthology are of performances I recorded during three visits to Norway (academic year 1988–89, summers of 1991 and 1993) or of tapes made at my request by the performers. The brief notes may include title, translation of title, and perhaps some information about the tune or performance that did not find a place in the general discussion of the music. In the indexing of the tapes, the first letter indicates performance venue (*i* stands for interview, *c* for contest or concert, *d* for dance, and *NV* for videotape made in any venue). The upper-case letters following *i* are the initials of the performer (e.g., *iME* refers to an interview with Mari Eggen), and following *c* or *d* the first letter of the location of the event (e.g., *cR* refers to a contest held in Røros). The remaining information refers to tape number, side of tape if applicable, and cut number.

1. "Springleik etter Amund Slåstugun," played by Mari Eggen. NV7.18 (July 15, 1993).

2. "Fel-Jakup Springleik," performed by Reidar Skjelkvåle; iRS1A.8 (July 11, 1991); "Springleik e. Loms-Jakup" (according to Helene Høye; cR5A.5, September 3, 1988); the transcription is of a near-identical performance by Mari Eggen, NV7.19, July 15, 1993; simply "Springleik" according to Leif-Inge Schjølberg; iLS.A9 (summer 1989).

3. "Springleik," played by Leif-Inge Schjølberg, learned from Ola K. Flaten; iLSB.3 (summer 1989), retaped as NV7.55 (July 15, 1993).

4. "Springleik etter Arnfinn Upheim," played by Ivar Schjølberg and others; cG2B.3 (May 6, 1989), retaped from Ivar Schjølberg as NV2.31 (July 5, 1993); "Springleik etter Fel-Jakup," played by Knut Kjøk; cR5B.3 (September 3, 1988), with bowings (only) from NV2.62 (July 6, 1993).

5. "Springleik," played by Reidar Skjelkvåle (learned from Pål Skogum); iRS1A.13 (July 11, 1991); same generic title, played by Leif-Inge Schjølberg, learned from Ola K. Flaten; iLS.A14 (summer 1989), retaped as NV7.58 (July 15, 1993). Another Gudbrandsdal fiddler, Øystein Rudi Ovrum of Sør-Fron, calls this tune "Springleik etter Pål Skogum."

6. "Vigstadmoin," played by Mari Eggen, iME1B.15 (spring 1989). She

learned her version from Knut Kjøk, and like him, has used the tune both in contests and to accompanying dancing.

7a. "Gammel-Husin," (Old man living on the small farm "Husin" in Skjåk), played by Amund Bjørgen, iAB1A.3 (July 22, 1991). Tune #7b is a *halling* played by Åse Østeraas, cR2B.9 (September 2, 1988).

8a. "Springleik etter Hans Teigplassen," played by Ivar Schjølberg, NV2.34 (July 5, 1993). 8b is "Gamel-Ringnes'n," played by Leif-Inge Schjølberg, on commercial cassette: *Storsagje*, side A, band 3, also taped as NV7.53 (July 15, 1993). 8c is "Rendalspolsk," played by Stein Bjørnsmoen, cR5B.8 (September 3, 1988).

9. "Bestamor" (Grandmother), played by Amund Bjørgen, iAB.1A1 (July 22, 1991).

10a. "Gammel-Køyllin i form etter Torger Iverstugen," played by Mari Eggen, iME1A.5 (spring 1989), taped again from her as NV7.20 (July 15, 1993). 10b is "Gråkøyllin," played by Ivar Schjølberg, iIS1B.3 (March 5, 1989), retaped as NV2.36 (July 5, 1993). "Gråkøyllin" exists under two titles in Sevåg and Sæta. These are "Stortuspen" (referring to a legendary hero) and "Gråkøyllin." The principal tradition bearer of a generation ago in Sør-Fron, Redvald Fjellhammer, played essentially the same piece under two titles, "Stortuspen"—Sæta gives this version—and "Gamel-Køyllin," which Fjellhammer had learned from Torger Iverstugen. Sæta does not give the latter piece, but I collected it from Mari Eggen. It does not come straight from Fjellhammer; Eggen learned it from her father, Ola.

11. "N'Eina Kveen," played by Leif-Inge Schjølberg (*Storsagje*, side A, band 5), retaped as NV7.58 (July 15, 1993). This title refers to one Einar Haugen, who was from a farm called Kveom in Vågå.

12. "Vigstadmogleda" (Fun at Vigstad; a farm), played by Reidar Skjelkvåle, iRS1A.4 (July 11, 1991). Mari Eggen plays a version of this (entitled "Springleik etter Ivar Storodden," iME1A.17, spring 1989) which has the strains reversed—the A major of her first strain seems to resolve to the d minor of her second strain.

13. "Springleik etter Ivar Storodden," played by Mari Eggen, cR6A.8 (September 3, 1988), retaped as NV7.31 (July 15, 1993).

14. "Fel-Jakupspringleik," played by Knut Kjøk, cR5B.2 (September 3, 1988), retaped as NV2.63 (July 6, 1993). Kjøk remarked in the 1993 interview that this tune is played "in a lot of ways."

15. "Fel-Jakupspringleik," learned from Pål Skogum, played by Knut Kjøk, NV9.19 (July 17, 1993).

16a. "Melovitte," played by Kristen Odde, NV3.2 (July 7, 1993); #16b, "Poldans fra Tomrefjord," played by Arild Hoksnes, after Hans Jelstein (a military and dance musician), iAH1A.5 (April 18, 1989), retaped as NV4.72 (July 11, 1993). "*Melovitte*" is local dialect for minuet. I first heard the tune played by Johannes Odde at the 1989 District Contest (as well as by an older fiddler, Ola K. Flaten of Vågåmo, at the same event). According to Valdres-based scholar Ånon Egeland, the tune appears as a minuet in several eighteenth-century Norwegian music commonplace books (though it is in none that I have seen). The tune seems rather awkward, not falling easily into three-beat measures, but has remained a widely known curiosity. It is now used as a *springleik* (though Kristen Odde said that his brother Johannes plays it as a *masurka*). Sevåg and Sæta gives two versions of this piece (1992, 2:432). The main difference between these is in the flashy figures in measures 10 and 12 (this is yet another piece in A major that ventures into third position). In a version by Ola K. Flaten (matching my recording of that fiddler almost exactly; cR1A.2, September 2, 1988), those figures are sets of four sixteenth notes, while they are triplets in a performance by Iver Krukhaug of Heidal, just as in a version I collected from Arild Hoksnes.

17. "Kvennhusbekken" (Mill creek; composed by Petter Eide), played by Leif-Inge Schjølberg (*Storsagje*, side B, band 1), retaped as NV7.57 (July 15, 1993).

18. "Springleik," played by Reidar Skjelkvåle (after the version of Mathias Bismo, who played this on the radio), iRS1A.2 (July 11, 1991).

19. "Riksbanken," versions played by Bjørn Odde (learned from Knut Kjøk), iBO.1A19 and 20 (March 5, 1989); Ivar Schjølberg, NV2.40 (July 5, 1993); and Rikard Skjelkvåle, NV7.12 (July 15, 1993). This last version, which Skjelkvåle said is reported to be how Fel-Jakup played the tune, follows the general contours of the other versions, but, since it is in D, must go to third, then even fifth position. This was the only time I heard this version.

20. "Flatmoen," played by Bjørn Odde, iBO.1A9 (March 5, 1989). See Sevåg and Sæta 1992, 2:366–69, for alternative versions bearing various titles.

21a. "Andre-Posisjon Springleik" (Second-position *springleik*), played by Leif-Inge Schjølberg, cLk12B.9, retaped as NV7.60 (July 15, 1993). This piece was performed (almost identically) in the 1993 National Fiddle Contest by Øyvind Eriksen of Dovre under the title "Springleik etter Pål Skogum," NV6.5 (July 14, 1993). 21b is "Springar etter P. M. Bolstad," played by Arne M. Sølvberg, of Stryn (in the far West), iAS.1B4 (May, 1989), retaped as NV7.3 (July 15, 1993).

22. "Springleik etter Pål Kluften," played by Mari Eggen, NV7.23 (July 15, 1993). I first heard this tune at the 1988 District Contest, played by Sør-Fron teenager Åse Østeraas. Åse did not tune down—her version can be extracted from Eggen's simply by eliminating the low f's. When I requested this tune from Eggen, she was willing initially to play it as Østeraas had, but she found this frustrating, and insisted on also playing the version given here.

23. "Halling," played by Leif-Inge Schjølberg, iLS.A11 (summer 1989), retaped as NV7.59 (July 15, 1993). See Sevåg and Sæta 1992, 1:86.

24. "Storhallingen hass Fel-Jakup," played by Leif-Inge Schjølberg, NV7.60 (July 16, 1993). This is nearly identical to a "Storhallingen hass Jakup Lom" (i.e., Fel-Jakup) played by Petter Eide of Vågå, after Øla and Pål Eide (Sevåg and Sæta 1992, 1:97).

25. "Bjønnhallingen etter Teodor Bakken" (Bear *halling* in the manner of Teodor Bakken), by Kristen Odde, after Knut Kjøk, NV3.14 (July 7, 1993). Second version played by Mari Eggen, iME1A.14 (April 1989), with bowings from her performance in NV7.33 (July 15, 1993). The performance of this tune transcribed by Sæta was that of the Teodor Bakken mentioned in the title of the two versions I had collected (Bakken's version is after Rønnaug Bakken, his mother; Sevåg and Sæta 1992, I, 43). It follows the modal scheme of the Odde/Kjøk version rather than that of the now more usual Sør-Fron form.

26. "Halling etter Martinus Helgesen," played by Helga Norman Møller, cR3A.6 (September 5, 1988) and iHM1A.2 (June 22, 1989), retaped as NV6.30 (July 14, 1993). This is one of the best-known *hallings* from the Southeast. Sturla E. Sundli, a virtuosic young player from Trøndelag, knows this piece under the title "Halling Dalakopa" (iSE.1A9; June 9, 1989; Dalakopa refers to an area of Sweden).

27. "Skomakarhallingen etter Paul Berstad," of Selje, played by Arne M. Sølvberg of Stryn, iAS1A.8 (May 1989), retaped in a somewhat different form as NV6.61 (July 15, 1993).

28. "Vals," played by Bjørn Odde, after a performance by Sigurd Eggen heard on tape, iBO1A6 (April 5, 1989; called "Fant-Kal Vals" when played by Jon Korstad of Sør-Fron, cR4B.13, September 5, 1989).

29. "Gammalvals," played by Ivar Schjølberg, NV2.43 (July 5, 1993). I first heard this piece played by Arild Rønningen of the Otta Spelmannslag (cR4A.11, September 5, 1988). Schjølberg said that while this piece was known in his home of Vågåmo, the next sizable hamlet up the valley from Otta, it was more closely associated with Otta, and the Vågå Spel- og Dansarlag often played the tune on occasions honoring Otta or in Otta.

30. "B-dur Vals," first recorded from Leif-Inge Schjølberg, iLS1B.6 (summer 1989), but transcribed here from Ivar Schjølberg, NV2.36 (July 5, 1993). This common tune is entitled "Vals etter Ivar Bråtå" roughly as often as it is called "B-dur Vals."

31a. "Finnvalsen etter Torger Iverstugen," played by Mari Eggen (learned from Bjarne Risdal), iME1A.2 (April 1989), retaped as NV7.28 (July 15, 1993), and two versions (31b–c) of "Finnjenta" (Fine girl), played by Arild Plassen, the first form as learned from Hans W. Brimi of Lom, the second as played in the Østerdal, NV2.19-20 (July 2, 1993).

32. "Holnurkjen," played by Reidar Skjelkvåle, iRS.1A12 (July 11, 1991), with bowings from Rikard Skjelkvåle, NV7.13 (July 15, 1993).

33. "Vals etter Hjalmar Fjellhammer," played by Øystein Rudi Ovrum, cR4B.5 (September 5, 1988). This rare waltz contains an interesting compression in measures 8–10, three bars that would seem once to have been five.

34. "Lomsvogga," played by Knut Kjøk, in the manner of his father, Erling Kjøk, cG5B.1 (May 6, 1989), retaped as NV2.64 (July 6, 1993).

35. "Springar etter Gamle-Lars Tomasgård," played by his great-granddaughter, Marianne Tomasgård, cR6A.2 (September 3, 1988) and iMT2B.2 (January 18, 1989).

36. "Gamle Kringelen" (Old Kringelen; a dancer who liked this tune), played by Bente Tomasgård, iBT1A.6 (May 1, 1989); bowings from Gunn Solvi Gausemel, NV1.1 (June 30, 1993). A more frequent title for this common tune is "Springar etter Magne Maurset" (e.g., when played by Marianne Tomasgård; iMT2B.1, January 18, 1989; Gunn Gausemel uses both names).

37. "Springar etter Samuel Bergset, i form etter Alfred Maurstad," played by Arne M. Sølvberg, iAS.1A5 (May 1989) and NV6.62 (July 15, 1993).

38a. "Springar etter P. M. Bolstad," played by Bente Tomasgård, iBT1A.2 (May 1, 1989). 38b is "Springleik," played by Leif-Inge Schjølberg, iLS.1A9 (summer 1989), retaped as NV7.52 (July 15, 1993).

39. "Springar av Anders Reed" (*Springar* by Anders Reed), played by Arne M. Sølvberg, iAS1B.7 (May 1989). According to Sølvberg, this common tune is the only one that Reed composed.

40. "Springar i C-dur etter Anders Reed," played by Arne M. Sølvberg, iAS1B.5 (May 1989), retaped as NV7.2 (July 15, 1993).

41. "Springar på oppstilt ters etter Magne Maurset," played by Arne M. Sølvberg, iAS1B.2 (May 1989) and NV7.5 (July 15, 1993).

42. "Napoleanmarsjen," played by Marianne Tomasgård, iMT1A.8 (January 18, 1989).

43a. "Bruremarsj etter Magne Maurset," played by Bente Tomasgård, cDk4B.2 (September 3, 1988). 43b is "Bruremarsj etter Samuel Bergset," played by Arne M. Sølvberg, iAS1A.9 (May 1989), retaped as NV6.40 (July 15, 1993). Sølvberg believes this is the oldest bridal march in Nordfjord. This claim is supported by the many versions that coexist and the variety of formal irregularities that they contain.

44. "Bruremarsj etter Bø-Mari," played by Gunn Solvi Gausemel, NV1.10 (June 30, 1993).

45. "Bruremarsj etter Anders Reed i form etter Moses Paulen," played by Arne M. Sølvberg, iAS1A.12 (May 1989), retaped as NV7.1 (July 15, 1993) and NV9.30 (July 17, 1993).

46. "Bruremarsj frå Fron," played by Mari Eggen, learned from Bjarne Risdal, iME1A.3 (May 1989).

47. "Pols etter Steffa Henningsgård" (title interchangable with "Steffa-leken"), played by Jens Nyplass, NV4.48 (July 10, 1993), with an accompanying part (actually for the Brekken version) below by Magne Eggen Haugom, NV5.17 (July 9, 1993). It should be clear that the second part played by Magne Haugom fits only approximately with Nyplass's version of the melody. Haugom's version of the melody can be almost precisely reconstructed by superimposing the rhythms of Haugom's accompaniment on Nyplass's melody.

48. "Brurleken åt Sulhusgubba" (Marriage tune for Sulhusgubba), played by Harald Gullikstad, iHG1A.12 (July 11, 1989), retaped as NV3.58 (July 8, 1993).

49. "Litjhurven" (Little mess), played by Harald Gullikstad, NV3.36 (July 8, 1993); Sven Nyhus, NV1.15 (June 30, 1993); Magne Haugom, NV5.16 (July 9, 1993); and Tron Westberg (July 8, 1993).

50. "Storhurven" (Big mess), played by Siw-Marit Johnson, iSJ1A.19 (June 11, 1989), and by Ivar Schjølberg, iIS1A.19 (May 4, 1989).

51. "Pols," played by Harald Gullikstad, iHG1A.2 (June 11, 1989), retaped as NV3.54 (July 8, 1993).

52. "Millom Abrahamsvolla og Køråsvollom (Bortover all veil)" (between these two farms, which border a lake between Røros and Brekken), played by Harald Gullikstad, iHG1A.2 (June 11, 1989), retaped as NV3.56 (July 8, 1993). The version transcribed is as Harald learned the tune from Peder Nyhus. Other local performances, such as that of Jens Nyplass (NV4.60, July 10, 1993) and Siw-Marit Johnson Nyplass (iSJ1A.20, June 11, 1989), are nearly identical to this.

53. "Tore Spranga," played by Harald Gullikstad, iHG.1A10 (June 11, 1989), retaped as NV3.39 (July 8, 1993).

54. "Sup-Leken" (Soup tune; played for the serving of soup during a traditional wedding), played by Jens Nyplass, NV4.51 (July 10, 1993).

55. "Forspellpols" (Prelude pols), played by Ivar Schjølberg, iIS1A.3 (May 4, 1989), learned from the Fjellhurven Spellmannslag of Ålen ca. 1980, retaped as NV2.45 (July 5, 1993). While a very short postlude, just a tag of a measure or two long, is common in the Røros area and associated areas in which pols is played, preludes are quite rare. This rare piece always has a prelude. I heard a prelude once preceding "Per-Persa Leken" (#64), and once before a "Pols etter

Henning Troen" (#70), though I heard both of these common pieces many times without prelude.

56. "Når 'n Olav Braut av Båggån" (The time Olav broke his bow), played by Siw-Marit Johnson, iSJ1A.24 (June 11, 1989).

57. "Pols etter Marta-Johannes," played by Magne Haugom, cB4B.4 (June 10, 1993), retaped as NV5.15 (July 9, 1993).

58. "Skejegge Loppe" (Beard flea), played by Harald Gullikstad, iHG1A.8 (June 11, 1989), retaped as NV3.40 (July 8, 1993).

59. "Sofie Råen," played by Siw-Marit Johnson, iSJ1A.15 (June 11, 1989) and by Magne Haugom, NV5.19 (July 10, 1993), with a version of the opening four measures played by Mary Barthelemy on *seljefløyte*, NV5.34 (July 10, 1993).

60. "Drommen av Sulhusgubben" (Sulhus's dream), played by Siw-Marit Johnson, iSJ1A.16 (June 11, 1989).

61. "Pols etter Henrik Møllmann," played by Jens Nyplass, NV4.62 (July 10, 1993).

62. "Kvernings-Anders," played by Harald Gullikstad, iHG1A.20 (June 11, 1989), retaped as NV3.42 (July 8, 1993).

63a–b. "Leken hass Nils Toresa," played by Harald Gullikstad, NV3.43 (July 8, 1993), Magne Haugom, NV5.14 (July 10, 1993), and 63c, by Tron Westberg, iTW.1A6 (June 10, 1989).

64. "Per Persa-Leken," played by Harald Gullikstad, NV3.47 (July 10, 1993).

65. "Pols etter Jørgen Wehn," played by Jens Nyplass, NV4.2 (July 10, 1993).

66. "Leken hass Gammel-Møllen," played by Tron Westberg, iTW1A.17, (June 10, 1989), retaped as NV5.9 (July 10, 1993); by Magne Haugom, NV5.25 (July 9, 1993), and by Ivar Schjølberg, NV2.48 (July 5, 1993).

67. "Leken hass Christian Dahl," played by Jens Nyplass, iJN1a.7 (June 11, 1989), retaped as NV4.46 (July 10, 1993). Nyplass learned this tune from Sven Nyhus, who, according to Nyplass, told him that the piece had come to the Røros area from the Gudbrandsdal over a hundred years ago. Perhaps it had been a mazurka there, he speculated. It does show earmarks of being from outside Røros—a rhythmically much denser melodic line, which is balanced by atypically few double stops. It is considered a hard piece in Røros; Jens plays it seldom, and Harald Gullikstad, although he can get through it, told me he disdains it as "more of an exercise."

68. "Pols," played by Jens Nyplass, iNJ1A.5 (June 11, 1989). Jens learned this irregular tune, like most in his repertoire, from Peder Nyhus; this one he characterized as being from the "Swedish" part of Peder's repertoire.

69. "Kvardagspols [Everyday *pols*] etter Henning Trøen," played by Tron Westberg iTW1A15 (June 10, 1993), retaped as NV5.11 (July 10, 1993), and by Jens Nyplass, NV4.47 (July 10, 1993).

70. "Pols etter Henning Trøen," played by Magne Haugom, NV5.29 (July 10, 1993).

71a. "Iver Kristesen Leken," played by Harald Gullikstad, NV3.61 (June 8, 1993). 71b is "Polsdans fra Lødingen," played by Suzanne Lundeng, from *Havella: Slåtter fra Nordland,* Heilo HK 7067, B12 (1991).

72. Set of *rundoms*: a. "Kjerringa med Stoven"; b. "Rundomen hinnes Tomine"; c. "Rundomen etter Saming Sørjoten" played by Bente Kvile Buflod, NV7.51–53 (July 15, 1993).

73. Set of *rundoms:* a. "Rundom"; b. "Rundomen hinnes Tomine" (exactly as in previous set, so not transcribed here); c. "Hussujo," played by Helga Normann Møller, iHM1A.3–5 (June 22, 1989), retaped as NV6.55–57 (July 15, 1993). Møller first played these tunes for me on June 22, 1989 (as iHM.1A3–5). I heard these three repeatedly in various combinations (including the grouping transcribed) and with other *rundoms* at the 1989 National Fiddle Contest, which, since it was held in Trysil, included unusually many rundoms.

74. Set of *rendalspolsks:* a and c are "Polsk fra Unset" (a village in the Rendal); b is a less-precisely named "Polsk fra *Rendalen,*" played by Stein Bjørnsmoen, NV9.9–11 (July 16, 1993). The middle tune seems to be a favorite of Bjørnsmoen. I first heard him play it at the 1988 District Contest, much more mannered rhythmically (transcribed as 8c in this collection). At the 1993 National Fiddle Contest, it was aired in the solo competition both by Stein in the A class and by his daughter Frøydis in the C class, and in several sets of *rendalspolsk* played by groups from Hamar to accompany dancers. *Rendalspolsks* seem little different from *rundoms* in how they are grouped, i.e., that they are now played in sets of three with few repeats.

75. "Åt Bønsa," played by Ivar Schjølberg, cR5B.11 (Sept. 3, 1988), and NV2.46 (July 5, 1993).

76. "Polsdans frå Åfjord," played by Sturla E. Sundli, cR2A.3 (Sept. 2, 1988), retaped as NV8.54 (July 16, 1993). Åfjord is north of Trondheim, across the Trondheim fjord and about sixty kilometers beyond. The generic designation *polsdans* is used in parts of Møre og Romsdal through Sør-Trøndelag up the coast into the north.

77. "Storpolsdansen fra Nordmøre," played by Torill Aasegg, cR2A.11 (Sept. 2, 1988).

78. "Rytmisk Polsdans," played by Arild Hoksnes on *Hørkelgadden* (1991, cut B4). The "Rytmisk Polsdans" represents the simple end of Nordmøre repertoire derived from Hallvard Ørsal. This tune is said to be by Hallvard's mother, Ane.

79. "Hund-dengar'n [Dog-beater]: Polsdans fra Nordmøre," played by Arild Hoksnes, iAH2B.3 (April 19, 1989), retaped as NV4.71 (July 11, 1993); also played in a solo accordion version by Tor-Erik Jenstad on Hørkelgadden (1991:B8). This rhythmically dense piece may be programmatic: according to Hoksnes, it is generally held that the many rapid triplets parallel the action of beating a dog. Pictorial or not, this dense fabric of triplets is hard for a fiddler to negotiate, and typical of this area only to the extent that Nordmøre has long been a crossroads full of intriguing and odd tunes. Hoksnes further notes that this piece has a cognate in the Gudbrandsdal, and speculates that it may well be from there originally.

80. "Polsdans etter Ivar Rognryggmo," played by Ståle Paulsen on *Slåtter fra Helgeland* (1993, band 21). The area called Helgeland is about 500 kilometers north of Trondheim. Ivar Rognryggmo ("Littj-Ivar," "Spellmanns-Ivar," 1864–1935), of Drevja (a bit north of Mosjøen, in the midst of Helgeland), is a principal source for Paulsen, who learned Rognryggmo's tunes through intermediary Nils Rognrygg or from the latter's pupils. This *polsdans* is among the most straightforward and linear tunes Paulsen knows. He asserts that, although there is considerable variety in both form and style in Helgeland fiddle tunes, certain characteris-

tics hold for most. They include measures that add or drop beats (in all genres; here see the end of each section). Such tunes feature unsystematic turns of phrase and forms (here, in the second strain), and are played rapidly and with very marked rhythms.

81. "Polsdans etter Marta Jønnso," played by Ståle Paulsen on *Slåtter fra Helgeland* (1993, band 25).

82. "Polsdans etter Konrad Hanssen Evensgård," played by Susanne Marete Lundeng on *Havella* (1991, side A, band 4).

83. "Kari Kluften," played by Leif-Inge Schjølberg, iLS1B.9 (summer 1989) and NV7.68 (July 15, 1993).

84. "Vals i form etter Einar Turtum," played by Kristen Odde, cR5B.7 (Sept. 3, 1988) and NV3.6 (July 7, 1993).

85. "Springleik etter Jakob Skogum," played by Leif-Inge Schjølberg, cR6B.1 (Sept. 3, 1988) and NV7.66 (July 15, 1993).

86. "Vals etter Petter Eide," played by Leif-Inge Schjølberg, cR6A.14 (Sept. 3, 1988) and NV7.67 (July 15, 1993).

87. "Kolagutt Springar etter Petter Paulen," played by Arne M. Sølvberg, cR5A.12 (Sept. 3, 1988), iAS1B.10 (May 1989), and NV7.8 (July 15, 1993). The West has just a handful of traditional pieces played in this tuning; Sølvberg knows of four. Sølvberg describes this tune as a *Tatarslått,* meaning that it is associated with Norway's traveling people, a specifically North European social analog for Gypsies (Rom).

88. "Hjulmaker," played by Harald Gullikstad, iHG1B.2 (June 11, 1989) and NV3.63 (July 8, 1993).

89. "Kjolstad Lek Nr. 2," played by Jens Nyplass, iJN1A.12 (June 11, 1989) and NV4.65 (July 10, 1993).

90. "Polsdans fra Drevja," played by Ståle Paulsen on *Slåtter fra Helgeland* (1993, band 14). Announced as "Polsdans etter Ivar Ronryggmo" when played by Paulsen at District Contest, cR4A.9 (Sept. 3, 1988).

91. "Solung Springleik," played by Mari Eggen, iME1B.5 (summer 1989).

92. "Havdalsslåtten," played by Arild Hoksnes, iAH1A.9 (April 18, 1989) and NV4.91 (July 11, 1993). "Havdalsslåtten" is an unusual example of imposing an awkward, probably old tuning on a *gammaldans* tune.

93. "Den der Nest" (The next one), played by Leif-Inge Schjølberg, *Storsagje,* Side B, band 7, and NV7.65 (July 15, 1993).

94. "Budeiehull" (Dairy maid's call), played by Mari Eggen, NV7.30 (July 15, 1993). I first heard this tune played by Amund Bjørgen at the 1989 National Fiddle Contest; Amund announced that this tune was "etter Erling Kjøk." Eggen said she had learned it from Knut Kjøk, who in turn had it from his father Erling. The versions by Eggen and Bjørgen largely match: hers has a few more ornaments. The version played for me in 1993 by Knut, the source who would be thought to be closest to his father, stood apart. He interpolated a new measure between the second and third measures of the other versions and used rubato more freely, so liberally that his third strain defied transcription in any meter. Fiddlers add more personal touches to listening pieces than to any other type. Knut, one of the most knowledgeable and also most creative fiddlers active today, seems once to have played his father's version—the version faithfully reproduced by Bjørgen and Eggen—then, as time passed, could not resist recasting this melody.

95a. "Gauken," played by Kristen Odde, NV3.7 (July 4, 1993). 95b is "Gauken, Springar etter P. M. Bolstad," played by Arne M. Sølvberg, iAS1A.3 (May 1989) and NV7.6 (July 15, 1993). 95c is "Gammal Gauken," played by Kristen Odde, NV3.8 (July 4, 1993). 95d is "Gaukmåtår'n," played by Kristen Odde, NV3.9 (July 4, 1993).

96. "Goroleikjen," played by Knut Kjøk, cG4B.5 (May 6, 1989) and NV2.67 (July 3, 1993).

97. "Hestleitaren" (The stable boy), played by Amund Bjørgen, iAB1A.7 (July 22, 1991).

98. "Folketone fra Hornindal," played by Marianne Tomasgård, iMT1A.6 (January 18, 1989); sometimes called "Gammal Folktone" when played by Bente Tomasgård, iBT1A.18 (May 1, 1989).

99. "Jenta ved Vogga, Bånsull etter Johan Hagen" (Girl rocking a cradle, lullaby after Johan Hagen), played by Mari Eggen, iMEB.4 (summer 1989) and NV7.32 (July 15, 1993). Eggen learned this tune from Amund Bjørgen and has played it in contests. A shorter version, without the dance section, is known in Møre og Romsdal. Arild Hoksnes plays it on Hørkelgadden: Ørsalmusikken, Heilo HK 7072, side A, band 5 (1991), in a version that begins and ends with singing of the tune of this lullaby. Hoksnes's source for the tune, ultimately Hallvard Ørsal, learned it during one of his many visits to the Gudbrandsdal.

100. "Bånsull etter Ola Rønningen," played by Mari Eggen, iME1B.16 (summer 1989) and NV7.29 (July 15, 1993).

101. "Ganlåt från Äppelbo," played by Ivar Schjølberg, iISA.24 (March 5, 1989).

102. "Førnesbrunnen" (Brown horse from Førnes), played by Annbjørg Lien on Hardanger fiddle, NV8.65 (July 17, 1993). Førnesbrunnen was "a horse that made its way alone across the mountains from Møsstrand to Rauland during the Black Death" (Gurvin 1960, 3:243; see also Hopkins 1986:89). Those locations are in Telemark, and older recorded versions of this common piece under this title are all from Telemark, the home of the most complex and highest-status Hardanger fiddle styles and tunes. More than a few players from there performed this tune at national contests during the early-to-mid-1950s, the only period for which it is easy to know which tunes were performed at the National Fiddle Contest, since the judges' comments were published in the Spelemannsblad.

103. "Hardingvals," as played by Knut Kjøk, cG1B.5 (May 5, 1989), retaped as NV2.47 (July 6, 1993), with cognates "Helgelands Jenta," performed by Arild Hoksnes, NV4.83 (July 11, 1993), and unnamed "Vals," played by Arild Plassen, NV2.2 (July 2, 1993). Many gammaldans tunes have at some point or in some versions been given texts. This may result in varying titles corresponding to different texts (here, the commonest title, "Harding Vals," reflects a text beginning "Jenta er mi"), and frequently also loosens any link a tune may have had to a specific key, since singers' ranges often inspire transposition.

104. "Jerusalemsvalsen," played by Knut Kjøk, cG1B.9 (May 5, 1989), retaped as NV2.52 (July 6, 1993). 104b is "Kjenner du, Kjenner du, Jenta på Lur?" (the incipit of a nonsense text), played by Arild Hoksnes, NV4.84 (July 11, 1993). According to Tor-Erik Jenstad, this piece is said to have been formerly in circulation both as a waltz and as a Pariser polka (in cut time!). Jenstad also noted that Kjøk's version was a "Gudbrandsdal version," while Hoksnes's version was just

as central to oral tradition on his home island of Aukre and to the repertoire of Andreas Nerbostrand, Hoksnes's first mentor.

105. "Godvalsen," played by Knut Kjøk, cG2A.5 (May 5, 1989), retaped as NV2.57 (July 6, 1993).

106. "B-dur Vals etter Pål Skogum," played by Knut Kjøk, cG2A.9 (May 5, 1993), retaped as NV2.61 (July 6, 1993).

107. "Masurka," played by Knut Kjøk, cG1B.7 (May 5, 1989), retaped as NV2.50 (July 6, 1993).

108. "Masurka," played by Knut Kjøk, cG2A.3 (May 5, 1989), retaped as NV2.55 (July 6, 1993).

109. "Kamper og ho Kari, Masurka," played by Knut Kjøk, cG2A.7 (May 5, 1989), retaped as NV2.59 (July 6, 1993).

110. "Skotsk," played by Knut Kjøk, cG1B.6 (May 5, 1989), retaped as NV2.49 (July 6, 1993). According to Tor-Erik Jenstad and Arild Hoksnes, this tune became widely known through being performed by Oddvar Nygård's quartet in the 1960s, as well as by Hans Brimi and his group.

111a. "Skotsk," played by Knut Kjøk, cG2A.1 (May 5, 1989), retaped as NV2.53 (July 6, 1993). 111b is "Galopp frå Otrøy," played by Arild Hoksnes, NV4.85 (July 11, 1993). When polka-type tunes migrate across geographical boundaries, they translate to a different dance genre. In the Gudbrandsdal, this tune is now a *skotsk*. Tor-Erik Jenstad knows it as a *galop* associated with the late Hilmar Alexandersen of Steinkjer, northeast of Trondheim. In fact, Kjøk learned the tune from a recording by Alexandersen.

112. "Skotsk etter Fel-Jakup," played by Knut Kjøk, cG2A.4 (May 5, 1989, retaped as NV2.56 (July 6, 1993). My consultants offered an interesting variety of opinions concerning who in this typical *skotsk* was "etter." Jenstad called it a "Gudbrandsdal *skotsk*," known to him through a Hans Brimi recording. Ivar Schjølberg called it "etter Sigurd Eggen." Kjøk wondered out loud if Per Bolstad had played it, perhaps because of the virtuosic exploring of positions in the third strain (Bolstad, from the West, was a major source for Arne M. Sølvberg). And Hoksnes called the tune "standard Kjøk stuff."

113. "Reinlender," played by Knut Kjøk, cG1B.8 (May 5, 1989), retaped as NV2.51 (July 6, 1993).

114. "Ringnesin Nr. 2," played by Knut Kjøk, cG2A.2 (May 5, 1989), retaped as NV2.54 (July 6, 1993).

115. "Reinlender," played by Knut Kjøk, cG2A.6 (May 5, 1989), retaped as NV2.58 (July 6, 1993).

116. "Reinlender av Harald Haug," played by Knut Kjøk, cG2A.8 (May 5, 1989), retaped as NV2.60 (July 6, 1993). Kjøk asserted that it was composed by Harald Haug, erstwhile leader of the Vågå Spel- og Dansarlag, and that he (Kjøk) had heard a Finn perform it in Denmark.

117. "Nordfjordvalsen," played by Marianne Tomasgård, iMT1B.5 (Jan. 18, 1989).

118. "Vals i C Dur," played by Arild Hoksnes, iAH2A.14 (April 19, 1989), retaped as NV4.77 (July 11, 1993).

119. "Bikkje Fredrik Vals," played by Jens Nyplass, iJN1A.27 (Nov. 6, 1989), retaped as NV4.58 (July 10, 1993).

120. "Randabygdaren," played by Bente Tomasgård, iBT1A.19 (May 1, 1989).

121. "Hamborger etter Teiga-Ola," played by Marianne Tomasgård, cR6A.3 (Sept. 3, 1988), with a second composed and played by Gunn Sølvi Gausemel, NV1.8 (June 30, 1993).

122. "Red Wing," played by Arild Hoksnes, NV4.79 (July 11, 1993). According to Hoksnes, this ubiquitous American square dance tune came to Norway both in the playing of returned immigrants and visitors from the United States and on early 78 rpm recordings. Accordionists knew it then as a polka or *Pariser* polka. It has borne the titles "Pariser frå Oppdal" (Sturla E. Sundli, who knew it without title, had learned it from the Oppdal Spellmannslag; iSE1A.20, June 9, 1989) and "Stockholms Polka," and has often gone without a title, although early Norwegian record catalogs listed it as "Red Wing." A *Pariser* is slower than a *skotsk.* Hoksnes's *gammaldans* group Nordafjells announces the tune as a *pariser.*

123. "Masurka etter Fel-Jakup," played by Reidar Skjelkvåle, iRS1A.11 (July 11, 1991).

124. "Masurka etter P. M. Bolstad," played by Arne M. Sølvberg, iAS1B.8 (May, 1989), retaped as NV7.4 (July 15, 1993).

125. "Jonsauk Draum" ("Dream on St. John's day," i.e., June 23), played by Arild Hoksnes, iAH2A.3 (April 19, 1989), retaped as NV4.80 (July 11, 1993). This tune was composed by Hans Gjeitvik in 1897 as the detached second half of a *reinlender* entitled "Frilynde," which also contains seven strains.

126. "Per Bergom, av Erling Kjøk" (Per Bergom was a fiddler in Lom), played by Bjørn Odde, cG5B.6 (May 6, 1989), with bowings from his son, Kristen Odde, NV3.10 (July 7, 1993).

127. "Pols på Rondeslåttet," composed and performed by Arild Plassen, NV2.15 (July 2, 1993).

NOTES

Preface and Acknowledgments

1. Norwegian is not a single language, but rather two main dialects and a host of local dialects. What may initially seem like inconsistencies in the spelling of Norwegian words in this book (e.g., "*Spelemannsbladet*" equals "the *Spelemannsblad*," and *vanlig* vs. *vanleg*), will generally result from my being faithful to how words were spelled in the sources from which I quote.

I have chosen to use an English plural form for Norwegian musical genres that do not already end in the letter "s" rather than taking the chance of confusing the reader by employing the various proper Norwegian plural forms. Thus, *springleik* becomes *springleiks* in the plural, while *pols*, which already ends in "s," will remain spelled *pols* in both singular and plural forms.

Chapter One

1. Today, a rural community is a hamlet or small town. The earlier *bygd* was simply a group of small farms gathered in a valley by the surrounding mountains: there was little or no center apart from possibly a church and a government building or two. There is no good translation for *bygd*; I will use the word *village*.

2. I will address just two of the many instances in which general evidence from nineteenth-century music notebooks may contribute to our understanding of the history of Norwegian folk fiddling. First, in contemporary *pols* repertoires in the area centered on Røros, a substantial minority of tunes begin on the second beat. The manuscript tune book that has been most thoroughly studied (in Aksdal 1988), that of the influential Smed-Jens (1804–88) of Røros, was begun in 1846. Smed-Jens quotes fourteen *pols* melodies, none of which starts on the second beat. In an anonymous manuscript that Aksdal dates 1870 (1988:54), seven of fifty nine *pols*, or 8.4%, begin late. In manuscripts from later in the century, by P. Wessel (begun 1877) and Smed-Jens's student Christen Johannesen Dahl (1827–1890; manuscript 1880s?), about 13% of a mounting number of *pols* have this characteristic. Interviews I conducted in Røros and nearby Brekken in 1989 yielded as many such *pols* as ones that started on the downbeat of the measure. This proportion shrunk to in the neighborhood of one-fourth to one-third during

dance evenings, but certainly remained much higher than in the nineteenth-century notebooks. This compelling mathematical progression would seem to indicate that the tendency to start *pols* on the second beat of the measure is a recent development. However, these are the *pols* known locally as *gammelpols* (old *pols*), and they do seem archaic in some ways, most obviously in that many of them are less easy to harmonize than *pols* that start on beat one. Were these *pols* common before the time of music notebooks, then out of style for awhile, then again in the mainstream as part of a reactionary or historic-romantic trend? Or were they so common in the middle of the nineteenth century that it was other sorts of *pols*, less easy to bring to mind, that were instead preserved in print? Other hypotheses are possible; none is especially plausible. More evidence is needed, and such evidence simply may not be forthcoming.

A second topic in style history is less confusing. Today, the Røros area and points south are the only places in the fiddle district where postludes are tacked on to tunes reasonably frequently. These do not, however, appear in the nineteenth-century music notebooks from this area. On the other hand, in a turn-of-the-twentieth-century manuscript from the West, that of Knut Stafset (facsimile and discussion in Aarset and Flem 1991a), nearly every *springdans* has a short coda. Is this a practice that has faded in the West, but burgeoned in the East? The problem here is noncongruence between sources. Stafset was an amateur with scholarly leanings, whose transcriptions are more descriptive than those in any other such notebook I have seen. The nineteenth-century Røros sources are prescriptive; if postludes then constituted a few short formulae, each used for many pieces (as is the case today), there would have been no need to write them down. The conclusion must be that the practice of postluding has indeed died out in the West, but survives in the East, although its strength in earlier times in that area remains unknown.

3. Dovre is modestly represented in Sevåg and Sæta 1992, since the recorded older material is scanty. Of eighteen tunes from Dovre that Sæta anthologized, he drew on the playing of Wigenstad for seven and on Andgard for the rest.

4. Weak areas foster such scholarship too. A short article on North Norway printed in 1956 was able to mention two strong fiddlers of the past, Jakob Iversa and his nephew Ivar Rognrygg, both of Drevja, and both of whom traveled all over the province of Helgeland to play weddings. When this article was written, almost no young people there were fiddling; the historic tradition was the area's only tradition (*Spelemannsbladet* 1956 [3–4]: 6–9).

Chapter Two

1. Bjørndal did not attend a university, but seems on his own to have acquired precisely the sort of education he would have received at the only Norwegian university of his day, that in Oslo, which followed the Danish model, which in turn drew on the German system.

2. To be more precise, *gammaldans* is particularly weak in the central Hardanger fiddle districts of Telemark and Setesdal. Hardanger itself is the home to plenty of what is there termed "*valsaspel*," this name referring to the oldest genre of *gammaldans*, the waltz.

3. I was unable to find information about Skarprud in the *Spelemannsblad* or

in appropriately dated Norwegian versions of *Who's Who*. My thanks to Johan Vaa and Tor-Erik Jenstad for providing details of Skarprud's life.

4. The hypothesis that many players of the normal fiddle might have been underprepared for contests is supported by a "Supplement to the Judges' Evaluations" (Tillegg til dommerkritikken) of the normal fiddle brackets of the 1955 National Fiddle Contest. The judges remarked that "both judges and the public have noticed that at contests, year after year, several of the [normal] fiddlers arrive with poorly maintained instruments." These men should, among other things, clean their pegs, and rub them with chalk and soap [a mixture with much the same consistency as modern peg soap], and remember to tighten the hair on their bows before they performed (*Spelemannsbladet* 1956 [5–6]: 18).

5. Less frequently, a *halling* can be a dance for a man and a woman; this can still be found in the Gudbrandsdal. This form is much less common than the solo male display dance.

Chapter Five

1. I thank Elizabeth Weis for mentioning the *gammaldans* controversy to me before I went to Norway. Her master's thesis (1989) provides the first summary in English of this debate (pp. 89–97 and 105–23).

2. To be more precise, *gammaldans* is particularly weak in the central Hardanger fiddle districts of Telemark and Setesdal. Hardanger itself is the home to plenty of what is there termed *valsaspel*.

3. In the summer of 1993, Bjørn Aksdal told me that another factor in Hoksnes's decision not to use the word "folk" was that the International Folk Music Council recently had taken this word out of its name.

4. The governing board of the National Fiddlers' Association appoints geographically balanced panels of judges for the National Festival for Gammaldans Music, just as for the National Fiddle Contest. At this festival, several of the most expert practitioners of *gammaldans* music from the Hardanger fiddle areas were unavailable for competition because they were judging. This was true for the normal fiddle area, too, but the benches are deeper there.

5. This strategy is not followed at the commercial and relentlessly jolly Titanofestival. For instance, the *gammaldans* ensemble Heidruns, which took third place at the 1991 Titanofestival, played meat-and-potatoes pieces very well at the 1991 *gammaldans* festival and placed much lower, twenty eighth.

6. I asked several people about the 1992 and 1993 festivals when I was in Norway for the 1993 National Fiddle Contest. The sound system at the 1993 National Festival for *Gammaldans* Music was roundly condemned, though the organizers felt it was good enough. Bjørn Aksdal mentioned that some of the original proponents of the festival were disappointed by their inability to attract a wider variety of *gammaldans* ensembles, performance styles, and perhaps thus historical layers. Like festival sponsors in the United States, they had cherished "the most persistent intellectual infirmity of science and magic, the illusion that what we conjure we can control" (Cantwell 1991:160).

Chapter Six

1. For example, a unison double stop consisting of the open *a* string and the same note stopped with the fourth finger on the *d* string would generally be pre-

ceded by a double stop of grace notes, the *g* produced by placing the third finger on the *d* string being invariably joined with the open *a* string. In such cases, I do not notate the grace note that is the open *a* string.

2. The octave *b*s found in the second strain of Magne Haugom's performance of "Pols etter Henning Troøen" (#70) constitute an exception, and require unusual skill. The difficulty of this series of double stops is recognized in the tune's performance by adding a prelude that helps the fiddler get his or her double stops in tune (the prelude reappears as a postlude). Haugom learned this tune, including the prelude, from a recording of influential older Brekken fiddler Post-Anders. Of three other performances of it that I heard, none had a prelude. Gullikstad and Nyplass ended with no fanfare, and Westberg appended only a simple tag. Perhaps today's fiddlers, who have much more time to practice than did their predecessors, don't need this "warm-up/tune-up" type of prelude anymore. In any case, this is one of just three instances of preluding I heard with tunes from the Røros area, and the only one with the function of practicing multiple stops.

3. The key of C major is home to a remarkable number of tunes with irregular strains. This key is uncommon today; several fiddlers suggested to me that the preponderance of irregular forms in C suggests that many such tunes are relatively old.

Chapter Seven

1. Sven Nyhus's published collections rely almost entirely on these two hamlets, drawing on his father, Peder, for Røros tradition, and on a few of Peder's contemporaries to represent Brekken.

2. Just as the style of Brekken is close to that of Røros, that of the Rendal, featuring the Rendalspolsk (see #74) is close to that of nearly Trysil, where the *rundom* dominates.

3. When I interviewed Kristen Odde, of Lom in the Gudbrandsdal, I asked him to play quite a few of the tunes his father, Bjørn, had performed for me four years earlier. After Kristen played "Gauken," he volunteered that there were two pieces that referred to the cuckoo apart from the main one, and played these. "Gammal Gauken" (#95c), although in the rare key of G minor, sounds like a form of "Gauken" between that now common in the Gudbrandsdal and that played in the West. Perhaps this "old" cuckoo is indeed the ancestor of the contemporary forms. "Gaukmåtår'n" (In the manner of a cuckoo, #95d) has been said to routinely follow "Gauken" in performance in the fairly recent past (Sevåg and Sæta 1992, 2:530). It is in the same key as the Gudbrandsdal "Gauken," but is formally irregular in a more symmetrical way (6 + 6 measures, then 4 + 4), yet less unified, and emphasizes the upper register more. It is a reasonably common piece.

4. Versions of these three tunes, as played by Knut Kjøk's father, Erling, are the first pieces anthologized in Sevåg and Sæta (1992, 1:57–59). Erling's titles are "Sinklarmarsjen" (corresponds to Knut's measures 1–18), "Så Svara Ho Guri" (Thus answered Guri; Knut's measures 19–35), and "Guri-Leik Nummer Tre" (Guri tune number three; Knut's measures 36–51).

5. A similar case is provided by Kjøk's "Jerusalems Valsen" (#104), which Arild Hoksnes knows by the incipit of a modern nonsense text, "Kjenner du, Kjenner du, Jenta på Lur?" ("Do you know, do you know, the girl on the wooden trumpet?"). According to Tor-Erik Jenstad, this piece is said to have been in circu-

lation formerly both as a waltz and as a *Pariser* polka (in cut time!). He said this was based on an apochryphal story related by Leif Halse, an older fiddler and scholar from Nordmøre, which tells of an old fiddler who used the same tune for all dances. A two-edged truth may be extracted from this tale, that some fiddlers of the past were content with very small repertoires, and that many tunes could indeed be recast into other genres with minor adjustments. Jenstad also noted that Kjøk's version was a "Gudbrandsdal version," while Hoksnes's version was just as central to oral tradition on his home island of Aukre and to the repertoire of Andreas Nerbostrand, Hoksnes's first mentor. Once again, the two versions are in different keys, marking the vocal connection for this tune and for much of *gammaldans* music.

6. Mazurka #108, the only tune in this set of fourteen that is in minor, is thought to be old. According to Arild Hoksnes, Hardanger fiddle player and scholar Ånon Egeland has found this tune in seventeenth-century notebooks listed as a minuet. Tor-Erik Jenstad has heard it played by the Hans Brimi Quartet under the modified generic title of "Gammal Masurka." Its uncharacteristically thin rhythmic texture and striking contour made the tune apt for the addition of text. Geir Lystrup nows sings lyrics to it that begin *"Kjære Tony Korporal,"* addressed to a young member of the British army in the Gudbrandsdal after the Second World War. The same sparse texture that allowed the addition of text left room for Kjøk to ornament freely during repeats. Mazurka #109, although in major, rather resembles the previous one. Jenstad called this a "Gudbrandsdal-type tune" known to *torader* players from that area. He has heard Hans Brimi (of Lom) play it, as well as Vågå fiddlers. It offers attractive variety between its three strains: the third arpeggiates, the second is linear, and the especially distinctive first strain does first one thing and then the other.

Arild Hoksnes and Tor-Erik Jenstad anchor a *gammaldans* group in Trondheim called Nordafjells. They play some relatively modern genres as part of a *gammaldans* evening in that city, i.e., the occasional fox-trot, two-step, tango, or western swing tune. But Hoksnes, after the group visited the Gudbrandsdal, said that the young people there "just wanted mazurkas."

7. The third version, a *Rendalspolsk,* comes from the Østerdal. Bjørnsmoen played it at the 1989 District Contest in Røros, with a rhythm so marked in the first strain that it seemed appropriate to transcribe it in 5/8. This and the previous set of pieces show connections from the Gudbrandsdal in the direction of Oslo. For an alternative reading of this "Rendalspolsk," see tune #74.

8. My general impression is that these various sorts of tune relationships may be found in the Hardanger fiddle repertoires, too, though the more organic tunes for that instrument will add new categories, in which tune versions and relatives shrink and expand. Some remarks concerning relationships among Hardanger fiddle tunes may be found here and there in Gurvin et al, especially in the last few volumes.

Chapter Eight

1. The tempo is 138 if the tape I audited at NRK is at the correct speed, which cannot be assumed, given the uneven performance of machines during that period, and the fact that these tapes have experienced generations of rerecording. If this tempo is right, Skavrusten and most of the other fiddlers at this event were

tuned approximately a half-step low. If, as I suspect, the tape is slow, then the tempo of his performance of "Vigstadmoin" would probably be in the mid-140s to about 150. The copy of this tape, consulted at the University of Trondheim, Rådet for Folkemusikk og Folkedans, is labeled L2623 (July 3, 1958).

2. This trend has not been limited to the Gudbrandsdal. Leiv Solberg, the primary folk music staff member at NRK radio as of this writing, related to me an episode from his work with Peder Nyhus, the nonagenarian fiddler who was the primary living source for fiddle traditions in the Røros area until his recent death. A few years ago, Solberg played Nyhus a cut that Nyhus had recorded for NRK in 1962. Nyhus's immediate reaction was that he was playing much too fast.

3. Less frequently, simple versions of tunes may be chosen for contests. For instance, Knut Kjøk chose the anthologized version of *springleik* #4 as one of his tunes for the 1988 District Contest. It is less interesting formally than the common version of the tune; in this case, the virtue of rarity briefly outweighed the liability of lesser complexity.

4. I made charts of the 1989 National Fiddle Contest much like those in Figures 11–12 for my own use, and have published similar charts for the 1988 District Fiddle Contest (1990). In both cases, the judging panels were unusual in that they were much less art-oriented than that for the 1993 contest. The correlation between complexity and score seen in both the A and B classes at the 1993 contest also held for the B and C classes at the two other contests charted, but not for the A class.

5. Entrants in the C classes are numerous, attesting to the general health of the milieu; their patterns of attendance reinforce the points just made. Competition in the B class is the least patterned, with the largest percentages of no-shows. This is acknowledged as a problem. The unjudged recruit class came into being to give the youngest fiddlers a chance to get on stage without as much pressure as the regular competitors face; then the category was eliminated to streamline the event.

6. In other attempts to streamline the event, a minimum age of twelve for competitors was instituted, and multiple participations in the dance categories by individuals restricted. Some have suggested that the best way to keep the National Fiddle Contest from bursting its seams would be to turn local contests into qualifying events, thus limiting the number of people allowed to participate at the national level (Arild Hoksnes, in *Spelemannsbladet* 1996[5]: 2).

BIBLIOGRAPHY

In this listing, American alphabetization will be followed. The letter Å will treated as A, Æ as AE, and Ø and Ö as O. Articles, letters, and other writings in the *Spelemannsblad* frequently are so short that it makes little sense to cite them individually. If no name is given in the reference in the text, the material in question was either editorial or for some other reason unsigned. In many cases I give, in the parenthetical reference, just the name of individuals quoted in such short remarks.

Aarset, Terje. 1991b. "Knut Stafset og Folkemusikken." In Terje Aarset and Erling Flem, eds., *Knut Didriksen Stafset: Mindre fra Forfædrene. Slåttar og Salmetonar frå Skodje og Vatne.* Volda: Sunnmøre Historielag og Møre og Romsdal Distrikthøgskule, pp. 197–220.

Aarset, Terje, and Erling Flem, eds. 1991a. *Knut Didriksen Stafset: Mindre fra Forfædrene. Slåttar og Salmetonar frå Skodje og Vatne.* Volda: Sunnmøre Historielag og Møre og Romsdal Distrikthøgskule.

Abrahams, Roger D. 1993. "Phantoms of Romantic Nationalism in Folkloristics." *Journal of American Folklore* 106:3–37.

Aksdal, Bjørn. 1982. *Med Piber og Basuner, Skalmeye og Fiol: Musikkinstrumenter i Norge ca. 1600–1800.* [Oslo]: Tapir.

———. 1988. *Spelemann og Smed: Smed-Jens fra Røros 1804–1888. Et Bidrag til Forståelsen av Rørosmusikkens Historie på Bakgrunn av hans Håndskrevne Notebok.* [Oslo]: Tapir.

———. 1990. "Samlinger av Eldre Danse på Noter-Typer og Kildeverdi." In *Norsk Folkemusikklags Skrifter Nr. 5.* Trondheim: Rådet for folkemusikk og folkedans, pp. 46–54.

———. 1991. "En Slåttesamling fra Skodje på Sunnmøre." In Terje Aarset and Erling Flem, eds., *Knut Didriksen Stafset: Mindre fra Forfædrene. Slåttar og Salmetonar frå Skodje og Vatne,* pp. 250–99. Volda: Sunnmøre Historielag og Møre og Romsdal Distrikthøgskule.

———. 1992. "Ensemble Playing in Norwegian Folk Music: A Historical Perspective." *Studia instrumentorum musicae popularis* 10:14–24.

————. 1993. "Generasjonsskiftet i norsk folkemusikk—et tidsskille?" *Spelemannsbladet* 1993 [11–12]: 8–9.

Aksdal, Bjørn, and Sven Nyhus, eds. 1993. *Fanitullen: Innføring i Norsk og Samisk Folkemusikk.* Oslo: Universitetsforlaget.

Bayard, Samuel P. 1939. "Aspects of Melodic Kinship and Variation in British-American Folk Tunes." *Papers Read at the International Congress of Musicology.* New York: Music Educators' National Conference, 122–29.

————. 1950. "Prolegomena to a Study of the Principal Melodic Families of British-American Folk Song." *Journal of American Folklore* 63:1–44.

————. 1982. *Dance to the Fiddle, March to the Fife: Instrumental Folk Tunes in Pennsylvania.* University Park: Pennsylvania State University Press.

Bjørndal, Arne. 1949. "Pietisma og fela: Ei liti Spelsoge." *Spelemannsbladet* 1949 [5]: 13.

Bjørnsmoen, Frøydis. 1993. "'Puss-Jo,' en Bygdespellmans Liv og Musikk: Særoppgave i Musikk." Typescript, distributed in photocopied form.

Bonus, Frantisek. 1980. "Polska." In Stanley Sadie, ed., *The New Grove Dictionary of Music and Musicians,* vol. 15. London: Macmillan, pp. 52–53.

Børdalen, Finger. 1968. "Døming og Domarer." *Spelemannsbladet* 1968[2]: 18–19.

Brynjulf, Alver. 1989. "Folklore and National Identity." In Reimund Kvideland and Henning K. Sehmsdorf, eds., *Nordic Folklore: Recent Studies.* Bloomington: Indiana University Press, pp. 12–20.

Cantwell, Robert. 1991. "Conjuring Culture: Ideology and Magic in the Festival of American Folklife." *Journal of American Folklore* 104:148–63.

Cowdery, James R. 1990. *The Melodic Tradition of Ireland.* Kent, OH: Kent State University Press.

Derry, T. K. 1973. *A History of Modern Norway, 1814–1972.* Oxford: Clarendon Press.

Elben, Otto. 1887. *Der volkstümliche deutsche Männergesang: Geschichte und Stellung im Leben der Nation: der deutsche Sängerbund und seine Glieder.* 2d ed. Tübingen: Verlag der H. Lauppischen Buchhandlung.

Feintuch, Burt. 1993. "Musical Revival and Musical Transformation." In Neil V. Rosenberg, ed., *Transforming Tradition: Folk Music Revivals Examined.* pp. 183–93. Urbana: University of Illinois Press.

Gans, Herbert. 1974. *Popular Culture and High Culture: An Analysis and Evaluation of Taste.* New York: Basic.

Gjellesvik, Henrik. 1956. "Norsk Rikskringkasting og Folkemusikk." *Spelemannsbladet* 1956[5–6]: 17–18.

Goertzen, Chris. 1986. Review of Samuel P. Bayard, ed., *Dance to the Fiddle, March to the Fife: Instrumental Folk Tunes in Pennsylvania. Ethnomusicology* 30[1]: 180–82.

————. 1990. "'Winning' Fiddle Dialects at the Røros *Distriktskappleik,* 1988." In *Norsk Folkemusikklags Skrifter Nr. 5.* Trondheim: Rådet for folkemusikk og Folkedans, pp. 33–41.

————. 1996. "The *Radiokappleik:* Regional Norwegian Folk Music in the Media." *Journal of Popular Culture.* 30:249–62.

Grimley, O. B. 1937. *The New Norway: A People with the Spirit of Cooperation.* Oslo: Griff-Forlaget.

Grinde, Nils. 1991. *A History of Norwegian Music.* Trans. William P. Halverson and Leland B. Saleran. Lincoln: University of Nebraska Press. [Originally published in 1981 as the third edition of *Norskmusikkhistorie.* Oslo: Universitetsforlaget.]

Groven, Eivind. 1964. "Domsgrunn for kappleikar." *Spelemannsbladet* 1964[3]: 4–6.

Gurvin, Olav, Arne Bjørndal, Eivind Groven, Truls Orpen et al., eds. 1958+. *Norsk Folkemusikk.* Serie I: *Hardingfeleslåttar.* 7 vols. Oslo: Universitetsforlaget.

Hald, Nils. 1950. "Prolog ved Spelemannsstemna 1948, Aulaen." *Spelemannsbladet* 1950[1]: 3.

Halski, Czeslaw, and Maurice Brown. 1980. "Mazurka." In Stanley Sadie, ed., *The New Grove Dictionary of Music and Musicians,* vol. 11. London: Macmillan, pp. 865–66.

Hoksnes, Arild. 1988. *Vals til Tusen: Gammaldansmusikken gjennom 200 år.* Oslo: Det Norske Samlaget.

Hopkins, Pandora. 1986. *Aural Thinking in Norway.* New York: Human Sciences.

Hørkelgaddan [musical group]. 1991. *Hørkelgaddan: Ørsalmusikken: Gammelt og nytt samspel etter Hallvard Ørsal frå Nordmøre.* Audio cassette (also available as CD). Heilo HK 7072, side B, band 4.

Jackson, Bruce. 1993. "The Folksong Revival." In Neil V. Rosenberg, ed., *Transforming Tradition: Folk Music Revivals Examined.* Urbana: University of Illinois Press, pp. 73–83.

Jenstad, Tor Erik. 1994. "Norsk Folkemusikk Terminologi, med Vekt på Feletradisjonen." Ph.D. diss., Dept. of Linguistics, Universitetet i Trondheim.

Jerdal, Ludvig. 1965. "Kappleikane har gjeve Spelet og Dansen ein Renessanse." *Spelemannsbladet* 1965 [3]: 3–5.

Jonassen, Christen T. 1983. *Value Systems and Personality in a Western Civilization: Norwegians in Europe and America.* Columbus: Ohio State University Press.

Kartomi, Margaret. 1981. "The Processes and Results of Musical Culture Contact: A Discussion of Terminology and Concepts." *Ethnomusicology* 25[2]: 227–49.

Kvideland, Reimund, and Henning K. Sehmsdorf. 1989. *Nordic Folklore: Recent Studies.* Bloomington: Indiana University Press.

Kvifte, Tellef. 1981. "On Variety, Ambiguity and Formal Structure in the Harding Fiddle Music." *Studia Instrumentorum Musicæ Popularis* 7:102ff.

Ledang, Ola Kai. 1990. "Magic, Means, and Meaning: An Insider's View of Bark Flutes in Norway." In Sue Carole DeVale, ed., *Selected Reports in Ethnomusicology.* Vol. 7: *Issues in Organology.* Ethnomusicology Publications, Department of Ethnomusicology and Systematic Musicology. Los Angeles: University of California, pp. 105–23.

Lewis, George H. 1975. "Cultural Socialization and the Development of Taste Cultures in American Popular Music: Existing Evidence and Proposed Research Directions." *Journal of Popular Music and Society* 4:226–41.

Lieberman, Sima. 1970. *The Industrialization of Norway, 1800–1920.* Oslo: Universitetsforlaget.

Lilleaas, Olav. 1947. "Prolog til Landskappleiken i Oslo 27/10/1946." *Spelemanns-bladet* 1947 [1]: 1.

Lindeman, Ludvig M. [1963]. *Ældre og nyere Norske Fjeldmelodier: Samlede og Bearbeidede for Pianoforte af Ludvig M. Lindeman.* [Originally in twelve parts, published 1853–67, and a thirteenth in 1907.] Facsimile edition. Oslo: Universitetsforlaget.

Linton, Ralph. 1943. "Nativistic Movements." *American Anthropologist* 45[2]: 230–43.

Lundeng, Susanne. 1991. *Havella: Slåtter fra Nordland.* Audio cassette, (also available as CD). Heilo HK 7067.

Mæland, Jostein. [1973]. *Landslaget for Spelemenn 50 År: 1923–1973.* Voss: Voss Prenteverk.

Marx, Leo. 1964. *The Machine in the Garden: Technology and the Pastoral Ideal in America.* New York: Oxford University Press.

Miljan, Toivo. 1977. *The Reluctant Europeans: The Attitudes of the Nordic Countries towards European Integration.* Montreal: McGill-Queen's University Press.

Myhren, Magne. 1967. "Landslag og Domarer." *Spelemannsbladet* 1967[1]: 7–8.

Neal, Mary Elizabeth. 1991. "Devil's Instrument, National Instrument: The Hardanger Fiddle as Metaphor of Experience in the Creation and Negotiation of Cultural Identity in Norway." Ph.D. diss., Indiana University.

Nordbø, Olav. 1952. "Den fyrste Kappleiken i Landet." *Spelemannsbladet* 1952[6]: 7.

———. 1955. "Dei fyrste Kappleikane." *Spelemannsbladet* 1955[11–12]: 24–25.

———. 1963. "75 År siden de første Kappleiken vart kalden i Landet." *Spelemannsbladet* 1963[4]: 27–28.

Nyhagen, K. 1949. "Spelemannslag og Landslag." *Spelemannsbladet* 1949[5]: 16.

Nyhus, Sven. [1973]. *Pols i Rørostraktom: Utgreiing om en gammel feletradisjon.* Oslo: Universitetsforlaget.

———. [1983]. *Fel'klang på Rørosmål: Fra Slåtter og Danser i Egen Familietradisjon til Nyere Samspillformer.* Oslo: Universitetsforlaget.

Örvik, Nils, ed. 1972. *Fears and Expectations: Norwegian Attitudes toward European Integration.* Oslo: Universitetsforlaget.

Øvsteng, Mathias. [1992]. *Vågå Spel- og Dansarlag, 1952–1992: Folkemusikk og runddans gjennom 40 år.* Otta: Engers Boktrykkeri A/S.

Paulsen, Ståle. 1993. *Slåtter fra Helgeland: På Gammelmåten.* CD. Heilo HCD 7082.

Peterson, Richard A., and Paul DiMaggio. 1974. "From Region to Class: The Changing Locus of Country Music: A Test of the Massification Hypothesis," *Social Forces* 53:497–506.

Popperwell, Ronald G. 1972. *Norway.* New York: Praeger.

Rønning, Tone. 1993. "Pris til ung felespiller." *Addressavisen* (*Kultur* section), July 5, p. 25.

Rosenberg, Neil V., ed. 1993. *Transforming Tradition: Folk Music Revivals Examined.* Urbana: University of Illinois Press.

Sandvik, Ole Mørk. 1950. *Lindeman og Folkemelodien: En Kildestudie.* Oslo: Johan Grundt. Tanum.

————. 1943. Osterdalsmusikken. Oslo: Tanum.

Sevåg, Reidar. 1980. "Norway §2: Folk Music." In Stanley Sadie, ed., vol. 13. *The New Grove Dictionary of Music and Musicians.* London: Macmillan, pp. 322–28.

Sevåg, Reidar, and Olav Sæta, eds. 1992. *Norsk Folkemusikk.* Serie II: *Slåtter for Vanlig Fele.* Bind I and II: *Oppland.* Oslo: Universitetsforlaget.

Turtenøygard, Jo. 1973. "Småglytt frå Livet til Fel-Jakup i Skjåk." *Gudbrandsdølen,* Dec. 9, 1972, quoted in *Spelemannsbladet* 1973[1]: 8–9.

Vemøy, Knut. 1991. "Spelemenn i Skodje og Vatne." In Terje Aarset and Erling Flem, eds., *Knut Didriksen Stafset: Mindre fra Forfædrene. Slåttar og Salmetonar frå Skodje og Vatne.* Volda: Sunnmøre Historielag og Møre og Romsdal Distrikthøgskule, pp. 191–94.

Weis, Elizabeth. 1989. "Contests and Conflicts: The Hardanger Fiddle in Modern Norway." M.A. thesis, University of Minnesota.

Wigenstad, Tor. [after 1983]. *Spellmenn og Folkmusikk i Dovre.* Lena: Østlandstrykke.

INDEX

Locators in **boldface** refer to tune transcriptions. In this listing, the letter Å will be alphabetized as A, Æ as AE, and Ø as O.

Lightning Source UK Ltd.
Milton Keynes UK
UKOW030034241012

201078UK00006BA/4

Ollscoil na hÉireann, Gaillimh

3 1111 40272 8628

9 780226 300504